Once Upon a Cross

Once Upon a Cross

Thom Lemmons

MULTNOMAH

ONCE UPON A CROSS
published by Multnomah Books
a part of the Questar publishing family

© 1993 by Thom Lemmons

International Standard Book Number: 0-945564-47-3

Cover illustration by Phil Boatwright

Printed in the United States of America

This book is dedicated to
Don Jacobson
who, in the words of Anne of Green Gables,
"inspired me with the idea in the first place."

Acknowledgments

The author gratefully acknowledges the assistance and encouragement given by the following people:

André Resner, Instructor of Old Testament and Preaching at Abilene Christian University: Thank you for clarifying my thinking about the milieu of the first century, A.D.

Dr. Bill Spencer, faithful minister of the church (and my next-door neighbor): Thank you for your guidance in current issues facing the church.

Christi Spencer: Thank you for reading the manuscript.

Robert and Pam Early, fellow deacons and friends: Thank you for serving as technical advisors on forty-two and dominos.

Characters

Anna — Matthias's wife

Annas — a Sadduccee, father-in-law of Caiaphas, the high priest who brought about Christ's death.

Caius — son of Anna and Matthias, Linus' younger cousin.

Caligula (Caius Caesar Germanicus)—great-nephew to Tiberius, later adopted as his son, who becomes his successor.

Claudius (Tiberius Claudius Drusus Nero Germanicus)—uncle and successor to Caligula, nephew of Tiberius.

Heracleia — Linus's wife, who dies in childbirth before the story opens.

Herod Antipas — son of Herod the Great, brother of Herod Philip and Herod Agrippa.

John of Gischala — a Zealot of Galilee.

Linus — a carpenter of Jerusalem.

Lukas — a physician of Antioch.

Matthias — Linus's older cousin.

Miriam — daughter of Anna and Matthias

Phoebe — a woman of Cenchrea (near Athens, in Greece), who becomes a follower of Christ.

Pontius Pilate — Procurator of Judea in the days of Christ's ministry.

Saul of Tarsus — a Pharisee who later becomes a believer, better known as the Apostle Paul

Tabit — a woman of Samaria.

Tiberius Caesar (Tiberius Claudius Augustus Nero Caesar)—third emperor of Rome, adopted son of Augustus Caesar.

Once Upon a Cross

"I fled Him, down the nights and down the days;
I fled Him, down the arches of the years;
I fled Him, down the labyrinthine ways
Of my own mind; and in the mist of tears
I hid from Him, and under running laughter.
Up vistaed hopes, I sped;
And shot, precipitated,
Adown Titanic glooms of chasmed fears,
From those strong Feet that followed, followed after.

"But with unhurrying chase,
And unperturbed pace,
Deliberate speed, majestic instancy,
They beat—and a Voice beat
More instant than the Feet—
'All things betray Thee, who betrayest Me...

"'...Whom wilt thou find to love ignoble thee,
Save Me, save only Me?
All which I took from thee I did but take,
Not for thy harms,
But just that thou might'st seek it in My arms.
All which thy child's mistake
Fancies as lost, I have stored for thee at home;
Rise, clasp My hand, and come.'

"Halts by me that footfall:
Is my gloom, after all,
Shade of His hand, outstretched caressingly?
'Ah, fondest, blindest, weakest,
I am He whom thou seekest!
Thou dravest love from thee, who dravest Me.'"

—from *The Hound of Heaven*
Francis Thompson
(1859-1907)

PART I

THE CROSS

1

There's a call comes ringing o'er the restless wave;
Send the light, Send the light!
There are souls to rescue, there are souls to save;
Send the light, Send the light!
Send the light, the blessed gospel light;
Let it shine from shore to shore!
Send the light, the blessed gospel light;
Let it shine forevermore!

For almost as long as I can remember, I've hated that song. When I was a little kid, wedged into the pew between my mother and one of my brothers, my legs dangling from the edge of the battle-scarred oak, I thought the song was about some woman named Cinda Light. Today, as the congregation trots out the saddle-sore old war horse one more time, I don't think the song makes much more sense with the right words than it did when it was about Cinda. The tattered tune lopes among the pews, a sterile gallop of righteousness. The pious horseman, his face in a grimace of duty and faith, brings a message of hope to the souls of the foreign unwashed. To the souls, I said; who cares about the bodies? And why do we send the light instead of taking it?

The last prayer is over now; time to go home. I shove the hymnal into the rack and stand, amid the relieved bustle of the released worshipers. I step into the center aisle, keeping my eyes on the slightly threadbare, sculptured cranberry carpet which leads me toward the back door. I'm trying to avoid eye contact with anyone, but not quite able to do so. An older woman, her hair pulled back in a severe, almost disciplinary bun, nabs me.

"Don't believe I've seen you here before, have I?"

"Well, I… ah…"

"My name's Barton—Maude Barton."

Maude. Why am I not surprised? She sticks her hand out, and I take it gently between my thumb and the first two joints of my fingers. How old will I be before someone starts shaking my hand this way, I wonder? I give her the most noncommittal smile I can muster.

"And who are you?" she asks, tilting her head back to get me in bifocal range.

"Janice Thompson." There. I've said it. Now can I go?

"Good to know you, Janice." Good to know you. She knows my name now, so she knows me.

"What brings you to these parts?" she wants to know.

"I'm teaching at one of the junior high schools in town."

"Oh, really? What subject?"

"Band." They never expect this. General music or choir, maybe; band, never. Maude digests this information with arched eyebrows, pouted lips and a slow, thoughtful nod of the head. I can tell she's giving me an opening, a chance to hold up my end of the conversation. So I let the silence widen, widen, and…

"Well, Janet—"

"Janice."

"Oh, yes, Janice, I'm sorry. Anyway, it's nice to have you here, and I hope you'll come see us again next Sunday."

"Yes, well… Thanks." I duck my head and make for a narrow opening in the aisle. A few more shuffling paces and I'm safely out the door and onto the sidewalk.

Why do I do this to myself? I wonder as I start my car and back out of the parking space. What twisted notion of duty or guilt forces me to get up early on a Sunday morning and drive to a boxy building filled with strangers to hear words that leave me—as far as I can tell—completely unaffected? Is this any way for an enlightened adult to act? And was it my imagination, or did I see faces around me in the pews this morning which looked just as confused, just as wistful to be somewhere else?

Maybe the human psyche is God's idea of a joke. Or maybe my ecclesiastical remorse is a vestigial throwback—like wisdom teeth, or the wings on ostriches—to something I used to be. Long on form and short on function. An evolutionary dead-end which creates intermittent discomfort and will eventually atrophy, since it is no longer needed.

Is that all church is for me—a habit which makes me restive if ignored?

What is it I'm looking for, anyway? And why do I keep expecting to find it despite repeated disappointment? Why do I keep going back to look in the same places, like a junkie searching for his next hit?

Boy, I'm really negative today. Maybe I'll do some work on the manuscript. That should take my mind off my ambivalence toward organized religion—at least for a while.

Going up the stairs to my apartment, I realize that next week is Dad's birthday. Guess I'd better find a card and get it in the mail. This is his first birthday since my move. At least you can't get in an argument with a birthday card.

Going inside, I glance at the mail on the kitchen table—still lying where I threw it yesterday. Unopened, except for another rejection letter from a publisher. I will myself not to dwell on this last in a long line of similar exasperations. One of these times, it's going to work.

There's still half a pizza left over from last night, waiting faithfully in its cardboard box on the countertop. Tearing off a stiff wedge of mozzarella-and-mushroom, I sit down in front of my word processor.

Heracleia's scream ripped through the closed door, shattering the air about Linus's head. His knuckles, already whitened in a death-grip on the bench where he waited outside the birthing-room, tensed even more. The sinews in his work-hardened forearms stood out like cords of steel. Matthias, the kinsman who kept watch with him, placed a calming hand on his shoulder.

"Steady, Linus," the older man urged. "Anna has been with many women in their travail—besides bearing our own four. She will care for Heracleia. All will be well—you'll see."

Linus, his eyes wide with helpless anguish, looked from the concerned, gently smiling face of his cousin to the door of the room where his wife was abed with the pangs of their first child. "Is ... is it always like this?" he asked.

"Yes, most times," nodded Matthias in sympathy. "And the first child is hardest. Once this one is born, Heracleia will have a much easier time."

Linus nodded, but remained shaken. "How can a woman ever think of bearing another child, if so much pain attends the birthing?" he wondered aloud.

Matthias chuckled. "Ahh, my kinsman! The Most High, blessed be He, has given a potent charm to the newborn. When the mother first holds it in her arms, much of the pain of the birthing-bed is forgotten."

"And the father?"

Matthias winked. "The father cannot speak, for the joy and pride he feels. And, in good time, I will be here once again, and Anna and Heracleia in there, and you and I will be laughing at the fears attending the birth of a young carpenter's first child."

Linus smiled weakly. "Perhaps, Matthias. I ... I hope so. Before the Eternal Himself, I hope so—"

The door opened and the flushed, worried face of Matthias's wife appeared. "Matthias! Run and fetch Lukas the physician! And Linus—send in Miriam. I need her help!"

Matthias was already dashing toward the open doorway, but Linus was tethered in stupefied shock to his place on the bench.

"Go, man!" Anna shouted. "The child is breech, and will likely die, but we may yet save your wife!"

In a panic, Linus leapt out the door and raced pell-mell across the bustling street to the door of Matthias's house. "Miriam!" he screamed, pounding on the door. "Come quickly! Your mother needs you! Miriam!" Again and again his fist smote the door.

"Miriam!" Linus sat bolt upright, staring wildly into the darkness of his shop. He looked about him, gulping air as he tried to return from the frenzy of his dream to the world where he lived.

The real world—not the paradise of the past, when he had loved Heracleia, and been complete. No; this was the present, and he lived and slept alone—here, on this workbench in his shop, with nothing but his tools and the smell of the wood to bring him comfort, such comfort as existed in a life devoid of love. Linus reckoned his life in two parts—the too-brief days when he had known Heracleia, and all other times. Her death was the dark star by which he navigated the dreary sadness of his days.

A pounding came at the door. For a maddening moment he thought the nightmare had invaded his waking, to grip him anew in its hopeless terror. But then he realized that someone was actually hammering at the locked door of the shop and shouting his name.

"Linus! Carpenter! Will you not awake and let us in?" the voice cried impatiently. Again the insistent fist thumped against his door.

Linus peered through a window at the star-filled night sky above Jerusalem. It could not be later than the third watch of the night! What fools came knocking at an honest man's door while the whole world was asleep? Blearily rubbing his eyes with the knuckle of a forefinger, he stood and stumbled toward the door.

"All right! I hear you!" he shouted as the impatient summons came again. "Calm yourself!" Laying a hand on the bolt, he asked, "And who might this be who comes and disturbs my sleep with such an unholy racket?"

"You need no names," the visitor answered haughtily. "Know only that we come from the High Priest."

Linus swallowed this bit of news with a grimace. Muttering under his breath, he drew aside the bolt and pulled open the door the space of a forearm, wedging it with his foot until he could see who was outside.

Standing in the street, with torchlight glimmering on his face, was a short, stoop-shouldered young man dressed in the garb of a Pharisee. Linus's eyes flickered over his features and peered carefully up and down the street. Seeing only the rabbi and a single torch-bearing attendant, he allowed the door to fall open, and the two men came inside.

"Since you have roused me from a sound sleep with your rude knocking, might I at least know how you are called, and what brings you on an errand which might have waited for a time when working men are not trying to rest?"

The Pharisee did not answer. He looked around the workroom, gathering his robes close about him, lest he should unwittingly allow his clothing to touch something in the carpenter's shop which would make him ceremonially unclean. When he had judged his contemptuous silence to have duly reminded this simple tradesman, this *am-ha'ares*, that he was in the presence of a teacher of the Law, the Pharisee replied.

"We need a cross, carpenter. A man is to be put to death before the next sunset."

"The centurion has already informed me of the event. I delivered the two crosses this morning past."

"There is to be a third."

"Why did the centurion not tell me?" demanded Linus. This Pharisee's high-handed manner was swiftly kindling his blood to a boil.

"The centurion did not know, carpenter," growled the Pharisee. "The condemned is a blasphemer, and the High Priest and Sanhedrin have only this night decided to put him to death."

"Without Pilate's authority?" interrupted Linus, incredulous. "I'll have no part of such folly! I have no intention to be a party to treason!"

"By sunrise, carpenter, Pilate will be persuaded of the necessity of executing this man," said the Pharisee. "He is a rabble-rouser, an inciter of rebellion. I do not expect such a simpleton as yourself to understand the intricacies involved—only to construct the cross, as ordered!"

By this time, the attendant was glancing nervously from the Pharisee to the carpenter. The two men glared at each other in a contest of wills whose outcome was not easily predictable.

Carefully, Linus turned away from the angered rabbi and looked about among the tools close to hand. Keeping his voice at a controlled level, Linus picked up a wooden mallet from a nearby bench. Rubbing his thumb along its battered face, he asked, "And who is this dangerous fool who angers not only the Almighty, but Caesar as well?" The implied threat in Linus's actions gave notice that it would be wise to answer his question.

Heaving an exasperated sigh, the Pharisee rolled his eyes and looked away. "Yeshua the Nazarene, whom the Greeks call Jesus."

Linus's head snapped up instantly. "The Galilean? The one who caused the stir in the Temple two days ago?"

The Pharisee studied Linus's surprised face for a moment. "Yes, that's the brigand," he smirked, realizing that he had unexpectedly scored a hit on the carpenter's emotions. "Why? Is he a friend of yours?"

Linus slowly put the mallet back in its place, shaking his head. "No... I don't know him at all. I just... didn't fancy him a dangerous person."

"Such decisions are best left to those who know the Law," snapped the Pharisee.

"But—the people!" insisted Linus. "The Nazarene is well-loved by them. There will be a riot if you arrest him."

"He is already arrested," interrupted the Pharisee, "and secured within the house of the High Priest. One of his intimates was a reasonable man, and delivered him to us in a quiet, secluded place—quite away from the press of the ignorant mobs."

Linus shuddered. He could well imagine the type of care the High Priest's hired ruffians were providing their prisoner.

"Now," continued the Pharisee, "will you provide the cross, or shall I find a more willing, less curious carpenter?"

Linus drew a deep breath, his glance darting about the room like a trapped bird seeking a way out. "I... I will build the cross," he said at last.

"Very well, then," said the rabbi brusquely, striding toward the door and motioning his attendant to follow. "We will expect the thing delivered to the Praetorium before the sun is over the walls of the city."

"Hold a moment more," Linus called out. The Pharisee paused, his hand on the door latch. "I demand to know who has ordered this done in the High Priest's name. I don't work for nothing."

The Pharisee cast a last contemptuous glance over his shoulder at Linus. "You may tell Caiaphas's servants that Saul of Tarsus ordered the work. Your silver will be forthcoming, never fear." With that, they were gone.

2

L inus hefted one end of the ash beam onto the sawhorse, grunting with the effort. Stooping low, he picked up the other end and set it on the horse's mate. Dusting his hands on his apron, he peered about the organized clutter of his shop to find his bronze hand saw. At last he spied it, gripping the smoothly worn oaken handle and eyeing the beam to find the proper spot to cut the joining groove.

The executioners of the fortress of Antonia usually preferred the *crux immissa,* with its vertical beam protruding above the victim's head, to allow a space for posting the placard describing the crime being punished. He assumed the same would be true this time.

Most carpenters would scarcely take the trouble to measure for such an implement as Linus was constructing, much less to cut and smooth the grooves which held the transverse and vertical beams securely together. "Why take such trouble," he had heard one fellow tradesman opine, "over something the user won't live to complain about?"

But to Linus's mind, the intended purpose of a piece of work had no bearing on its quality. He found a kind of virtue in making a thing as precisely as human hands could fashion it. It was a means of salvation for him; a mandate for his existence.

The death-moans of his beloved Heracleia, the tiny, bluish-white body of a child who had never drawn breath still haunted his sleeping and his waking. But wood was hard and durable. A man could lean on wood, could rest his weight on it. Wood, well-wrought, would not splinter and rend, as the failure of flesh had done to him. His shop was his home, his tools his only trusted allies, the works of his hands his only offspring. He had decided it was best. Besides—might there not be beauty even in a death-instrument, if it was perfectly fashioned?

He thumbed the serrated edge of the tool in his hand. He had been intending to obtain an iron-bladed saw, but iron was more expensive and harder to come by than bronze. He would sharpen this blade a few more times before parting with hard-earned silver for a piece of iron. Linus leaned over the wood, then realized that he was in his own light. Straightening, he turned to move the oil lamp from its place behind him to a window sill in front of his work area. With a final imprecation on the arrogant Pharisee from Tarsus who had forced him out of bed at such an hour, he bent to his work.

* * * * *

Linus had first taken notice of the rabbi from Nazareth during the Festival of Sukkoth, in the third year after Pontius Pilate became procurator. Linus had been in the Temple precincts, like thousands of other pilgrims at festival-time, to walk among the throngs, perchance to see those who might bring him news of his former home in Syrian Antioch and the friends he had left there. But mostly, he wanted to hear the teachers and experts in the Law propound and justify their intricate interpretations of Moses and the prophets.

Well might the Greeks call his people "a nation of philosophers," for surely few other clans under heaven spent as much time debating over the interpretation of words, the precepts and nuances of meaning suggested by this prophet or that teacher. And this was an employment not limited to the scribes and scholars; any boy or man past his *bar-mitzvah* might, if he wished, take part in the debate swirling about the rabbis and teachers who competed with one another for listeners in the Temple courtyards. Many were those from distant places who journeyed to Jerusalem to test their mettle, their mastery of the Torah among the learned atop the Temple mount.

As Linus walked among the crowds of worshipers and onlookers, peering this way and that, he collided with someone coming from an unseen direction. "I'm sorry, brother," he began, turning about, then halted in mid-sentence.

A Sadducee, his patrician features locked in an expression of perpetual disdain, glared at Linus as if he were a cur dog who had darted across his path. Presently the priest— for so Linus assumed him to be—backed away, shaking his gold-embroidered outer robes as if Linus's presence were a dust he sought to remove.

Linus watched him disappear, striding away among the bone-white columns of Solomon's Portico toward the Gates of Huldah. The fellow was probably a son or nephew or cousin of the high priest's family— as were many of the Sadducees. These few households, descended from a handful of wealthy land-owning clans with old, aristocratic blood, held a virtual monopoly on the Temple offices.

Pharisees, though outnumbered in the Sanhedrin, were by far the favorites of the common people—in part because of their elevation of the place of oral tradition in interpreting the Law. In so doing, they had made life easier for the common men and women who were not as able as the wealthy Sadducees to adhere to the strictures of the Levitical ordinances.

But, as Linus watched the rabbis of the Pharisees teaching their audiences, it seemed to him that their words were more for each other than those who squatted to listen. The fluid eloquence of their expositions soared above the heads of their hearers, and Linus felt within himself that they intended it to be so. They seemed far more interested in impressing one another with the cleverness of their arguments, with maintaining ritual cleanliness and circumspection in tithing, than with providing their followers any useful teaching, any comfort for the bleakness of their lives.

To the Pharisees, the common folk were a great mob of religious know-nothings, a dirty, unsavory crowd of foolish children to be threatened or cajoled, as the situation dictated. And in this way, they maintained a secure place among the powerful in Judea and Galilee—for without the influence of the Pharisees, the common folk would never endure the edicts of the Sanhedrin. The Pharisees gave the semblance of freedom with one hand, and stole it away with the other—or permitted Caiaphas and his kin to do so. As bad as the Sadducees were for their self-serving political machinations, Linus wasn't sure the Pharisees weren't worse for the religious manacles they kept firmly, if inconspicuously clamped about the wrists of the adoring, ignorant Jewish masses.

He felt a hand on his shoulder. Turning away from the babble of learned discourse in the courtyard, he felt himself wrapped in a bear hug, huge hands pounding painfully against his back in a frenzy of greeting. Managing to get his hands on the shoulders of the other, Linus levered himself backward far enough to see the face of his enthusiastic attacker.

"Caius!" he shouted in joy, recognizing the adult outlines of a face he had last seen in its youth. "You've grown to a man!"

"Aye, cousin!" grinned the son of Matthias, "I have! Mother and Father send their greetings!"

Linus smiled, remembering Matthias and Anna and their many kindnesses to him when he had still lived in Antioch. "Well then, Caius, tell me of your mother and father—are they well?"

"Yes, Linus, they are. And Father told me to say, should I find you while I am here, that his offer still stands. He said you would take my meaning." A questioning look followed Caius's words, as he peered into the face of his older cousin.

Linus nodded. "I do, indeed," he said wistfully. *Someday, your heart will lead you back here,* Matthias had said to him at their parting, *just as it now leads you away. And when it does, remember: there will always be a place in my shop for a good carpenter.* Smiling at the memory, Linus said, "It's good to know that a ready welcome awaits me in Antioch, should I ever decide to return there. But how can I go back," he continued softly, more to himself than to Caius, "and face all the memories—all the familiar sights which give them added power? Too many voices from other times."

He realized Caius was looking at him strangely. "I'm sorry, lad," he chuckled, shaking his head. "I was wandering among bygone days, I'm afraid. Woolgathering over old times, as I do too much." He clapped Caius on the shoulder and smiled into the wide eyes of the younger man. "It's truly good to see a face from Antioch, and to hear Greek unsullied by an Aramaic accent." He squinted one eye, carefully studying the face of his cousin's son. "But this is your first time in Jerusalem, isn't it?"

Caius nodded.

"When did you arrive?"

"Early this morning."

"By what route did you come? Land or sea?"

"Ah, cousin Linus!" exclaimed Caius. "My father's shop prospers, it is true; still, I am but a carpenter's apprentice! I could scarcely save the money to make the pilgrimage by foot, much less pay fare for a sea passage!"

Linus chuckled. "So! The cock grudges even the down in his own chick's nest, eh?"

Caius nodded emphatically, then pitched his voice in a low, raspy imitation of his father's: "Don't get airs, boy, just because you're the son of the shop owner. You'll learn the trade from the ground up—"

"—the same as I did," Linus finished for him, in the same burred growl. As both men laughed, Linus said, "I got the same speech from him when I started. And I'll tell you, Caius," he finished, raising a finger to emphasize his next words, "kinsman or no, there isn't a better master carpenter in Antioch than Matthias, son of Demas."

Caius nodded, pleased into embarrassed silence by such lavish praise of his sire.

"Tell me, then," Linus went on, "what do you think of Jerusalem, after having spent all of"—he squinted at the sun—"a half-watch within her walls?"

Caius said softly, "You remember, cousin, how sometimes we of Antioch laugh at those of our people who have never been out of Judea. We scorn them as yokels, backward knaves who know nothing of the wide world. But when I first looked across the Kidron valley, and saw the Temple shining gold and white in the sun, I thought that to have lived in Jerusalem all my life might not be such a bad thing. I realized that perhaps a little less knowledge of the wide world would be a small enough price to pay."

Linus made no reply as he reflected on the awe in his younger kinsman's voice—an awe he himself had felt once, but nearly forgotten. Perhaps he had been too long in this flawed, holy city, this venerable, crowded cradle of his heritage. Perhaps the residues of Sadducean avarice, of Herodian cruelty, of Pharisaic dogmatism had so silted over the ancient glories of Jerusalem that new eyes were required to reawaken him to their luster.

"What am I thinking of, Caius?" he exclaimed presently. "You have as good as told me that you traveled all night to get here, and I have failed to offer you the hospitality of an innkeeper, much less a relative! You must come with me to my house! You need rest and food. Please forgive my poor manners, won't you?"

Caius shrugged, smiling. "I was in such a hurry to get to the Temple, and then, to chance upon you so quickly on arriving—truly, I had not thought of my fatigue until this moment. But now that you mention it," he yawned, massaging his neck, "I would welcome a chance to rid myself of the dust of the road."

"Come then," said Linus. "My house is not far from here. And I have a jug of good Galilean wine freshly laid in. Not quite as fine as the Syrian vintages you are accustomed to, but it makes no mean cup, for all that."

The two men worked their way through the crowded Court of the *Goyim* toward the Sheep Gate. Already, the early summer sun was warming the masonry, driving many of the celebrants to their homes and lodgings; many were observing the old custom of sleeping on the roofs in booths woven of olive, acacia, and sycamore boughs. But in the heat of the day, they would be inside, where the sun could not so easily reach them.

From the terrace above the balustrade separating the Court of the *Goyim* from the inner courts, the *shofarim* blew, announcing the beginning of the midday sacrifice. Linus and Caius were nearing the gate when their attention was distracted by a small group of people, sitting raptly at the feet of a rabbi who stood by the wall just inside the entrance. Most of the other crowds were dispersing, but these showed no sign of leaving; their eyes were fastened on the one who taught them, and they seemed oblivious to everything but his words. Linus slowed to hear what the learned one taught that commanded such respect.

"When you have lifted up the Son of Man," he was saying in a quiet, authoritative tone, "then you will know who I am and that I do nothing on my own..."

The Son of Man! A thrill rippled through Linus as he heard this phrase. The term, arising from the prophecies of Daniel and the chronicles of the Maccabean revolt, was often used as a cipher for the Messiah—that One whose coming would free Israel from the yoke of the foreign oppressor.

Though the Sadducees and Herodians tried with all their might to dissuade the revolutionary tendencies engendered by such talk, the Messianic hope was an ember burned deep into the hearts of many in Judea and Galilee. Was this fellow a Zealot? How dare a Zealot teach openly in the Temple, practically beneath the eyes of the Antonia garrison? And why would the Sadducees permit such a radical doctrine to be promulgated under the very eaves of the Temple? But the man was speaking again.

"If you will hold to my teaching, you are really my disciples. Then you will know the truth, and the truth will set you free."

"What's the matter?" Caius murmured in his ear. "Why are we stopping?"

"That fellow there," whispered Linus, pointing at the rabbi, "what impression does he give you?"

Caius studied the features of the soft-spoken man with the flashing eyes. "His dress is rough and soiled, like one who spends much time in the wilderness, with no roof over his head."

"True," agreed Linus. "Not like any rabbi I've ever seen before. Yet see how his followers hang on his words!"

"Rabbi," one of them was saying, a troubled look on his face, "you speak of freedom. Yet we are Abraham's descendants, and have never been slaves of anyone. How can you say that we will be set free?"

With a small sardonic smile, the teacher glanced from the disturbed face of his listener to the turrets of the Antonia fortress, looming ominously above the Temple grounds.

Here it comes, Linus thought to himself, *the Zealot rallying cry!* He began edging toward the gate, anxious to avoid the rush of guards that was sure to come. And then the teacher made his reply.

"I tell you the truth, everyone who sins is a slave to sin. Now a slave has no permanent place in the family, but a son belongs to it forever. So if the Son sets you free, you will be free indeed."

A Pharisee had drifted to the edge of the rabbi's audience. Linus'sdiscomfiture grew even greater, but he could not leave while the strange, utterly self-possessed man continued speaking.

"I know you are Abraham's descendants," he was saying, "yet you are ready to kill me, because you have no room for my word. I am telling you what I have seen in the Father's presence, and you do what you have heard—from your father."

"Abraham is our father!" the Pharisee announced impatiently.

"If you were Abraham's children, then you would do the things Abraham did. As it is, you are determined to kill me, a man who has told you the truth that I heard from God. Abraham did not do such things. You are doing the things your own father does."

"We are not bastards!" the Pharisee protested, amid nods of agreement from some of the teacher's listeners. "The only father we have is God himself!"

Linus looked over his shoulder. A handful of Temple guards and Pharisees were headed in their direction. Clearly, matters were about to take a hostile turn. "Come on, Caius," he urged, moving toward the gate, "we'd better leave."

"Yes," agreed Caius nervously. "It's getting too hot to be out, anyway."

3

There. The last cut was made. Blowing away the sawdust and placing his saw to one side, Linus reached for his adze. A final time, he measured the width of the beam which would become the transverse piece, or *patibulum*, with his thumb and palm, matching it against the area he had just finished working. Satisfied that the span of the cuts was a perfect match with the width of the beam, he began carefully chipping out the space between each parallel cut he had made into the *simplex*, or vertical beam. The adze thunked firmly into the ash, where he levered the blade back and forth, splitting the sawed sections loose with crisp, splintering noises. He would repeat this process on the *patibulum*, making a perfectly matched socket at the intersection of the two pieces. In this way, the implement would be much stronger, much more capable of withstanding the load it would be called to bear.

He had seen crosses slapped together without any such care—the two beams simply nailed across each other without any thought to the justness of the fit. In one such case, the poor wretch being crucified had writhed so that the spikes holding the beams together had torn loose. The pitiful creature pitched forward onto the ground, cruelly tearing the flesh of his feet. He lay there, face-down in the dust of Golgotha, his hands still pinned to the *patibulum*, screaming in agony as the soldiers of the execution detail cursed and kicked him for the trouble he would require to be nailed up again. Linus vowed that, if he must build crosses, his would hold, and would do the job cleanly and without complication.

The lamp was guttering—time to add more oil. Carefully he poured some olive oil from a horn flask into the basin of the lamp. The flame flickered once more, then strengthened and brightened. Linus leaned out the window and peered upward, toward the slice of sky visible above the narrow, twisting street. Dawn had not yet begun tracing its pale line above the rooftops. He should have enough time to finish the job properly and deliver the goods to the Praetorium as agreed.

Turning again to his work, he thought of the one who would be nailed to this cross. For a moment his blows to the wood paused, his grip weakened on the adze. Jesus the Nazarene! How could he have been so wrong about him? He felt the beginnings of a sigh, as the feelings and intuitions he strove to hold in check slipped their bonds for the briefest of moments. The Nazarene... a rebel? He could scarcely credit such talk as truth. But the Pharisee from Tarsus seemed so sure, so confident in his appraisal.

It wouldn't do for Linus to become unfavorably entangled in the affairs of the scribes and Temple officials. Much less did he desire to attract the attention of the Roman officials at Antonia. Pontius Pilate had shown himself all too eager to vent his spite on those he was sent to govern, and his lieutenants were no better. Let them all look to their own affairs, and the less notice they paid him, the better.

Not that he didn't have his own opinions on such matters. Had he not been born and lived most of his years in Antioch of Syria, one of the three greatest cities of the Roman world? Only Alexandria, and Rome herself, ranked ahead of Antioch in grandeur, influence, and significance to the Empire. And were not the schools and gymnasia of Antioch scarcely less renowned than those of Athens?

To Jews who had never ventured out of the shadow of Jerusalem and the Temple, the pronouncements of the priests and Pharisees were tantamount to words from the Almighty Himself. But for Linus, and for many Jews living among the far-flung cities of the Empire, it was not so. Though almost every Jew Linus had ever met sent the yearly half-shekel tax for the maintenance of the daily sacrifices, and although the Temple mount was the earthly embodiment of their spiritual aspirations, not all entertained the same instinctive awe of the religious authorities. Linus had even heard old men in Jerusalem mutter behind their hands about Annas, father-in-law of Caiaphas, buying the priesthood from Pilate's predecessor.

Linus remembered enough of his schooling in the Greek philosophers to know that not all ideas which originated in gentile minds were invidious or evil. Many of the most ardent supporters of the synagogues in Antioch had been gentiles who were earnestly seeking a better knowledge of the Eternal; "God-fearers," they were called. Despite their lack of circumcision and laxity about restricted foods, their moral qualities and respect for the Torah had commended them to many.

No, Linus could not look at humanity the way many of the chief priests and Pharisees did—as either Jews or filth. His experience had shown him too many contradictory examples.

He had finished roughing out the notch in the *simplex*; now he reached for a pumice stone to smooth the gouges and uneven places left by the adze. After numerous brisk strokes of the raspy stone, he ran a hand slowly over the sides and bottom of the notch. He grunted in satisfaction; smooth as a child's cheek. Leaning the beam against the nearest wall, he hefted the shorter crossbeam onto the sawhorses. Measuring with his arms, he found the center, and marked distances to either side of the line. Again taking up his saw, he began the perpendicular cuts.

Perhaps it was no coincidence that, shortly after that fateful Sukkoth-tide, Linus began hearing numerous folk about Jerusalem whispering about the enigmatic teacher from Galilee. Apparently the fellow had angered many of the synagogue leaders in the north country with his strange teachings and casual attitude toward many of the legal obligations insisted upon by the Pharisees. And there was hearsay of other things; lepers cleansed, sight returning to blind eyes—even miraculous provision of food in the Galilean wilderness.

Linus scoffed at such talk. But one thread which ran through the gossip swirling about the Nazarene could not be dismissed so easily: he constantly invoked, so it was said, the coming of the Son of Man, and urged his followers to prepare for the imminent onset of the Kingdom of God. This teaching was what made the Pharisees most uncomfortable, and what attracted to the Nazarene the deadly attention of Caiaphas and the rulers of the Temple.

Further, it accorded with what Linus had heard from the teacher's own lips that day in the Temple, and this disturbed him deeply.

Not that this was a new notion; far from it. Many a freedom-loving Jewish heart had been kindled by the imagery of Daniel's vision since the day, almost two generations past, when the Roman general Pompey lodged his hobnailed boot within Israel's threshold. Once the Roman eagle glimpsed the strategic benefits of Palestine, her keen eye never blinked. And where her eye roved, her talons were soon felt.

But Linus knew, with a chilling certainty, what horrors would be unleashed if the Zealots had their way. Nation after nation had fallen before the resolute efficiency of the Roman legions. What could a few thousands, or even tens of thousands of ill-equipped, poorly-organized patriots hope to accomplish against such a seasoned, patient, and remorseless adversary as the Romans had proven themselves, time after time, to be? Rome ran full-sail before the winds of history, it seemed to Linus, and opposition to her rule, regardless of how righteous the motive, must surely fail.

Still the tide of resentment toward Rome ran deep and strong; little provocation was needed to goad the Zealots to violence. Linus dreaded the day when the dry tinder of Palestine would at last receive the fatal spark, kindling the conflagration which must surely consume the whole land. Yet, despite his dread, he felt the day would come, as surely as death. Men like this Galilean rabbi who went about with Messiah-talk on their lips would see to it.

And yet...had not the rabbi sidestepped an invitation to raise the banner of revolt? When his listener had broached the subject of Jewish subservience, the teacher from Galilee had chosen to talk about bondage to sin, not to Rome. Was this the creed of a Zealot? And if not, why the persistent mention of the coming Day of the Lord?

The next festival had been Chanukah, and once again thousands of pilgrims had flocked into Jerusalem to commemorate the Maccabean victory over Antiochus, the Seleucid defiler, and the subsequent rededication of the Temple. This time, Linus had searched avidly for the mysterious teacher from the north. He was anxious to know more, to evaluate for himself the threat posed by the shadowy Galilean.

Linus found him, as before, in the courts of the Temple, walking among the crowds. He was in the company of a nondescript band of twelve followers, along with an odd assortment of women, beggars, half-grown boys, and other strays. As the Galilean walked among the crowds, he spoke, or answered questions from his followers, or from those he passed along the way.

As Linus worked his way near the rabbi, one of his followers was describing Pilate's vicious reprisals against a group of Galilean pilgrims who had protested the procurator's appropriation of resources from the Temple treasury to construct an aqueduct which would bring fresh water from the Ephrathan highlands into the city. Linus had heard of the event, as had all of Jerusalem: the pilgrims, devout men all, had loudly remonstrated against the diversion of sacred funds for such a secular purpose. And though these were Galileans, who were properly subjects of Herod Antipas, Pilate had taken it upon himself to storm the crowd with troops from Antonia, spilling the protestors' blood on the very pavement-stones of the Temple courts.

Linus leaned as near as he could to hear the teacher's reply. What better opportunity could the Nazarene have to inveigh against the brutal despotism of Rome's procurator, to fan the blaze of religious fervor to a white-hot pitch? The rabbi halted, turning to face the one who had just spoken.

"Do you think," he replied quietly, "that these Galileans were worse sinners than all the other Galileans because they suffered this way? I tell you, no! But unless you repent, you too will all perish."

More talk of repentance, where rallying cries might be better expected! Indeed, the teacher seemed to be discouraging those present from taking actions similar to those that had precipitated the Galilean pilgrims' misfortune. But there was more.

"Or those eighteen who died when the tower in Siloam fell on them; do you think they were more guilty than all the others living in Jerusalem?"

Linus knew this tale, as well. Eighteen Zealots had forced their way into an arms magazine located near the pool of Siloam, in the southeast corner of the Lower City, barricading themselves inside and defying all entreaties to surrender peaceably. Pilate had ordered the foundations undermined by his engineers, and the entire structure had crumbled, killing all eighteen of the insurrectionists.

"I tell you, no!" the Galilean went on. "But unless you repent, you too will all perish."

His eyes flashed among them for several heartbeats. And then, for one breathless instant, Linus met his gaze. To his astonishment, he felt as if the Nazarene recognized him—

impossible! As he stood still, the teacher turned and strolled slowly away through the crowds, his motley followers trailing behind him.

* * * * *

Linus put down the saw, staring thoughtfully into the farthest corner of his shop. The eyes. That eagle stare, glinting like the Galilean sun on a burnished shield of gold—it was in that instant that the Nazarene became for Linus a sort of obsession, a quest whose urgency sprang from some hidden source within him.

The sky_was brightening; the grayness of dawn had seeped even to the bottom of Linus's narrow street. He put down the saw and reached again for his adze. There should be just enough time to smooth the notch and make certain of the fit between the two beams. Then it would be time to load the donkey and go to Antonia.

* * * * *

Among certain of the people of Jerusalem, murmurs had persistently run back and forth—of things happening in the outlying areas of the Transjordan out-country, the same areas from whence the Baptizer Prophet had launched his tirades against Antipas's incestuous marriage to his brother's wife. Apparently, the Galilean gathered a large following to himself.

Linus had heard people tell of multitudes gathered to hear his teachings. Sometimes, it was said, these took the form of common, earthy allegories sprung from the soil of everyday life—of mustard seeds and grapevines, of judges and suitors, of wedding feasts and shepherds and sheep. But others were more ominous, more dire in tone and portent. Linus heard tell of comparisons with the days of Noah and of Lot when God had visited the earth in wrath and judgment. There was a day coming, taught the Nazarene, whose onset would flash like lightning, would wring cries of terror from those who saw—a day when vultures would gather, and feast.

Linus could not decide what to think. If the rabbi was a rebel, then he was surely the most dangerous man in Palestine. Such teachings, coupled with the aura, the presence Linus had experienced in the Temple, could not fail to incite the discontented masses to rise up against the powers and authorities—including Pilate and his masters—which had held them in thrall for so long. And in such a rising, Linus knew, the vultures might well rejoice.

The Nazarene was a potentially disastrous leak in the dam that the Sanhedrin, reinforced by the Roman threat, had built against the swelling current of Jewish nationalism. They could be counted on to use whatever means they had to stanch it, to avert the flood which must surely sweep them all away. For once, Linus realized, he found himself in agreement with the authorities.

But still... something about this analysis seemed incomplete. It was as if the rabbi consciously avoided the role the crowds were eager to thrust upon him; as if mere freedom from Roman rule were irrelevant to his purpose. As if, in fact, he were about something infinitely more important, which his listeners had not yet grasped. Linus remembered the strange feelings he had had in the presence of the teacher—and the puzzled looks on the faces of those who followed him. They too, it seemed, were perplexed, upset, challenged by the threatening innocence of this man of Galilee.

The month of Nisan had arrived, as spring broadened in the land. And from all over Judea they had come, ingathering to Jerusalem for Passover, that most ancient observance which defined for Jews throughout the world what it meant to be children of Israel. Even from beyond Judea they came, from Galilee, from Mesopotamia in the Parthian hegemony, from Egypt. From Asia Minor and Africa, from Macedonia and from Achaia. Even from as far away as the distant trading outposts of Transalpine Gaul they came, their eyes eagerly straining forward for their first glimpse—for most of them, the only glimpse they would have in a lifetime—of

Jerusalem, the holy mount, the city of David and Solomon, the age-old home of their spirits, the object of their yearnings.

And even amid the festive, sacred hysteria swirling through the streets of Jerusalem, Linus heard talk of the Nazarene. That he would come to Jerusalem at Passover, Linus never doubted. What would happen when he did, Linus was loath to imagine.

The gossip ran thus: he had passed through Jericho on his way up to Jerusalem from the Jordan valley, and had performed signs and wonders—some said he had healed a blind man, others that he had instantly cleansed lepers. There was even a wild tale that a prominent merchant of Bethany, a man who had sometimes given aid to the teacher and his followers, had died, then been summoned alive from his tomb. And wherever the teacher went, crowds lined the roads to wave and shout and beg for a favor, a benediction, a miracle.

One could scarcely hear such stories from the exhilarated tellers without hearing, in the next breath, the title Messiah imputed to him. Jews from the farthest reaches of the Empire who, a day before, had never heard of the rabbi from Galilee, could scarcely enter the city without hearing of one of the many astounding feats he was supposed to have performed. A groundswell was building among the throngs in Jerusalem, a tidal wave of adulation for the inscrutable Galilean. The enthusiasm of the mobs was impossible to contain—even the arrival of Pilate from Caesarea at the head of a cohort of a thousand Auxiliary infantrymen could not dim the growing, dangerous passion of the people.

* * * * *

A final time, Linus ran a hand carefully over the notch in the *patibulum*, then inspected its mate in the *simplex*. Both perfectly smooth. He hoisted one end of the longer vertical beam across the horses, with the groove facing upward, then slid the transverse piece over it and maneuvered the joining notches together. The pieces slid solidly into place—a tight, strong joint. Nodding in satisfaction, he hefted the shorter piece up again, disconnecting the beams. By now, the orange-and-blue mingling of the morning sky was clearly visible. Time to load up and leave for the fortress. But first, one final touch, without which no work left his shop. Taking a small chisel and a mallet from a nearby bench, he bent over the *patibulum*. Carefully he engraved into the wood, close beside the central notch, his identifying mark: the simple line-shape of a bird in flight, with a similar, smaller shape beside and above:

It was his own private message to himself; at once a form of homage and a proclamation. "For you, Heracleia," he whispered, "and you, my little one. I have made it as well as I know how. For you."

* * * * *

Linus remembered the day—had it really been only two days ago?—when the Galilean had finally arrived in Jerusalem. How could anyone who saw forget ? He came in along the road from Bethany and Jericho, and a crowd spontaneously lined the path along which he traveled. They laid palm branches before their prophet-champion, who rode on the back of a young donkey, surrounded by a nervous handful of his followers. Standing at the back of the throng, Linus carefully studied the face of the rabbi: unlike his followers, he seemed far from surprised at the adulation of the people, nor yet particularly pleased. His expression was oddly composed. As the procession drew alongside Linus and began the ascent of the Kidron valley's western ridge, he noticed that the Nazarene's eyes were fastened on the walls of Jerusalem, outlined white against the blue sky ahead. Tears glistened on his cheeks.

Linus trailed along at the back of the mob as it strung out behind the Galilean, craning his neck to keep the teacher in view as he neared the Shushan Gate, and prepared to dismount. He was ringed about with a circle of admirers, still chanting the psalm of praise with which they had saluted his progress along the Bethany road. As Linus neared the dense mass of people about the rabbi, they began to pass inside. Linus squeezed through, and found himself within the very Temple, among the columns of Solomon's portico.

Even here, a crowd of enthusiastic supporters gathered about the Nazarene as he took in the scene which had become a common feature of Passover Week: long lines of tables sat end-to-end along the walls of this outermost courtyard, the Court of the *Goyim*. Bankers, who had bid eagerly for this concession from the chief priests, waited to assist travelers from afar in exchanging their profane Roman denarii for the silver tetradrachmae of Tyre, or some other mint suitable for mingling with the sacred store of the Temple treasury. Merchants, with bleating, cooing inventories of preapproved sacrificial beasts at hand, were ready to provide the eager worshipers with an offering for the Lord of the Passover.

Normally this courtyard would be open to people of all nations, whether Jew or gentile, as a place of prayer to the Eternal, a place where even an uncircumcised God-fearer might seek to draw near to the holiness of the Presence. But during Passover Week, other considerations predominated. The courtyard was truly the only place in the vicinity large enough to accommodate the crush of traffic the visiting worshipers created. And, after all—business was business.

As Linus looked on, the teacher strode through the onlookers, who parted before him as water before the bow of a Roman trireme, to the nearest table, that of a banker. The Galilean stared for a moment into the wide, surprised eyes of the money changer seated behind the table, his coin-filled hand poised in midair.

Then the Nazarene stepped around to the end of the table and, seizing it with both hands, flipped it suddenly on its end. Gold-and-silver coins cascaded onto the flagstones of the courtyard and into the lap of the banker, who stared, slack-jawed, into the stormy countenance of this unknown, silent assailant from Galilee.

Without a word, without a hint of explanation, the rabbi continued to the next table in the line, also a banker's booth, and repeated his actions. By now, the stuttering, red-faced bankers were on their knees, hastily scooping coins into their skirts, casting dumbfounded glances at the Galilean, who was striding away toward the tables of the livestock sellers. Ripping the tether lines loose, he began dispatching the lambs and kids with loud noises and swats to their hindquarters. He broke open the cages of the doves, and flung them, white and fluttering, into the clear, blue sky.

Linus glanced at the upturned table nearest him. He saw his two-birds trademark on its underside. With a detached sense of satisfaction, he noted it had not been greatly harmed, despite the rough treatment it had just received. The Galilean was speaking.

"Is it not written, 'My house will be called a house of prayer for all nations?'" His voice rang out clear and round, each word a pearl of fire in the ears of his listeners. His tones rose, effortlessly it seemed, above the confused bleating of the beasts, the rustle of the doves' wings, the distant hubbub of the city outside the Temple compound. Now he gestured about the Court of the *Goyim*, littered with overturned tables, straying sheep, and wide-eyed spectators. Even the bankers had ceased their hurried scrabbling after coins and sat, all but helpless in the urgent glow of his holy indignation. "But you," he shouted, jabbing a finger toward the bankers, the animal-sellers, and the Sadducean officials who had come onto the steps of the terrace to observe in shocked silence the carnage in the outer courtyard, "you have made it 'a den of robbers!'"

"A prophet quotes the prophets," muttered an old man at Linus's elbow. "In the words of Isaiah and Jeremiah, he upbraids the high priest and his accomplices."

"Who knows?" whispered another. "Perhaps he himself is Jeremiah, returned from Sheol for this very day."

The first speaker nodded sagely, his eyes never leaving the commanding figure of the Nazarene.

An old scribe limped toward the solitary figure of the northerner, his face clotted with rage. Linus recognized the man; his name was Berechiah, and he was of kinship with the houses of both Annas and Boethius. He shook a finger in the face of the rabbi, then gesticulated wildly about the courtyard. "By what authority," he sputtered, "in what name have you done all this?"

A semicircle of Sanhedrin members gathered behind old Berechiah, waiting for the Nazarene's reply. He waited long before speaking, staring at each of them in turn, as if taking their measure. When he spoke, it was not to them he directed his eyes, but to the crowds gradually moving toward them.

"I will ask you one question! Answer me, and I will tell you by what authority I do these things."

The teacher had issued a challenge the officials would be hard-pressed to refuse. Linus could see their eyes, flickering back and forth between the silently approaching throng and the erect, calm figure of their adversary. After several false starts and much huffing, Berechiah gave a disgusted shrug, looking away as he waited for the Galilean to propound whatever infernal riddle he proposed.

"The baptism of John—" said the rabbi in a voice calculated to be heard from the gateway to the terrace on which the Sadducees stood—"was it from heaven, or from men? Tell me!"

For anyone living in Judea, the dilemma the teacher presented was clear. John, son of Zechariah, had been widely hailed by the common folk, and tacitly recognized by the authorities, as a prophet. Indeed, the Temple establishment had secretly delighted in the bizarre wilderness preacher's attacks on Antipas's forbidden marriage, though they would never publicly endorse such a nonconformist as the Baptizer Prophet. But because of the passions he stirred in the people, most of the Sadducees, at least, were less than sorry to see his death. Anything approaching armed rebellion would clearly display to Rome their inability to keep a rein on the emotions of the Jewish nation, and they could scarcely afford the risk posed by such a one as John, son of Zechariah. For them to now publicly concede his divine charter would be tantamount to an admission of cravenness at best, disloyalty to God at worst.

Yet, to repudiate the Baptizer as having no more than mortal authority—and to do so here, in front of this crowd of the very sort of people who had most loved John's words—this was not precisely palatable, either. Linus heard them mumbling among themselves, searching frantically for a way out of the impasse. At last, Berechiah muttered, "We... we don't know." The words trailed off into his beard, and a great hush fell as the crowd awaited the Nazarene's answer.

He looked about at the faces in the throng, and smiled broadly. Looking back at the officials, he announced, "Neither will I tell you by what authority I am doing these things!"

Linus felt his breath escaping in a sigh of relief, followed swiftly by an amused admiration for the clever trap the teacher had constructed for the scribe and his cronies. Then he heard a low, appreciative chuckle from somewhere behind him. He turned about, seeking the source of the sudden sound, and spied a woman, robed in an Athenian style, seeking to stifle her merriment by pressing her hand tightly against her mouth.

The veil she wore covered her face, but what drew Linus's gaze were her eyes— so dark as to be almost black, and yet bright, with an inner, joyous light. He peered at her for several heartbeats. Finally, she must have felt his eyes on her, for she pulled her gaze away from the Galilean prophet, casting about in discomfiture, until their glances locked.

Her eyes widened, as if in alarm. Bowing her head and turning away, she disappeared from his view, into the unheeding crowd. Only when the ranks of the throng closed behind her did Linus come to himself, with a startled, awakening sensation.

He peered about. An attentive circle of listeners had gathered close about the Galilean by this time, and the scribe and his allies were allowed—much to their relief—to melt back through the ranks of the forward-pressing crowd. Linus heard the rabbi begin speaking.

"A man planted a vineyard. He put a wall around it, dug a pit for the winepress and built a tower…"

Linus's glance fell upon a knot of Sadducees and priests standing on the terrace above the crowd. Even from this distance, he could sense the fear and hatred in their faces as they watched the Galilean teaching his followers. Woe to the lone prophet, Linus realized, if the rulers of the Temple were able to come upon him without the protecting phalanx of the common folk gathered about him.

4

The bell rings, and I sigh with relief—the school day is over. The last-period beginners start disassembling their instruments with an inexpert vigor barely short of vandalism. Sometimes I feel guilty inducing hard-working parents to spend inordinate sums of money on complicated, delicate band instruments which are destined, alas, to be placed into the hands of twelve- and thirteen-year-olds.

"Remember guys, the scale test is Monday," I say, raising my voice to carry over the sounds of escape. "You'd better take your horns home and practice." Jenny Galway nods at me, beaming. I have absolutely no doubt that she will take her flute home and practice diligently. Jenny is the same sort of over-achiever I was at her age. She will probably play flawlessly on Monday—as flawlessly as a beginning flutist can be expected to play—and retain her iron grip on first chair. Throughout her life, Jenny will be first chair, or doing whatever it takes to get there. It's always that way with the Jenny Galways of the world. Unless they grow up to become frustrated authors. I make a mental note: try not to get too attached to Jenny. We probably wouldn't be good for each other.

The last-period bell on Friday has a different sound than any other signal. If you listen you can hear, mingled with the electric clattering, faint strains of Handel's "Hallelujah

Chorus." It's a phenomenon never officially acknowledged, but well-known to every teacher who ever lived. Like UFOs.

Eventually, the last students filter through the band room. Out of habit, I check the instrument storage room to see who is and who isn't going to be practicing this weekend. This early in the school year, the ratio of practicers is fairly high. As the term goes by, however, the number of instruments left at school generally increases, inversely proportional to the number of days left before summer vacation. Sighing, I turn out the lights, check the practice rooms one more time for stragglers, and lock the doors.

Getting into my car, I try to decide whose music I'm in the mood for. Wagner? No, too heavy; like a banana split with a chocolate malt chaser. Mozart? Too sprightly. Right now I don't feel much up to sprightliness. Bach? Hmmm… yeah. Just the right balance. Light in texture, but no gymnastics. I dig through the cassettes in my console, find the recording I'm after and insert it in the slot. The "Little Fugue" in G-minor blooms from the four speakers, filling the interior of my Toyota with the crystalline, mathematical mazes of Bach's counterpoint.

It crosses my mind that Johann Sebastian Bach was an intensely religious man. He is supposed to have said that music should be for "the glory of God and the refreshment of the spirit." Or words to that effect. Not surprising, since so much of his material was based on Lutheran hymn tunes. I'll bet it was something to see when the Bach family went to church. Of course, Johann had to be there early, since he was the organist and choirmaster. So Mama Bach—his cousin Maria Barbara, wasn't she?—had to get the seven little children fed, dressed, and into the pews before the first chorale prelude. No wonder she died at such an early age. But then came Anna Magdalena, more fecund by half than his first wife—they had thirteen children together. Of course, less than half survived him. Lots of baby-sized coffins in those days.

I wonder if Bach had any daughters. What am I talking about? With twenty kids, of course he had daughters. What would it have been like to be a child of the greatest keyboardist and composer in Germany? No doubt the boys, at least, spent a lot of time at the kitchen table and the keyboard, slaving over counterpoint and harmonization assignments. It must have worked out okay; Johann Christoph, Carl Philippe Emmanuel, Wilhelm Friedemann and Johann Christian went into the family business when their turns came.

But what about the girls? Did they ever get any counterpoint assignments? Were they ever challenged, coached, admonished to become anything other than housekeepers and brood mares or, at most, intelligent, God-fearing adornments to the husbands selected for them? I wonder if they got into fights with their father. Or were they in such a distant orbit that his actions and attitudes toward them were irrelevant—or, worse, nonexistent? If they survived their father physically, did any of Bach's daughters survive him emotionally and spiritually? Or, were their dreams and ambitions doomed to stillbirth?

I called my folks last night. When pressed, Dad acknowledged receipt of the birthday card, with a reluctant thanks. He wanted to know if I was going to church anywhere regularly. I told him no, not really, and that effectively ended his part of the conversation. Mom wanted to know if I was dating anybody, and I told her no. Ditto for Mom. Their worst fears for me confirmed, the call limped toward an anemic goodbye. Just before she hung up, Mom said, "Janice, honey... you know—" I could almost hear her looking over her shoulder, making sure Dad was out of earshot— "you know your father loves you, don't you?"

"Yeah, Mom. I know."

"He just has trouble—expressing his feelings."

Right. "Yes, Mom. I understand, don't worry. I love you, okay?"

"I love you too, honey." Dial tone.

No mail in my box at the apartment, except for my electric bill. Oh, for the days of "all-bills-paid" apartment living! But those went out with the energy crisis of the mid seventies.

Ahh, the weekend! I luxuriate in the feeling of Friday evening, I exult in the long, plush comfort of the next fifty-five hours; I soak in them like a hot, scented bubble bath after the cold, damp exertion of the week. Time to do as I like, to go at any pace that suits me. Time to find out what sort of trouble Linus has gotten himself into. With relish, I flip on my word processor.

Hold still, you!" Linus commanded, jerking the donkey's halter rope. The beast tossed its head, shuffled its front feet, and obeyed. Linus tugged on the ropes, tightening them across the beams until they were snug, then took two half-hitches in the line, securing the load for the trip to the fortress. He waggled the burden to assure himself it was centered and secure, then pulled on the halter rope, coaxing the donkey out of its stall and into the morning street.

Though the hour was still quite early, the traffic was relatively heavy. After all, this was the morning of Passover Eve, and folks were busy securing the traditional foodstuffs and making other preparations necessary for the celebration that would soon begin. Linus and the donkey picked their way among the crowds rushing to and fro among the winding streets of the Bethesda district. Linus had sited his shop strategically almost exactly halfway between the Antonia fortress and the Temple complex it guarded, and the wood sellers market just outside the city's north wall. Thus, he was roughly equidistant from the source of his raw materials and the military commanders and Temple officials who represented much of his trade.

He trudged up the incline toward the main gate of Antonia, a huge, bronze-clad oaken door set in the bare wall between two of the hulking, sullen towers of the stronghold. As usual, a squad of Judean Auxiliary infantrymen stood guard in front of the entrance to the fortress.

The commander of the squad eyed Linus suspiciously. "What's your business here?"

Linus kept his voice even, his eyes lowered. It was folly to provoke four armed, already hostile men. "I have been ordered to bring this—" he motioned toward the beams strapped to the donkey's back—"to the Praetorium this morning. I am told that a representative of the High Priest will accept the goods."

The sergeant studied Linus and the donkey for several moments. Finally, without taking his eyes off Linus, he gave a terse order. "Aureus, go inside to the Praetorium. See if anyone there can substantiate this Jew's story." A foot soldier saluted and spun away, opening the massive door and disappearing inside.

Waiting under the unfriendly stares of the guards, Linus found himself remembering more of the events of the past two days.

The morning after the tumult in the outer court, he had been again in the Temple courts. He sensed this would be the setting for whatever drama unfolded between the Galilean prophet and the Temple authorities he seemed so ready to antagonize. Linus was not disappointed, because no sooner had he arrived than a man rushed through the gate into the Court of the *Goyim*, shouting, "He comes! From Bethany he comes!" No one in the courtyard had to guess who was meant.

Soon the noise of the enthused devotees rose over the walls, its volume steadily increasing as the joyful mob progressed up the rise from the Kidron valley. Listening to the approach of the Nazarene and his followers, Linus was stricken with the strong premonition that the flood of emotion released by this visionary preacher from the north would not dissipate without some harm, some dire distress befalling... whom? Perhaps the Temple officials. Perhaps the Galilean himself. Perhaps, Linus realized, his heart racing, all of Judea.

The throng just outside the gateway was chanting his name as if it were an incantation, or a paean of victory. Linus could see nothing, for the entire space about the gate was jammed with close-pressed bodies, each one craning his neck uselessly to catch the first glimpse of this man who had so captured the imaginations of the masses.

And then, the Galilean strode into the Temple courtyard, encompassed by the handful of rough-looking men who were usually seen with him. The crowd crammed through the gate, following him inside; a confused, greedy tangle of hands reaching toward him for blessing, a babble of eyes and voices pleading with him for notice, for healing, for some hint that life would be better tomorrow than yesterday. "Save us, Lord!" they cried. "Give victory!" "Remember us, son of David!" It was awe-inspiring, and pathetic. It was frightening.

Looking back over his shoulder, Linus saw a man detach himself from a knot of Pharisees and Temple officials and begin working his way through the crowd toward the prophet. As the Pharisee's agent approached, the Galilean turned toward the man, raising his hand to quiet the crowd.

When the noise had died down, the man asked a question in a voice that seemed, to Linus, intended to carry to the edges of the audience.

"Teacher, I know that you speak and teach what is right," the fellow began, his face a portrait of earnest inquiry, "and that you do not show partiality, but teach the way of God in accordance with the truth."

A low mumble of assent greeted these fair words. The fellow went on.

"Is it right for us to pay taxes to Caesar, or not?"

If the crowd had been quiet before, it was now positively holding its breath. Linus felt his chest swelling in apprehension. What a time to ask such a question! With the mood this crowd was in, any hint on the Galilean's part that Caesar's impost was unjust would surely be greeted as a call to arms. Linus began to wish he had stayed at home this day, and minded his own business.

The Nazarene studied the face of his questioner, then smiled, looking toward the small group of Pharisees and officials who were standing at a slight remove, busily engaged in appearing disinterested in the events unfolding in the courtyard. When the silence had stretched to the breaking point and beyond, the Galilean turned to someone standing close by.

"Show me a denarius," he said. Everyone in the vicinity, even the Pharisees' agent, fumbled in purse and wallet to comply with the teacher's request. Soon a coin was handed to the teacher, who glanced at it, then handed it to the questioner.

"Whose portrait and inscription are on it?" he asked, needlessly. Even the children in the streets of Jerusalem knew the bull-necked, small-chinned profile of Tiberius Claudius Augustus Nero Caesar which appeared on the coin, and most could recite the Latin motto: *filius divi Augustus*— "son of the deified Augustus."

For a long moment, the fellow stared at the silver coin, as if feigning uncertainty of his answer. Finally he muttered, "Caesar's."

"Then give to Caesar what is Caesar's," the Galilean replied, still smiling, "and to God what is God's."

Some of the people around the prophet began to smile and nod at the simple elegance of his answer. But Linus also noticed scowls among the faces in the crowd. Apparently, there were many who, far from enjoying the way the Galilean had sidestepped the trap laid for him, wished for an open, unambiguous declaration of war. They yearned for this man, who had so much popular support at his beck and call, to declare himself plainly, and raise the banner of David. They wanted a Messiah, a savior of the stature of this man's namesake, Joshua. They longed for a commander of hosts, not a whittler of words.

But now the prophet moved off, ambling in the direction of the bronze collection urns which held the freewill offerings of the people. On any given day, a score or more of prosperous merchants, landowners or other members of the wealthier classes could be seen standing before these urns, carefully pinching stacks of silver tetradrachmae between thumb and forefinger, holding them at a suitable angle to be seen by any chance passersby. Then they would toss them onto the very lip of the urns, so that the loud clanging of the numerous coins would announce to all within hearing the munificence of the giver.

Today was no exception. Especially at Passover-tide, eager donors lined up at the urns to make such demonstrations of their expensive devotion to the Eternal and His Temple. The din of the coins was, from this close range, almost deafening.

But among the embroidered linen robes and silk-stitched tunics of the rich stood a threadbare, stoop-shouldered woman dressed in the somber habit of a widow. Carefully keeping her veil over her face, she edged toward the nearest urn. Quickly, she dropped two tiny copper *lepta* into the urn's mouth, and turned away.

But the Nazarene, having watched the people as they gave to the temple treasury, said to those who had followed him toward the urns, "I tell you the truth—this poor widow has put in more than all the others."

A few of the donors, hearing these words, stared at the rabbi as if to say, "Are you blind? Did you not see the generous handful of heavy silver coins I just tossed into the urns?" And then the prophet continued:

"All these people," he said, gesturing toward the indignant benefactors, "gave their gifts out of their wealth; but she out of her poverty, put in all she had to live on."

* * * * *

The door of the fortress creaked open, and the soldier, earlier dispatched by the sergeant, stepped outside. He saluted his leader and said, "It is as he says, sir. The cross is needed in the Praetorium for the Nazarene."

"Oh, for that one, is it?" grunted the sergeant. "Very well, then. You can go in," he said, jerking his chin toward the gateway. "Aureus, you'll take this baggage to wherever it's supposed to go."

"Yes, sir," saluted the soldier, ducking back inside and striding off across a paved courtyard while Linus urged the donkey through the arched gate. He shuddered, hearing the door thud closed behind him. Even though he came here only to deliver a parcel and then depart, the finality in the sound chilled him to the bone. The soldier guiding him paced quickly forward, uncaring whether Linus followed. "Come on, you!" he whispered tersely to the donkey, jerking the halter rope as he hurried after.

* * * * *

The next morning, the Nazarene prophet had come again to the Temple, surrounded by a crowd, as usual. Linus noticed a group of men, clearly from Achaia by their dress, speaking earnestly with one of the prophet's disciples. This man nodded and moved through the bystanders toward his master.

The men shifted slightly, revealing a woman, similarly garbed, standing slightly behind them. On seeing her, Linus felt a thrill of recognition. It was she! She of the black, glowing eyes, the ready laugh! The woman of Athens who had so unaccountably drawn his gaze on the day of the thrown tables!

Sternly, he checked his surging emotions. What was he thinking of? In the first place, the woman was a gentile. And after his uncouth stare of the other day and the sudden, wary manner of her departure, how could he possibly entertain the thought of approaching her again—assuming that such was his aim, which was certainly not the case.

Even as his mind was forming such denials, his feet carried him nearer to the group of Greeks. What am I doing? he cried silently. This is improper! It is mad! I cannot speak to a gentile woman—who is probably married to one of these, her countrymen!

And he took another pace toward them, then two.

Just as he came within two arm-lengths of the mysterious woman of Achaia, the disciple returned, the Galilean rabbi in tow.

"Here, master," he said, gesturing toward the group of Greeks. "These people are the ones who asked to see you." He stepped aside, and the teacher stepped forward, his eyes silently greeting each of the Achaians in turn. One of the men—Linus assumed him to be the leader of the group—stepped forward hesitantly, and bowed toward the Nazarene.

"Honored one," he began in heavily Hellenized Aramaic, "we have come many leagues to see you. We are of Athens, but are diligent seekers after the true and only God, the one named in your tongue as 'El Shaddai,' The Almighty."

The effort of communicating in an unfamiliar language was clearly taxing the speaker. He paused long between words, agonizing over expressing in Aramaic the ideas cramming themselves onto his Greek tongue.

"Some have come from Judea to the synagogue where we study, speaking of you as a great... as a great..." Frustrated, he turned to his countrymen, shaking his head in consternation. Linus overheard him muttering the word *"didaskalos"* —"teacher." Having been reared in the thoroughly Hellenistic city of Syrian Antioch, Linus realized that *rabbi* was the term the speaker was searching for. Even as his tongue wrapped around the first syllable, the voice of the woman broke in upon the awkward silence.

"Rabbi, Anaximedes," she prompted in a low voice, her eyes flickering from the Galilean to the man she addressed. "The word you want is rabbi!"

The man glanced his thanks at the woman, and turned again toward the Galilean. "A great rabbi," he said, relieved. Turning back to the woman, he said, "Phoebe, could you speak for us? You have the best Aramaic."

Even with the veil shielding her face, Linus could see the color rise in her cheek. His heart turned a handspring at the sight. You fool! he shouted silently at himself. Get a grip on yourself! He had been in Jerusalem long enough to be embarrassed by the dubious propriety of a woman speaking for a group of men. Then, in the next heartbeat, he was testing the sound of her name: Phoebe—the Latin title for Artemis, the moon goddess. It fit her well, he reflected, before he again clamped a fist about his imagination.

She stepped forward, her head lowered deferentially. Her eyes questioned Anaximedes for what he wished her to say.

"Tell the teacher that we have heard many wondrous things about him—things which, if they are true, are far too amazing for any man of flesh and blood."

In smooth, idiomatic Aramaic, the woman relayed the message. Anaximedes cleared his throat and said to the woman, "Ask him if... if these things are true. Ask him if he is the one of whom the prophets speak. The one the Jews call *Kristos* —The Anointed One."

She repeated the question in Aramaic. When she pronounced the last word—*mashiach*— his gaze lifted above their heads in a stare as focused and single as the aim of an archer.

"The hour has come for the Son of Man to be glorified."

Linus felt the hair lifting on the back of his neck. Here again was Daniel's world-end language spoken by the prophet from the north!

"I tell you the truth," the Galilean continued, "unless a kernel of wheat falls to the ground and dies, it remains only a single seed. But if it dies, it produces many seeds. The man who loves his life will lose it, while the man who hates his life in this world will keep it for eternal life."

Death and burial! How many graves, Linus wondered, would be needed to hold the corpses, the victims of the conflagration the Nazarene would kindle with the torch of his eyes, the fire of his words?

"Whoever serves me must follow me; and where I am, my servant also will be. My father will honor the one who serves me."

Who was this father? Linus wondered. Was there truly some pretender in Nazareth so mad as to send his son into Jerusalem to rally an army to a banner which did not exist, could never endure? What honors could this man's father bestow, to compensate his son's followers for the doom they would surely bring on themselves? Who was this man, and whence his origins? But he spoke again, and as he spoke, Linus sensed the prophet's awareness shifting from the people gathered about him to a wider presence, an unseen ear; as though they, his listeners, had become merely eavesdroppers on a conversation which had been continuing, unabated, for time out of mind.

"Now my heart is troubled," he went on, "and what shall I say? 'Father, save me from this hour'?" His brow furrowed with true consternation, the outward mark of some deep, struggle raging. Then his forehead smoothed, as if, for the moment at least, a truce was called or a battle won. "No," he said, "it was for this very reason I came to this hour." And then, with the expression of one who has seen his enemy flee before him, who has won a respite from the onset of an adversary, he shouted in an exalted voice, "Father, glorify your name!"

From the clear sky above them, a sudden peal of thunder ripped like a gash torn in the sailcloth of the firmament. All over the courtyard, Linus could see startled faces glancing upward, then at those about, each one asking, "Did you hear that?"

The prophet's gaze dropped then; fell back to earth, it seemed. An expression of weary patience had replaced the victorious fervor of moments before. Now, when he spoke to them, it was truly they whom he addressed. "This voice was for your benefit, not mine," he said. "Now is the time for judgment on this world; now the prince of this world will be driven out."

Linus's breath again caught in his throat. So! He had announced himself at last! He had just made a direct threat upon Caesar, had he not?

"But I, when I am lifted up, will draw all men—" he gestured toward the listening Greeks—"unto myself."

* * * * *

The butt of a spear jabbed rudely against Linus's chest. "Hold it there, you fool!" a soldier spat into his startled face. "You can't take that jackass into the Praetorium!"

Linus stared about, then realized he had reached his destination. The ponderous, iron-hinged doors of Antonia's inner fortress stood before him, guarded like the outer doors by a contingent of Auxiliaries. Instinctively, he lowered his head in deference. "I have brought a—"

"I know why you're here, wood-butcher," interrupted the spear-wielding guard. "Wait here."

The trooper went inside for a moment, then returned, followed by a very nervous young under-scribe, his face blanched and beaded with cold sweat. He gestured toward Linus. "You have brought the cross?"

Linus nodded.

"This way, please."

"Tie your beast over there," directed a guard, pointing toward an iron ring set at chest-height in the stone wall, several cubits distant. Linus led the donkey to the place and looped the halter rope through the ring, then loosed the cords binding the load. He slid the beams to the ground, and made as if to heft them both in his arms, when the scribe spoke up.

"No, not the long one—just the shorter one."

Linus shrugged, leaning the *simplex* against the stone wall and lifting the *patibulum* onto his shoulder. He came back to the doorway and followed the scribe through the opening, which led into yet another, smaller courtyard. As the heavy door closed behind them, the cleric said, over his shoulder, "You will take the other part of the cross to Golgotha. The prisoner will carry—"

"I know the usual practice," said Linus, impatiently. "But no one said a word about my transporting anything for your masters! I was told to build it and bring it here—nothing more!" The threatening air of Antonia was stifling him; the prospect of having anything more to do with this business filled him with panic. "Always before, the auxiliaries have managed these things themselves! Why must I do their work for them today?"

"There wasn't time," the official said. "The prisoner was just taken before Pilate early this morning, and is still being questioned by the procurator."

Linus stopped in his tracks, his eyes wide with consternation. "Are you telling me that I built a cross for a man who has yet to be condemned?" His voice rose as he spoke, "What is Caiaphas trying to do—make all Jerusalem accessories to the murder of an innocent man—perhaps a prophet?" The crossbeam slipped from his shoulder, clattering loudly to the flagstone pavement.

The scribe spun about, looking at Linus with a mixture of loathing and fright. "I am the emissary of Caiaphas himself!"

he half-whimpered. "You will stop saying such things or—or someone shall hear about it!"

Linus, his lip curled in contempt, glared at the quailing scribe.

"Besides," the scribe gibbered, "your payment is to be given you only when you have delivered the goods to Golgotha! And... and if you strike me, I shall... I shall have them withhold a third of your money!" As he said these words, the scribe's voice pinched into a squeal of alarm and his arms came up to fend off the blow he feared.

At that moment, the doors behind them burst open, and an angry knot of men crowded into the courtyard, led by the High Priest and Annas, his father-in-law. Paying Linus not so much as a glance, Caiaphas shouted at his trembling minion, "Go and fetch Pilate! He has delayed us long enough!"

"But... but master!" the scribe pleaded, "if I go inside, I will be ceremonially unclean, and the Passover begins—"

"Go!" shouted the frenzied High Priest. Whimpering, the scribe turned and fled toward the entrance to the procurator's quarters.

Moments later, the scribe returned, scurrying ahead of a phalanx of bodyguards. Pontius Pilate strode in the midst of them, his face an impassive mask of authority. And yet, there were creases at the corners of his eyes, a drawn, tense set to his mouth. Despite his outward reserve, the procurator appeared to Linus as a man with a burdened mind.

The phalanx halted in stiff discipline, and the procurator stepped quietly between two of his men, standing with his right hand hanging loosely beside his thigh, his left hand properly hidden beneath the careful, precise drape of his toga. His eyes roved the restless, angry group ranged before him.

The Imperial Procurator of Judea was a man of average height and slender build, with the close-cropped hair—steely gray in color—typical among the Roman nobility. He was clean-shaven, his eyes hooded beneath a perpetually half-lidded, almost indolent gaze. His toga displayed the thin purple stripe denoting equestrian rank, and he carried no weapon, nor wore any armor. The authority and might of Imperial Rome were the only protection he required. His level stare now focused on Annas and Caiaphas as he waited calmly, almost haughtily, for the priests to speak. The silence drew taut, like a leather cord pulled between two oxen.

And then it snapped.

"Well?" demanded Caiaphas, ceding the contest of wills, for the moment, to the procurator. "Have you given the order?"

"What order do you mean?" Pilate asked.

"You know very well what he means!" shouted Annas. "The death-warrant for the rebel, Jesus of Nazareth!"

Pilate looked at the two men for several breaths, then parried with a question of his own. "Why didn't you tell me this man was a Galilean? As you know, I have no authority over citizens of Antipas's domain. Why did you bring him to me rather than an *ethnarch* of your own blood, whose subject the Nazarene is, in any case?"

"You cannot escape your responsibility that easily," Caiaphas grated. "Do you think us blind? Do you imagine we don't know that you and Antipas twitch on the end of the same Imperial string?"

"You cared little enough for the principate of Antipas," Annas scoffed, "during the demonstration in the Temple courts last Chanukah-tide."

Pilate shrugged off the reference. "Be that as it may, Herod Antipas questioned the man and sent him back to me. Apparently, he was as hard put as I to find anything culpable in the Nazarene's words or actions."

"The man is a blasphemer!" hissed Annas, eyes bulging. "He threatens the Temple! And besides—he is an inciter of rebellion against Caesar! You cannot ignore such a threat to the peace of Rome!" The handful of men behind the two leaders nodded and grumbled their assent.

"I trust I am not the only man here who is solicitous of the peace of Rome," said Pilate, his voice dripping with sarcasm. His icy gaze flicked toward Caiaphas, then back to Annas. "High priests can be deposed, as you, Annas, should know better than most. And besides," Pilate continued, "from this man I have heard nothing to make me anxious to such an end. As to the charge of blasphemy against your religion and temple, I am not qualified to judge. Take him and try him yourselves according to your Jewish laws."

"We have no authority to put a man to death!" shouted Caiaphas and Annas together. Linus thought that this lack of authority was what most chafed the High Priest and his allies. Though they might spout piously about their devotion to the Temple of the Almighty, it was earthly power they most craved. And it galled them to come begging Caesar's procurator for permission to do away with this Nazarene threat to their spiritual domination of the hearts and minds of Judea and Galilee.

Now Annas crept a half-pace closer to Pilate, trembling with barely suppressed wrath. He raised an old, gnarled finger in the procurator's face. One of the bodyguards put his hand on the hilt of his short-sword, but Pilate stayed him with a gesture. Then the old man spoke.

"If you allow the Nazarene to go free, it will be proof that you are disloyal to Caesar. And do not think that such news will be slow to arrive in Rome."

Pilate's eyes widened ever so slightly. This was a threat the procurator could scarcely ignore. And this would by no means be the first complaint of his tenure in Judea. The one thing Caesar prized above all in the governance of his provinces was efficiency. And a procurator who generated a steady stream of plaintiffs to Rome was hardly efficient. How would Pilate respond to this accusation?

"I will bring my tribunal to the *Lithostratum*," Pilate said, finally. "There I will announce my decision." He nodded at the commander of the bodyguard. The troopers wheeled about, fell into rank around the procurator, and marched back inside the stronghold, leaving the Temple officials sputtering and cursing in the courtyard.

5

B y the time Linus could deliver the *simplex* to Golgotha, receive his payment, and return to the city, the sun was striding toward midday. He set his face sternly toward his house, determined to avoid the vicinity of the Temple and Antonia Fortress. He had no intention whatever of being drawn into the storm gathering about the Galilean prophet. The tensions, voiced and unvoiced, that he had witnessed in the courtyard of the Praetorium had shown him the folly of placing oneself under the unwelcome scrutiny of Rome and the Temple. Having seen the naked malice on the faces of Caiaphas and his father-in-law, Linus was hard put to say which was worse—to oppose the empire, or the leaders of his own people.

One thing was certain: the Galilean's reluctance to grasp the reins of power had served him ill. Again and again, Linus had heard the common folk of Jerusalem and the surrounding countryside testify to their awe of the wandering preacher from the north country. That the Galilean had gripped the imaginations of the masses, Linus could never doubt. Why, then, had he failed to properly use this one weapon that the Sadducees and Pharisees most feared and could least withstand? Linus had felt the eyes, the mind of the prophet boring into his own. The Nazarene, whatever else one could say about him, was no simple-headed vagabond. Linus knew this in the core of his soul. Even the Achaians in the Temple court had sensed his power.

Why had he now allowed himself to be trapped within the clutches of the High Priest and his accomplices? For months he had moved cannily about Judea and Galilee, preaching to crowds, drawing such a following as made him impossible to ignore, surpassing even John the Baptizer in the adulation of the throngs. He came into the very Temple courts, surrounded by an adoring mob, throwing down his challenges, unhindered and unanswered, before the feet of Caiaphas and the others. How could a man this astute in the ways of power, this aware of the self-serving greed of the Temple establishment, this attuned to the moods, the dreams, the desires of those around him, allow himself to be snared like a sleeping bird, captured by the betrayal of one of his deputies?

Linus tied the donkey in his stall, tossing a few handfuls of straw into the manger. He slouched into his shop, scattered the half-dozen silver coins—the payment for his work —onto a table, and set about convincing himself that his involvement in the affair was ended.

He should be busying himself, he knew. After all, was this not Passover Eve? Linus had not gone completely without friends since coming to Jerusalem; usually, he would keep the first night's feast with some household or other. No doubt he should be out checking to see who might have a spare place at the board. And besides—ought he not go to the market to buy the unleavened *matzah* which he would eat with his meals for the rest of the week? There were plenty of things he needed to be doing.

But his eyes kept returning to the coins lying on the table. On one closest to him, Linus could clearly see the profile of Tiberius Caesar stamped in the silver of the denarius.

Give to Caesar what is Caesar's... and to God what is God's...

He picked up the coin, rubbing his thumb thoughtfully over the emperor's image.

The words of the Nazarene haunted him, echoed relent-lessly in his memory like a challenge—or a promise. It came to Linus that the reason for the prophet's misfortune was his unwillingness to be cast in any of the familiar molds. Was he a Zealot? A popular, military champion of the people, like the long-dead Maccabees? No. He might stride to the cliff's edge of rebellion, but he would step aside at the last, and turn his attention to other things. Indeed, outside of the rowdy demonstration in the Court of the *Goyim*, Linus had never seen or heard of the Nazarene offering violence to anyone. Was he an Essene? Hardly. He came willingly to the Temple at feast-times, gladly embraced the occasion to teach such as would listen to his words. His was not the austere isolation, the unforgiving rigidity of the Qumran hermits, which drove them to forsake mankind in favor of some remote, sterile, comfortless vision of truth.

But neither was he compatible with the Pharisees, and still less the Sadducees. For he seemed to genuinely love the dirty, crippled, work-bent masses who flocked to him, who hung on his words, who begged him for healing and—some said—were made whole. Not for him the haughty ambition of the Sadducees, nor the manipulative platitudes of the Pharisees.

So—in what mold was the Galilean cast? Linus stared at the coin in his hand. Whose image was stamped upon the Nazarene? Would anyone ever know, or would the puzzling prophet from Nazareth carry the secret to his tomb?

More to the point, Linus wondered: whose image was stamped upon himself? Until the Nazarene had come along, he had generally avoided such deliberations. For Linus, identity had long been a matter of the tallying of losses. He defined himself by what was left behind—which was little enough, he thought.

And what could account for Caiaphas's hatred toward the Galilean, or the Temple leaders' adamant clamoring for his blood? They had never so troubled themselves over other, more conventional troublemakers. Even the Baptizer Prophet was secretly applauded by them.

Decisively, Linus slapped the coin to the table and stood. He would see the thing to its finish. For good or ill, the Nazarene still maintained a purchase on his mind, still tugged and nagged at his long-dormant sense of wonder. For the sake of that, at least, Linus would follow the course to whatever end it might lead.

He strode out the door and turned uphill, toward Fortress Antonia.

By the time he arrived at the *Lithostratum—Gabbatha,* as it was called in Aramaic—a large, ugly crowd had already gathered. Pilate's tribunal sat upon the raised platform, ringed about by armed guards, but the procurator was nowhere in sight. Entering the large walled square, Linus could hear the angry rumblings, see the clenched fists. He didn't need to observe the taut faces of the guards to know that this mob was close to its kindling point.

Toward the back of the crowd, close by an open archway, stood a clump of priests and other Temple officials. Nearby gathered a knot of influential Pharisees, although not so close to the Sadducees as to openly admit the uneasy alliance that had brought them here. Linus saw them murmuring among themselves, and now and again one of the members of one group would glance at the other, as if to be assured of their continued complicity.

A man was weaving his way among the throng, stopping now and then to speak a few words to those within earshot. Linus fancied something familiar about the man as he worked his way through the crowd, closer and closer to Linus's position. At last, the fellow came so near that Linus could overhear the message he passed among the uneasy assembly.

"Pilate will offer to release one of two prisoners in observance of the festival. One of them will be Bar-Abbas, the other will be the Nazarene, Jesus."

Bar-Abbas—Son of the Father! Would Pilate actually release a known insurrectionist? How could the Nazarene possibly be more dangerous than a proven killer with Roman blood on his hands? But the man was saying more.

"The Galilean has many words, but few deeds. We need a man whose actions send a clear message."

The men gathered about the speaker nodded their agreement.

"So, then—for whom will you speak?" he asked.

"Bar-Abbas!" gritted one of them, pulling aside his cloak to reveal the haft of a dagger. "And I will speak for him with this, if need be!"

The others muttered their agreement. The speaker moved on, and as he passed Linus, the carpenter realized where he had seen the man before. He was the one who had posed the dilemma about taxes to the Nazarene in the Temple, only two days past—the agent of the Pharisees and officials.

So! The Sanhedrin were willing to play a reckless game to rid themselves of the Galilean. They were willing to incite the crowd's anti-Roman fervor if such would insure the prophet's death! In so doing, they betrayed the true nature and depth of their malice, for Caiaphas and the other Sadducees would normally be far from sorry to see an agitator like Bar-Abbas nailed to a Roman gibbet. Though they had little enough to gain and much to lose by an armed revolt, they preferred to risk even this, rather than permit the Nazarene to go free. Linus wondered what could spawn such desperate hatred, such relentless, remorseless rancor.

And then, Pilate entered from the doorway at the back of the platform and seated himself ceremoniously upon his tribunal. The crowd quieted.

A party of soldiers appeared in the doorway to the platform, herding with them two prisoners, both of whom were brought before the procurator and forced into a kneeling position, facing the crowd.

Linus's eyes briefly noted Bar-Abbas, but his attention quickly riveted on the Nazarene. Looking at the teacher, he winced in sympathy.

As a cruel jest, his captors had bent a sprig of acacia thorns into a circlet whose cruel points were jammed onto the Galilean's head. Crusted blood, mingled with sweat and dirt, streaked his forehead and cheeks. There were dark bruises on his face, as though fists had struck him repeatedly. One of his eyes was swollen almost shut. A dirty, ragged cloth was thrown over his shoulders, but Linus could clearly see the fresh blood oozing from the whip-gashes on his back.

Pilate spoke. "I will have it known, before every man here, that I have questioned this man—" he gestured toward the Galilean, on his right— "and have found no basis for accusation against him."

The procurator's words were lost among a chorus of enraged shouts, led by the voices of the Sadducees. "Crucify him! Crucify him!"

The soldiers surrounding the platform shifted nervously, their knuckles white upon the shafts of their lances. Pilate raised a hand, waiting until the tumult had died down, before speaking again.

"Some of you have asked me to follow the usual custom of releasing a prisoner in honor of your Passover feast," the procurator said. "I have brought out two men, as you see. Now you may choose. Whom shall I set free? Jesus of Nazareth; or this man, known as Bar-Abbas?"

"Give us Bar-Abbas!" shouted the dagger-man standing near Linus. He thrust an angry fist into the air as he said it, and the cry was taken up by dozens of throats in the courtyard. "Bar-Abbas!" "Release Bar-Abbas!" "Bar-Abbas!" they chanted.

Linus wanted to retch. From his own observations and from the evidence of Pilate's own lips, the Nazarene was guilty of nothing other than poorly chosen words and opposition to the Temple establishment. Yet this mob clamored to see a hot-headed murderer go free instead. Whether they knew it or not, they were once again playing into the hands of the chief priests who, despite their hypocritical machinations, had less desire than anyone to see Rome evicted from Palestine. Once more, the Sanhedrin used the passions of the masses as a tool to further their own ends.

When the furor had again died down, Pilate raised his voice to address them. "What crime has this man committed," he asked, indicating Jesus, "to make him worthy of death?"

A belligerent roar was his only answer: "Crucify! Crucify! Crucify!"

Pilate shouted above the din, "This man says he is your king! Will you have me crucify your king?"

"We have no king but Caesar!" screamed Annas.

Some of the men glanced darkly at the high priest, but most continued their chanting, some calling for the release of Bar-Abbas, some crying for the blood of Jesus of Nazareth. The captain of the guard leapt upon the dais beside Pilate, gesturing urgently from the crowd to his men and himself. It was evident that he feared matters might quickly come to blows. Pilate looked out at the hostile mob, then at the Nazarene. At last, he stood, raising his hands to signal his intention to speak. By degrees, the chanting quieted, until the procurator could again make himself heard. He turned to a guard and gave an order. The man dashed into the Praetorium, soon returning with a bronze basin from which water splashed as he carried it toward Pilate's tribunal.

The procurator stood before his tribunal and carefully dipped his hands in the water. He then turned to the crowd, holding his hands above his head, palms outward, and announced, "I call upon you and all the gods to witness that I am innocent of the blood of the man you call Jesus of Nazareth."

At the back of the square, the voice of Annas crackled once again. He swore a terrible oath, and said, "His blood be upon us, and upon our children!" The crowd, unthinking, quickly echoed the cry.

"Very well," said Pilate, finally. "It shall be as you have said." Turning to the commander of the guards and pointing at the Nazarene, the procurator said, "Take this one, flog him, and crucify him. As for the other—" the half-lidded eyes flickered toward Bar-Abbas, out to Annas and his allies, then back to the captain— "set him free. Doubtless he and his patron deserve each other."

Linus was standing near the west gate of Antonia when it opened. Because of the volatility of the crowds at Passover-tide and the furor swirling about the Nazarene, Pilate had ordered the usual size of the crucifixion detail doubled: twenty-five Auxiliaries, armed to the teeth, strode out of the fortress along the Tyropoeon Valley road, their short-swords loosened in the sheaths and their lances at the ready.

The three condemned men were in the middle of the formation, ringed about by their guards. Each of them had the *patibulum* of his cross strapped across his shoulders with rawhide thongs, so that all whom they passed would know of their imminent fate. Parading the victims through the streets of Jerusalem was considered a deterrent to those who might be contemplating similar crimes.

The three men, weak from loss of blood and the beatings they had received prior to this grisly promenade, staggered under their unwieldy burdens. But the Nazarene seemed the most feeble of the three. Several times within a few paces of the fortress, he fell so far behind the others as to receive prods and curses from the guards bringing up the rear. He staggered blindly under the weight of the beam, slapped to and fro by the blows of the soldiers.

As the group neared Linus's position, the captain, seeing the slow progress made by the Galilean, called a halt. The rabbi fell to his knees.

"We'll never get this lout up the other side of the valley, much less up the side of Golgotha," he groused, spitting disgustedly at the feet of the bleeding, panting Nazarene. "You, there!" he called to a tall, swarthy-skinned African who had been striding past, "Come here!"

The man looked at the captain with a puzzled, surprised expression.

"Yes, you!" the commander said, summoning the man with the jerk of a forefinger. "I need someone to carry this fool's cross to Golgotha. If you'll do it, there's a denarius in it for you."

The African slowly approached, staring guardedly from the soldiers to the pathetic figure lashed to the beam. For a long moment, his eyes took in the defeated form bound to the cross. Then, hesitantly, he glanced at the captain, and nodded.

"Cut him loose," snapped the commander. A soldier strode toward the Nazarene, unsheathing his short sword. He swiftly hacked through the leather thongs and, released at once from his burden and his support, the Nazarene collapsed to the ground.

The African bent and, with the gentlest of touches, raised the condemned man to his feet. As he stood, the Galilean grasped at the beam to gain a purchase on his balance. His bloody hand swept across the place where Linus had carved his trademark, leaving a dirty crimson splash across the two-birds emblem.

Linus gasped involuntarily as a wave of sudden shame swept over him, leaving a dull pain in his throat. The sharp juxtaposition of the prophet's blood with the symbol of what remained of his honor was almost more than he could bear. The image brought into acute relief the emptiness, the abject futility of his life.

He trod the path to Golgotha in the wake of the soldiers, his vision fogged by the darkness in his soul. In a daze he gathered at the crest of the barren hillock with the small group of curious onlookers, die-hard supporters, friends and relatives of the three victims.

The sounds and sights of the crucifixion entered his consciousness as echoes, visions which scarcely penetrated his cloak of confusion. He saw, and yet did not see the dejected, half-dead prisoners looking on as the guards nailed together the beams of their death-racks. From some far-distant place, the thought reached him that the joints of the gibbets were, at least, tight and secure. As if in a dream, he saw the soldiers roughly wrestle the three wretches backward onto the crosses, saw the prisoners struggle feebly as their limbs were bound tightly in place with leather thongs. Through a numbing curtain of pain and perplexity, he saw the hammer rise high above the cruel spike held in place on the Nazarene's wrist, saw its downward stroke. He saw the spine of the prophet arch, heard the weak, ragged scream of pain which tore from his tortured throat as a ringing hammer blow—then another and another—drove the iron pin fiercely home.

At last, the crosses were raised upright and dropped with dull thuds into the holes prepared for them. Most of the spectators began to drift away, leaving behind only those whose loyalty or spite held them fast. Even the sight of the Athenians walking slowly past, their faces reflecting their sad puzzlement, did not rouse Linus from his stupor. For a moment, the woman, Phoebe, glanced at him, her dark eyes registering the briefest instant of recognition. Then she was gone.

The sound of keening came from a knot of bedraggled peasants gathered near the foot of the Galilean's cross. In their midst was an old woman, wailing, "My son! My son! Why, oh why, my son?"

Then, a sound reached him which, even in his present state, jangled his nerves with its incongruity. It was the sound of snickering, and it came from a group of Sadducees and chief priests. "Look at him!" one of them was saying as he pointed at the Nazarene, writhing in pain upon the cross, "the Messiah! What a deliverer he is! If he truly saved others, let him use his power on himself, now!" The others laughed in a smirking, self-satisfied way, and added similar insults.

It was too much. Overcome at once by shame, confusion, anger, and fear, Linus wheeled and ran pell-mell down the side of Golgotha, blindly fleeing the looming wall of emotion which threatened to fall upon him, to crush his sanity in its rubble. He gave no conscious thought to the direction of his flight, simply bolting wherever his feet took him; bounding past surprised passers-by, even colliding with those unable to avoid him. The city walls passed in a blur, and he darted like a wild thing among the narrow, twisting streets surrounding the Temple Mount.

Only when he entered the mouth of the street where his shop was located did his senses begin to rein in the runaway horses within his mind. Panting heavily he entered his shop and sat heavily on the nearest bench. The silver denarii still lay on the table where he had tossed them earlier in the day. Now he scooped them in a fist and flung them through the doorway, scattering them in the dust of the street.

He seized upon the thought that he must leave Jerusalem. He had believed, years ago, that by coming here, to the spiritual axis of his forefathers, he might regain something of the heart-center he had lost with Heracleia and the child. But he felt that Jerusalem was, instead, strangling him, crushing him beneath the weight of her centuries of unfulfilled expectations.

Somehow, the tragic death of the Nazarene had shown him that there were no answers here; only questions and disappointments. Even in Jerusalem, a life of unadorned purity and truth did not suffice: the cross crowning Golgotha's summit gave mute, stark testimony to that. And still in his mind's eye he could see the blood smeared across the trademark on the crossbeam he had made. Was his guilt truly less than that of the crowds in the *Lithostratum* who had begged for the Nazarene's death?

He found his leather bag and began tossing into it the tools of his trade. Chisels, awls, bow-drills, mallets, whetstones; they followed one another in rapid succession into the bag. He found himself moving more and more rapidly, so desperate was he to be away. The thought that this day was Passover Eve made not so much as a dent in his haste. He would travel as soon as he was packed, and he would continue to travel even after sundown had ushered in the *Shabbat* and the beginning of Passover Week. His sudden obsession to distance himself from Jerusalem would not permit him to do otherwise.

As he cinched the pack tightly on the donkey's back and led the beast out of the stall, a gust of cool wind made him look up at the sky. Though the sun had been shining brightly when he had entered his house, a sudden storm had gathered over Jerusalem in the past few moments, clabbering the sky with thickening clouds. Fitting, he thought. Even the sun is ashamed to look down on this city of broken promises.

The unnatural gloom settling over Jerusalem matched the twilight in Linus's heart as he turned north up the oddly quiet street. Walking past the Pool of Bethesda, he left by the northeast gate, along the Damascus road. He trod steadily northward, and did not look back.

I slump in my chair and look at what I've just written. As I read, I feel tears stinging my eyes. Is this maudlin or what? A skeptical child of the Me Generation, wooed to repentant sighs by her own recounting of the crucifixion. Camera closes to full-frame shot of the wet-streaked face of Our Heroine, then a fade-in of an open Bible. Samuel Barber's *Adagio for Strings* hums poignantly in the background. Fade to black and roll the credits.

Make all the fun you like—I still have to go find a box of tissues.

I realize as I wipe my eyes and blow my nose that, try as I might, I don't have it within me to jest about the death of Jesus. It's the one thing I truly want to—wish I could—

believe in. Even when I was in high school, going through my most rebellious times (on the sly, of course)—trying out all the swear-words, drinking and smoking and acting cooler than I felt around the drugs and sex that seemed to be everywhere—I could never, unlike most of my friends, use his name as a curse or a joke. Even then it seemed... disloyal. After all, if the Bible is true, he became one of us, even though he didn't have to. That's worth something, isn't it?

No, I very much want to believe in Jesus. The problem lies with the people I meet who expect me to believe they believe in him. I could see myself trusting somebody like Jesus, but there's no way I can ever trust the church. Not after being on the business end of some of its tender mercies.

It's tough when you're a kid who asks all the wrong questions. Those who are snug and warm inside the house dislike any insinuation that there might be a leak in the roof. Especially from a snot-nosed girl with an attitude. Especially when she's the preacher's daughter.

So, Linus— where do we go from here? Like ol' Thomas Wolfe said, you can't go home again. And they probably don't want you back anyway. They moved, or you did, and left no forwarding address. Oh, well... I guess we'll burn that bridge when we get to it.

PART II

THE QUEST

6

Linus shaded his eyes against the shimmering heat of the midday sun, squinting ahead at the sides of Mount Gerizim, clad with cedar and scrub oak. The winding road twisted in and out among the contours of the venerable hill, disappearing at last over its northern shoulder to descend into Shechem and Sychar.

The donkey shook its mane and heaved a fluttering sigh through its nostrils. "Me, too, old friend," Linus smiled, wiping his forehead with a corner of his cloak. "But to get rest and water, we must get over old Gerizim to the towns beyond." He scratched the donkey behind the ears. "And I am as loath as you to spend another night without a roof over our heads."

The first night of his journey was passed in Bethel, an easy day's walk north of Jerusalem. But last night he had made a fireless camp in a sheltered ravine just off the road, which ran up the spine of Judea and Samaria. A few leagues north, the road wandered down along the western marches of the Plain of Esdraelon. After crossing into the district of Galilee and through Nazareth, the way angled west and north toward the shores of the Sea of Galilee. Once the lake was left behind, however, it was a long trek across the grasslands of Trachonitis and Ituraea until the walls of Damascus came into view.

But such thoughts were best left to another day. For now, it was enough to concentrate on reaching such comfort as might be found in the nearby towns of Samaria. Linus shook his wallet; he had little silver remaining to him, since he had thrown away his fee for—

Enough. He stepped forward along the road, tugging on the donkey's halter rope. Surely someone in Sychar or Shechem would need the services of a carpenter. He would stay long enough to earn some money for the road, and then be on his way to... where?

For the thousandth time since he passed Jerusalem's northern gates, he wondered to himself what, exactly, was his final destination. His urgency to escape Jerusalem had impelled him to depart without taking much thought for his eventual journey's end. It was enough to be going, to be away from the menace which crouched among the alabaster-and-gold finery of the Temple, the surly gray stones of Fortress Antonia.

But he still didn't know precisely where he was bound. He had the vague thought of sojourning in Damascus for a time, then perhaps faring on north. It was even possible that he might return to Antioch one day... when he felt strong enough.

He leaned into his uphill strides as the road wound back and forth across the flanks of Gerizim. Despite the burning in his calves and the sweat running beneath his clothing, Linus felt exhilarated and alive. The green pungency of the surrounding cedar filled his nostrils with a glad, expanding satisfaction; he reveled in the simple beauty of this sun-washed day in the hills of Samaria. It was enough, he decided, to be abroad on such a day, to be able to exult in the blood coursing through one's veins, to feel the healthy stretch of muscle and sinew and the gratification of honest sweat. Such uncomplicated joys made the contemplation of a drink of cool water, or of a bed at day's end, the more pleasurable for the anticipation.

At last he crested Gerizim and began his descent. Looking at the valley spread below, he could see a rambling city wall and the rows of earth-colored houses it enclosed— the town of Shechem. A bit further along and to the west, a haphazard clutter of dwellings marked the smaller village of Sychar. The road jagged from one place to another, but the focal point of its meandering was a small, irregular green circle between the two settlements which denoted the reason for the first human habitation here: the Well of Jacob. Linus could barely make out the clump of stones which identified the location of the actual well. But already he could imagine the cool comfort of the drink awaiting him.

A thread of unease unraveled from the fabric of his thoughts. While he was not, unlike some of the more pious Jews of Judea and Galilee, a hater of Samaritans, he was not sure how many of those he would encounter here were as tolerant of Jews. There had been more than enough bad blood between the two peoples to justify resentment on both sides. Linus had heard many stories from travelers to Jerusalem who had been, at best, treated inhospitably and, at worst, openly harassed by the residents of Samaria. On the other hand, such Samaritans as were foolish or unfortunate enough to venture into Galilee or Judea were frequently scorned or taunted as unclean half-castes.

As he neared Jacob's Well, he decided to speak Greek while in Samaria. Perhaps any Judean overtones his speech had acquired during the years in Jerusalem would be easier to mask in Greek than in Aramaic. No sense in borrowing trouble.

By now the sun rested on the peak of Mount Ebal. Wincing as he eased his shoulder pack to the ground, Linus reached inside the well to grasp the well-worn cord tethering the drinking-gourd. He hauled the gourd up hand-over-hand, grasped it gratefully in both hands, and tilted it to his mouth, slaking his dry throat in deep, satisfying gulps. The water ran in a cooling rush through his beard and down his chest, and when he had finished drinking, he poured the remainder of the gourd's contents over his head, eagerly rubbing the dust of the road from his face.

As he drew another draught to pour in a nearby trough for the donkey, a woman padded softly to the well and waited patiently for him to finish with the gourd.

As Linus poured the water in the trough and the donkey pressed eagerly forward to drink, the stray thought wandered into his mind that she could possibly direct him to some chance of earning a coin or two. He cleared his throat and took a half-pace toward her, still holding in his hands the now-emptied gourd. "May I help you draw the water for your pot, good woman?" he offered in what he hoped was a helpful tone of voice.

Her eyes darted toward him in the flinching manner of one who is more accustomed to receiving blows than offers of aid. "I am a journeying carpenter," he explained quickly, "from... the south, and I would be happy to find some work—that is, if you know of anyone who might need my services." His voice trailed into dejection as he observed the flat, vacant stare with which the Samaritan woman regarded him. Tired from the long day's walk and despairing of getting useful information from her, he dropped the gourd into the well, hearing the faint splash as he turned away.

"Once, not so long ago, I came to this well," the woman said to his back, "and spoke with another man who had come from the south..."

Slowly he turned again to face her, confused by her words, but still hoping she might direct him to a place where he could look for work.

But the silence grew so long that Linus again became discouraged. Of all the people of Samaria, he had the misfortune to run into a madwoman! And then she spoke again.

"He came from the south, and he asked me for a drink...me, of all people!" Her face brightened as she spoke, and as she looked at Linus, something like happiness breathed faintly on her cheek. Then, as if suddenly realizing that he couldn't possibly know what she was talking about, she looked down and began dragging the urn toward the well.

Linus had walked slowly back toward the well. Now he found himself pulling on the cord, hauling the gourd up to fill the pitcher of this woman whose face had been so profoundly—even if briefly—transformed by a distant memory. "Here. Let me help you," he offered. "The well is deep."

She hesitated a moment, then nodded, still without looking at him. "Thanks," he heard her mutter softly, "You are kind."

"Odd" he heard her continue, in that same hushed tone which seemed more for herself than for him, "I have spoken with but two men of the south at this well—and both of them offer water." Linus heard a soft, self-mocking laugh.

He looked at her in frank puzzlement as he poured the water into her jar. "Why should this surprise you? What else would one expect to get from a well but water?"

She shot him a glance. "Yes. What, indeed?"

She stared into the distance as she said it. The water jar was still half-empty. Again he dropped the gourd into the well.

"Living water!" she said quietly. "Who could imagine such a thing?" She shook her head and smiled at the memory. "What a simpleton I was!" she laughed, then pulled up short, a look of embarrassed awe on her face. "But how… how could I have known?"

Linus poured again into the pitcher, filling it within two fingers' breadth of its top. He was oddly disturbed by the strange, meandering words of this indrawn woman of Sychar. Each time her mind wandered down the paths of whatever strange memory drew her on, her face changed, softened. If seemed to Linus that this recollection was, for her, the one oasis in a lifetime of dry wandering.

"Living water," she whispered. "Oh, that I might have drunk deeper—far deeper from his well." A single tear spilled from her right eye and made slow, glistening progress down her cheek.

Linus felt the hair prickling on the back of his neck. Listening to the words of the Samaritan woman, he suddenly recalled a day in the Temple. A day of strange, disturbing words, and the eyes of a stranger who seemed to know him instantly, to his very core.

He bent low and raised the water jar as she arranged the pad on her head. When she had the jar balanced, he started to turn away. Then, quickly he turned back to her. Catching her sleeve, he spoke low, as if he were suddenly afraid of being overheard.

"I have seen him, too. I have heard his voice and looked into his eyes."

She looked at him then, a new recognition dawning in her eyes. For several slow breaths they regarded each other.

"Who was he?" Linus asked quietly.

"He said he was the *Taheb*," she replied in a voice even softer, but rigid with belief.

Taheb—the Samaritan "Restorer," equivalent to the Jewish *Mashiach*. The Coming One. The Awaited, the Anointed. Somehow, Linus was not surprised. It was of a piece. If only it could be true. But no! He was dead, and all such hopes had died with him.

"What of him?" she asked now. "When did you last see him? Will he—" a breathless expectation bloomed on her cheek. "Will he come this way again?"

Seeing the resurrected hope in her eyes, Linus felt himself dying inside. How could he tell her? How could he bring to this woman, this one whose very life was wound about the center of a single encounter with the Galilean, the news that her savior was dead—slain as a common criminal on a cross that he himself had built?

"He... he was in Jerusalem. It was Passover-tide..." The words dropped to the ground between them and lay there, inert.

"You are a carpenter, you said?" she asked at last.

"Yes" he said, surprised to realize that she had heard his earlier inquiry. "Do you know of anyone who needs such work?"

"Perhaps..." She looked at him more carefully. "Where have you come from—exactly? Who are your kin?"

He could not bring himself to lie to her. "I am—I am come from Jerusalem. I am a Jew." He held his breath and stared at the ground, awaiting her response.

When he looked up, her eyes betrayed the smile beneath her veil. "So was he," she replied. Linus had no need to guess who was meant.

"I have a kinsman in Sychar who has an inn," she went on. "He is not overly fond of your people, but he is a fair man, and will not permit any harm to you. That is," she chuckled, "as long as you pay in silver—and, perhaps it would be better if you spoke no southern-tinged Aramaic while hereabout."

Linus smiled with relief. "Greek I have, and silver, but unless I find work, not enough of the second for a long stay with your kinsman."

"Come, then," she said. "We should go into the village. I will show you the place."

Retrieving the donkey's halter rope, he followed the strange, damaged, hopeful woman of Sychar as she led him toward the town.

———

I discover, much to my dismay, that the public library has taken out its nice, comfortable card file in favor of a computerized system. Great. All I wanted was to quickly check a couple of references, but instead I'm going to be in here all evening learning how to use this high-tech terror to find the two or three books I need.

I'm standing at the terminal, pecking helplessly at keys selected at random. Instructions keep popping up on the screen, and although they are in English, they might as well be in Aramaic. You'd think a person my age, living in the Computer Era, would be reasonably conversant with such things, but I'm getting more and more frustrated by the error messages and derisive electronic hoots issuing from the machine in front of me.

"Can I help you?" The voice comes from just behind my left shoulder. "Well," I reply, "I seem to be having a little trouble—"

I glance at the librarian. It's Maude, from church. Perfect.

"Oh, hello, Janet!" she exudes.

"Janice."

"Yes, of course, Janice, I'm so sorry. Here, let me show you what to do—" She reaches around me for the keyboard. With an evenly divided mixture of gratitude and chagrin, I move aside and allow her free rein. As she pecks and taps at the computer, she keeps up a running barrage of comments, helpful hints, and questions.

"This thing is really not as hard to use as it might seem at first. See here, all you do is enter your choice from this menu here—" (tap) — "then go to the next screen and do the same thing—" (tap)— "and just tell it what you're looking for. See?" she beams proudly at me, "it's as easy as that."

Something about my face must betray my skepticism, and she turns back to the screen. "All right, now. What *specific* information are you interested in?"

Okay, Maude you asked for it. "Social norms and customs of the Hellenistic world of the first century A.D." I admit it; I relish the amazed look on her face when I lay that tidbit on her.

Maude's countenance takes on a grim, determined look to replace the good-natured, see-how-simple-it-is expression of a moment ago. She attacks the keys in short, business-like bursts, and the word "sociology" appears on the screen. She tabs down to a field which is labeled something like "x-ref?" and types in "Corinth." Then, with a triumphant *coup-de-grâce*, she punches the "enter/send" key, and the terminal begins muttering to itself in small electronic chirps and wheezes.

As Maude turns back to me with a patient, slightly patronizing look, I realize she is not an opponent to be trifled with. "What I've done," she explains as if lecturing an elementary school tour, "is cross-reference your main topic, 'sociology,' with your secondary topic, 'first century Greek culture.' I assumed information listed under 'Corinth' would be fairly representative of the general thing you're after?" Her arched eyebrow, her up-tilted chin invite me to put her to the test again, if I dare.

With a final, satisfied beep, the screen displays a list of three titles. Maude and I look at the results of her digital safari. "The first one," she says, "is on microfiche, in the basement of the library. I can show you how to—"

"No, thanks," I interject quickly. "I'd like to be able to take the sources home, if at all possible."

"Well, then," she continues crisply, "the other two books are in the 900 series, on the third floor."

I admit to a grudging admiration of Maude's mastery of her *milieu*. The lady deserves some sort of acknowledement, as badly as I hate to say so. She turns to leave. "Umm, Mrs.—ma'am?"

She turns back toward me.

"I really appreciate your help. Sometime when I've got more time, I need to get you to show me how to put this thing through its paces." I gesture toward the terminal and make a sincere attempt at a smile of gratitude.

Her expression softens a trifle. "The name is Maude, honey," she says. "And I'll be glad to help anytime."

"Okay, well… thanks."

As I approach the circulation desk, Maude finds me again. There's a wrinkle of puzzlement above the bridge of her nose. I tense inwardly, sensing the question she will ask.

"By the way—Janice, is it?"

"Yes, that's right." Finally.

"I'm just curious about something. Are you taking graduate courses, maybe? I haven't had many requests for this sort of information—" She nods toward the books tucked under my arm.

I knew it. The Moment of Truth. That instant, viewed with aversion by all aspiring writers, when they must admit publicly the disparity between the dream and the likelihood of its realization. At best, the one to whom you reveal yourself will think you quaint or stylishly offbeat—like a favorite old-maid aunt who's just crackers enough to be interesting. They'll arch their eyebrows, bend their mouths in a caricature of impressed surprise, and say something like, "Oh, really?" And the next words in their minds, if not out of their mouths, will be —"and what have you had published?"

It is this moment, if no other, that teaches you either to yearn deeply for that first publication and dig all the harder, or to despair and take up a more harmless hobby. Because until that first hurdle is overcome, you can prove nothing about yourself other than being a dabbler, a pretentious scribbler self-doomed to a future of pathetic, fruitless ambitions. They may ask you good-naturedly, "How's the manuscript coming?" But to themselves they're saying, "Poor sap." And you have no rebuttal. Until you're published, you are merely Doing Some Writing. Only afterward can you say you are A Writer.

For some unfathomable reason, I tell Maude the truth. "I'm... I'm working on a book." The words come out in an apologetic mumble, and I half-hope she doesn't hear me. No such luck.

"A book!" she exclaims. I assume that every library patron within thirty feet of the circulation desk is now gazing curiously at the blushing pretender being accosted by Maude, Librarian and Town Crier. And then something happens for which I am quite unprepared.

She hugs me. A firm, enwrapping, welcome-home kind of hug. Then she puts her hands on my shoulders and holds me at arm's length, like a favorite niece she hasn't seen in months. I am at once embarrassed and—to my own great surprise—oddly touched by this spontaneous exhibition. And to my further amazement, when I reluctantly raise my vision to her face, I see tears in her eyes, shimmering like melted glass. "That is just wonderful," she says in an enthusiastic stage whisper. "And don't ever let anyone tell you you can't do it—because you can!"

We stand like that for maybe five seconds, before she gives me a final squeeze and walks away. I sense that there is more, much more she would like to say to me, but can't, just now. Bewildered, abashed, and inexplicably elated, I proceed meekly to the circulation desk and fish my library card out of my handbag. Still marveling at the bizarre oracle I've just received, I leave the library and walk to my car in the crisp air of the October evening.

7

Linus half-squatted as he eased one end of the rough-cut door post to the ground, tilting it carefully from his shoulder to lean against the baked-clay wall of the inn. Slowly he straightened, wincing from the kinks in his back. He massaged his shoulder and rotated his arm as he critically studied the post and the nearby doorway it would soon occupy. Tomorrow he would chisel the ends of this piece to match the lintel and threshold sockets in which the current splintered and dilapidated door now swiveled. With the new door post in place, he could set about the task of framing and fitting the door. Doubtless the innkeeper and his patrons would sleep sounder for knowing that a stout new door guarded their slumber.

Linus had made good progress today. Arising at first light, he had hiked up a draw between two of the low hills surrounding the town, and had located a straight, strong oak suitable to his need. He felled it and shaped it to its present form, and had also managed to rough out several of the planks he would need to fashion the rest of the door. Tomorrow brought the promise of the job's completion, and payment. Well might he anticipate that, since he had barely enough coin left in his wallet to provide for this evening's board and bed. It was lucky, indeed, that the kinsman of the woman at the well had such acute need of his skills. The innkeeper had spied the carpenter's tools in his pack, and was quick to accept Linus's offer of assistance at a price that was mutually agreeable. If his ear detected anything of a Judean accent in Linus's voice, he had given no sign. Linus was pleasantly surprised to find work so quickly—even without the woman's aid.

Again Linus thought of Tabit—he had learned her name. As they approached the village, she had turned aside, pointing the way to her kinsman's hostelry. He remembered the withdrawn, shamed look in her eyes, the downcast tone of voice in which she had explained why she went no further. "It would be better for you not to be seen entering the town in my company," she had said. "I am... I have acquired a reputation." And she had walked away, leaving him to find the inn alone in the gathering darkness.

He went around the inn to the small lean-to at its back, where the guests' beasts were tethered for the night. The donkey was there, munching placidly on a mouthful of straw. Linus scratched the animal between the ears, checking again to see that he was properly secured and provendered. Hoisting his leather pack across one shoulder, he returned to the front and entered the inn.

Linus nodded once to the innkeeper, who was piling loaves into a basket for the evening meal. The carpenter carried his pack, the tools inside clanking softly, to the small cubicle which was his room. He laid it across the straw-stuffed pallet which took up most of the meager floor space in the tiny compartment, then returned to the common room. The innkeeper, his wife, and their half-grown son were gathering for the meal, along with two other travelers who had arrived during the day. A single tallow lamp sat on the table, which consisted of a rude plank, about a cubit-and-a-half in width, laid across two beams which the son had earlier dragged to the center of the room. When the meal was over, this simple fixture would be disassembled and stacked against the wall to allow the innkeeper and his family to make their beds on the hard-packed dirt floor.

As he approached the table, Linus's eyes quickly took the measure of the two latest arrivals to the inn. One was a portly, red-cheeked fellow with a ready grin and a loud voice. He reclined easily beside the board and bantered in a casual, natural manner with the innkeeper as the final preparations for the meal were being made. A merchant or peddler of some sort, thought Linus. The type of fellow who never meets a stranger.

But the other was as far removed from his companion in behavior as he was in build. A thin, slight man, he seemed withdrawn, gathered apart. Though he, as well, reclined by the board where the meal was being laid, an aura of aloofness enveloped him, isolated him.

Linus dropped a single denarius—his last—into the waiting hand of the innkeeper, then lowered himself to a straw mat beside the table.

The wife now shuffled toward them, holding a basket in either hand. One contained the loaves of yeast-bread which Linus had seen the innkeeper sorting earlier. The other held a few double-handfuls of dried dates and figs. She placed them on the table and, without ceremony, they all helped themselves to the contents of the baskets and began to eat.

After a few moments of silence, the innkeeper turned to one of the more outspoken of his guests and asked, around a mouthful of bread, "What news from the north?"

The traveler shrugged and chewed a moment more. "As usual, there is strife with the Zealots," he answered after swallowing. "They make trouble in Galilee, then run from the legions and hide among our hills. More than a few of our people have been set upon by one of their bands while traveling through the countryside. A locked and bolted door is scarcely defense enough against their thievery."

"A pox on all Jews," muttered the boy, seated beside his father. The innkeeper scowled darkly at his son, then glanced at Linus, who kept his gaze studiously averted. "Quiet, boy," the father growled. "These men aren't interested in your opinions."

"Not on all Jews," the other traveler interjected unexpectedly, breaking his silence. "I have met one, at least, who did me more good than harm."

His companion gave him an irritated look. "That isn't the first time I've heard you start down that path," he fumed, "but I have yet to hear you finish the tale of this mysterious, benevolent Jew." The quiet man gave no sign that he had heard. After a moment, the speaker shook his head in resigned disgust.

"How long have you known him?" asked the innkeeper softly, peering curiously at the still-silent man across the table.

"We met only yesterday," the first traveler explained. "I was coming south on the road from Caesarea, and met this fellow coming down from Ginaea. We were both southbound, so I suggested traveling together. But little enough comradeship he has provided. I might as well be walking with a deaf-mute." The other man still showed no evidence of having heard anything, so lost was he in whatever memory shrouded his awareness.

"Anyway, as I was saying," he continued, "it was a dry winter, so I fear the grain will be sparse and dear. Some have spoken of applying for relief to the procurator when he returns to Caesarea from Jerusalem."

"And well he should do something," snorted the innkeeper scornfully. "With all the tax money Pilate collects, surely he could spend a little of it for the aid of those whose sweat continues him in office! I doubt that the emperor would notice the lack."

"True enough," grinned the traveler ruefully as he selected another handful of fruit.

As the two men prated on about this and that, Linus surreptitiously studied the strange, silent traveler. He sat, picking absently at the food he cupped in his hand, in that solitary contemplation which even the hearty familiarity of the loud-voiced man beside his elbow could not penetrate. To Linus, he seemed as one who had lost the habit—perhaps from disuse—of ordinary communication with other humans.

The meal concluded with as little ceremony as it had begun: as soon as the food baskets were emptied of their contents the innkeeper, his wife, and son wordlessly rose and began putting away the utensils and removing the table for the night.

Linus went outside to relieve himself before lying down to sleep. Picking his way carefully back toward the inn in the starlit evening, he spied the slender form of the silent stranger, apparently returning from a similar errand. His curiosity was aroused as to what unexpected currents might roil beneath the remote, motionless exterior of this wanderer from the north. "You, there!" he called. "Wait a moment, won't you?" The other obliged, standing still in the darkness as Linus, still unsure of his footing, stepped cautiously forward.

"I am called Linus," the carpenter began as he drew even with the waiting stranger. "I journey north, toward Damascus. And you hail from Ginaea, near the Galilean border, isn't that so?"

The man nodded silently. Linus waited for him to speak, to no avail. "And what is it men call you?" Linus persisted, even deciding to risk switching from Greek to Aramaic; perhaps the more familiar tongue would loosen the other's voice. For several steps, Linus thought the man had chosen not to answer. Then, surprisingly, he spoke.

"I have been called many things by men. Once, so long ago now that it seems to have happened to another, I was called Janneus, son of Bannias. But then, for many years, no one used that name. Instead, I was called unclean, out-cast...leper."

Linus felt his skin crawl. Either this man was deluded, or he was deliberately exposing everyone about him to the most hideous death imaginable. Linus took a step backward involuntarily. "You... you cannot be... you don't look—"

"Oh, I'm healthy enough," the stranger said through a tense grin, "now." He stretched out a hand, baring his arm from beneath his tunic. He thrust the limb into Linus's face. "See? Not a blemish." He wiggled his fingers under Linus's nose. "As fine a hand as you'd ever want. Not so much as a fingernail missing. Not at all like before."

Linus knew now that he was surely confronting a madman. Would this fellow attack him? Was he dangerous as well as insane?

"You think me mad," the stranger stated flatly, looking away. "Not that I can blame you. There are moments, sometimes days, when I question my own sanity." He gave a mirthless chuckle. "Sometimes I think it might have been better, easier, had the Nazarene ignored our pleas..."

Before he could think, Linus gripped the other man's shoulder and spun him about. "Nazarene? Of what Nazarene do you speak?" He had the eerie sensation that he already knew the answer.

Instead of replying, the Samaritan stared back at Linus, as if he attempted to read some unconcluded tale in the face of this one who had accosted him. Finally, he said, simply, "You, too, then?"

Then the man, standing motionless in the darkness, began to tell his tale.

"I could not have been more than sixteen seasons old when the disease took me," he began in a cold, toneless voice. "For a time, I could hide it; the abscesses were small at first, and in places normally concealed by clothing. But eventually, as with all lepers, a cut on the hand becomes a running sore, then a rotting stench. And I was driven out. I suppose they really had no choice.

"An amusing thing happens when you have leprosy. In being cast out of your own family, your own country, you acquire a new family, a different nationality. You become a kinsman of every leper you meet, be he Jew, Samaritan, Syrian, or Greek. You become a citizen of a land with no borders, no cities, no houses. A land whose population is not augmented by births, but by deaths.

"I soon fell in with a band of nine other wretches. I think four of our number were Jews of Galilee, the rest Samaritan. It's easier, you see, with companions, because ten throats can make more noise than one. Ten lepers create a greater discomfort, a more immediate and acute uneasiness; the populace of almost any town will quickly open its purses to buy the absence of such a hideous congregation as we were.

"We had been wandering the border country between northern Samaria and southern Galilee for several seasons. That's the worst thing about leprosy; it can take years and years to kill you. A finger rots off one year, an ear the next, the nose the next, and so on—all with such patient, unhurried misery. And all the time one's belly requires filling, one is chilled by the rains of winter and roasted by the sun of summer. One is cursed and feared, shunned and hated and pitied and dreaded. I was a leper, and I knew that was all I could ever be."

He looked at Linus in the cold starlight, and his chin quivered as he said, "Do you have any idea what it is to squat in a gully at night and smell the reek of your own putrefying body? To see the decaying, shredded face of one of your fellows and know that yours is as bad, or worse? To see the same expression of disgust and horror in every single person you meet—and to feel in your soul that you deserve nothing else? To hold no higher aspiration upon awakening than that you will be able to scavenge enough of humanity's refuse to extend your miserable, pathetic existence for another night's sleep, another hopeless awakening? This," he said, his chest heaving with emotion, "this is leprosy. This is what I was. Until he came."

"At any rate, we were wandering the outskirts of Ginaea, staying close to the road that runs from Nazareth through Samaria to Jerusalem—the road which brought us to this very place, tonight. We would importune travelers as they came along the road, or beg from merchants as they made their way into or out of Ginaea. Oh, did I mention—" he asked, interrupting himself— "that Ginaea was the place of my birth? Not, of course that that made any difference. A leper has no home, no mother or father. One place becomes quite as good as another. Ginaea was simply where we were at the time. It might as well have been any other town in the area.

"When we saw the band of thirteen men traveling on foot, we suspected who they might be. Even the lepers had heard tales of Yeshua of Nazareth, the Jewish wonder worker who went about Galilee with his twelve comrades. They were walking toward the south, approaching Ginaea. I suppose they were on their way to Jerusalem for one of the festivals of the Jews. Why they chose to travel through Samaria, I will never understand…

We saw them, and began to shout, 'Rabbi Yeshua, Rabbi Yeshua! Have mercy on us!' Who knew? Perhaps they would at least give us a few coppers to buy our silence—" He broke off, trembling at the memory. After several swallows, he resumed.

"It was not difficult to see that we had guessed correctly, nor to determine which of the men was the teacher. When the others saw us, they fell back from him, as if to permit him room to work. Or, perhaps, to see what he would do. And he did—nothing! Nothing at all, except to cup his hands and shout back at us, 'Go and show yourselves to your priests!'

This was harsh comfort, indeed! As if the priest of any god would welcome the sight of ten lepers straggling into his temple, trailing their tatters of stinking flesh behind them. Go to the priests! I thought. As well might he say, 'Go to the Garden of Paradise and get a drink from Father Abraham's fountain!' I turned away, realizing that we would get nothing of value from this band of travelers.

"As I dejectedly walked away, I suddenly felt my eyes bulge from my head. I stared down at my right foot: five toes, where before there had been but four, and an oozing, wound where the fifth had been! And my ankle! The place which had been an open sore, running with pus, was now covered by skin as healthy and smooth as that of an infant!

"My breath coming in gasps of mingled hope and dread, I raised my sleeves to look at my arms. Clean! Not so much as a scar to show where the cankerous boils had been! Ripping my cloak in a gathering frenzy of delight, I stared at my chest, my belly. In a silent thunderclap of amazement, I realized that my leprosy was gone; vanished without a trace—as if the last years of relentless torment were but a horrible dream from which I had just awakened!

"As if from far away, I heard shouts and cries of joy coming from my nine companions. Without really knowing what I did, I turned and raced pell-mell toward the road into Ginaea, screaming, 'Yeshua! Master! Wait!' I caught up with them, and fell at his feet, embracing his ankles and blubbering like a child. I don't remember what I said, but I know that my heart contained but a single thought: 'Thank you! Thank you!' Over and over and over again..." These last words came in a husky, choked whisper, and Janneus fell silent.

Far off in the darkness, the yips of a wild dog racketed in staccato bursts up toward the silent stars. Linus contemplated the story he had just heard; a tale which, despite the undeniable authenticity of Janneus's anguish, strained the bounds of credibility. How was it possible for a leper to appear before him as Janneus of Ginaea now appeared; a man outwardly sound in body, even if scarred and limping in spirit? And how could anyone who had experienced such a miracle, bear a countenance and manner which spoke far more eloquently of grief and silence than of joy and celebration? There were pieces of the puzzle Linus could not quite juggle into place.

"Forgive me," Linus began softly after several moments, "but should you not be joyful and thankful for the wonder of your restored health? I should think you have much—"

Janneus peered at him with an odd, indefinable expression that silenced Linus instantly. "Much to rejoice over?" he queried, finishing Linus's sentence. "Much good news to share with those who waited at home, grieving over my misfortune? Much to tell of the wandering Jewish wonder worker who had saved the life of a Samaritan leper?" A harsh, short, bark of a laugh escaped him. "I fear that such an easy conclusion is not the way of this tale, my friend. My body was healed, true enough; but, you see, I no longer fit the place to which mankind had relegated me—indeed, to which I had relegated myself.

"When the leprosy took me, I was counted as one who had already died. Indeed, the one condition always produces the other, does it not? A recovered leper is an impossibility, a cipher who does not fit the world as we know it.

"Don't you see?" Janneus demanded in a tormented voice. "Though my body was cleansed, I was still—to others as well as myself—Janneus the Leper, a source of discomfort for anyone who had known me before. I was a living, breathing perplexity, a bothersome enigma which could not be put out of sight. When I was cast out, my place was vacated, smoothed over, occupied by other persons, other matters. And now I had returned, asking to be let back in the same position as before—but that position no longer existed. There was no longer room for me among my people, because no one imagined my space would ever again be needed. Worst of all, I was a nagging suggestion that reality does not always operate according to the customary rules. For those who are comfortable with the world they know," he said, staring pointedly at Linus, "miracles are unwelcome intrusions.

"And so," he finished wearily, "I left Ginaea, traveling south. Though the leprosy has left my flesh, it yet clings to my heart, sucking the marrow from my spirit. It seems that I must seek another healing—one which only the Nazarene can give. I will go to Jerusalem, or wherever he has gone, and ask him if the inner affliction may be banished, as well as the outer."

Linus's spirit sagged. He had encountered a broken one, an outcast whose life had been touched forever by the prophet from Galilee. He found himself lacking the heart to reveal the prophet's death.

What would Janneus do when he reached Jerusalem and learned of the death of his last refuge? As crippling as his delusion was now, what would happen to him when even that scanty shelter was snatched away?

"It grows late," he said finally. "We should be going in, before the innkeeper bolts his decaying door against us."

Janneus shrugged and turned to go with Linus. The two men, each nursing very different thoughts about the man from Nazareth, walked to the front of the inn. Glancing a last time at the night sky, Linus felt a sudden chill, as if the stars themselves breathed a cold indifference down onto the heads of benighted mankind. He shuddered and stepped quickly inside, closing the door behind him.

8

Linus probed the socket in the lintel above him, measuring with his hand both its depth and volume. As he peered upward to gauge the size of the opening, he blinked sweat from his eyes. Though it was scarcely midmorning, the sun was already promising far more warmth than the carpenter needed for his work.

The old door lay in splintered fragments at his feet. As soon as the dawn had given him sufficient light, Linus had begun dismantling the flimsy door of the inn.

Next, he would chisel the ends of the new post to fit the sockets in the lintel and threshold, creating at once the support and hinge for the door. He withdrew his hand from the hole above him and bent to study the end of the door post. He picked up his adze and made a dozen carefully placed strokes. He flicked the loose splinters away and lifted the post into place, socketing first the top end, with its longer taper, then settling the bottom end in place. He swiveled the post to and fro, simulating the motion it would make when in use. Assuring himself of the justness of the fit, he removed the door post from the sockets to begin the next phase of construction.

Removing a knotted leather thong from his tool bag, Linus measured again the size of the opening. Measure twice, cut once, he reminded himself. Walking to the nearby pile of rough-cut lumber, he selected two pieces which looked to be about the proper dimensions to serve as cross-beams, and dragged them over to where the door post lay.

A shadow fell across him as he worked. Linus looked up to see a large-boned, lantern-jawed man standing above him, arms akimbo as he critically eyed him and the work in progress. "I need a carpenter to build a bench and a table," the fellow blurted in a loud voice. "When you finish here, come to the stone house beside the large acacia tree." He jerked a thumb over his shoulder to indicate the place. "I'll show you what I need."

The man had spoken Aramaic. Linus nodded hesitantly and replied slowly, in Greek, "I will be happy to come to you as soon as I am able." The large man grunted once in satisfaction and strode off. Linus turned back to his work with a pleased arch of the eyebrows. As he had hoped, the sight and sound of his labor had given notice to the community of his availability for hire. He needed several more jobs to earn the silver required to carry him on his way toward Damascus.

Linus rummaged in his tool sack for the bow drill and its iron bit. He would drill through all the points where the framing pieces would join and pinion them tightly together with wooden pegs. This done, he would be ready to fasten the planks across the sturdy frame he had fashioned.

He twined the wooden shank of the bit into the thong of the drill and felt it stretch taut. Positioning the bit at the point on the crossbeam he had selected, he began manipulating the bow in a back-and-forth, sawing motion, as chips and shavings of oak twirled out of the hole he was drilling.

A motion in the doorway attracted his attention. The innkeeper's son stood in the opening, affecting nonchalance. Linus smiled inwardly. "Could you help me hold this steady?" he asked in Aramaic, noting the eager way the boy stepped forward to grip the beams in the place Linus indicated.

"Thank you," the carpenter said, receiving the lad's grateful nod in return. Linus turned back to his work. "What is your name?" he asked over his shoulder.

"Damon," the boy replied.

Linus finished the first hole, and moved his drill into position for the second. "Will you run an inn one day, Damon—like your father?"

"No," the boy answered quickly, to Linus's surprise. "When I am of age, I will leave Sychar, and I will travel as much of the world as I can. I don't ever expect to come back to this place." Long moments passed, with only the grinding and squeaking of the drill bit to break the silence.

"Tell me," the boy began shyly, ending the hush, "about the places you have seen. Where have you traveled?"

Linus thought long before replying. How much should this stripling, who had expressed such strong anti-Jewish sentiments, know of his origins and past? "I... I was born in Syrian Antioch," he began carefully. "I lived there for most of my life..."

"Antioch!" the boy breathed excitedly. "The capital! Did you ever see the legate, or any of his tribunes? Did you ever see the Syrian Legions on parade?"

"No, no," Linus laughed, "the legate doesn't commonly show himself in the precincts I frequented. And when I did see the legions, it was merely as a member of the roadside crowd watching some procession or other."

"I'd really like to see the legions one day," Damon said. "I've even thought, sometimes, that I might join. I'd only be able to get in one of the auxiliaries, of course. We don't have the citizenship..." His voice trailed off into a despondent silence.

Linus remembered the virulent spite of the Judean Auxiliary troops toward the people of Judea. It saddened him to think of this decent, simple boy amid such a vengeful, violent atmosphere. And again he realized the implacable wedge of mistrust which time and creed had driven between his blood and that of Damon.

"Why did you leave Antioch?" the youth now asked, as the carpenter prepared to drill the second hole at the intersection of the two crossbeams. "And whatever brought you to Palestine? Nothing exciting ever happens here."

With more care than was strictly necessary, Linus placed the bit on the wood. Just before he began drilling, he risked a quick glance at his companion. "What makes you think I crave excitement?" he asked, his voice a trifle sharper than he intended. "I left Antioch for... for reasons which are my own," he muttered, bending toward his work.

"I'm sorry," Damon said. "I didn't mean—"

Linus dismissed the apology with a shake of his head. "Never mind. Over there," he pointed, "by that pile of wood, are some round, slender rods. Bring two of them to me." The boy stood quickly, and strode off to do as ordered.

Linus blew the sawdust out of the hole he had just finished. Damon's last question had pricked him deeper than the lad could have imagined. Why, indeed? he asked himself. Why did I think that leaving Antioch would salve my pain, or that going to Jerusalem would answer my questions?

Damon returned, holding out two rods of peeled oak, branches trimmed from the same tree Linus had felled to provide the door post. "Yes, those will do," he said, taking the rods from the boy. "In my sack, there should be a large wooden mallet, and a hand axe. Bring them here." Damon rushed to comply.

Axe in hand, Linus held one of the rods against the place where the upper crossbeam lay across the door post. Marking the proper length with a scratch of his thumbnail, he chopped the rod into a peg long enough to join the two pieces, then another of the same length. Turning to Damon, he asked, "Did you see how I did that?"

The boy nodded.

"Good. Take the axe and chop pegs for here, here, here, and here," the carpenter said, indicating the remaining holes he had drilled. Eyes widening with delight, Damon reached for the axe.

Linus tapped one end of the peg into the crossbeam, then drove it, squeaking and protesting, through the beam and into the door post. The two pegs went home with a satisfying stubbornness that assured Linus of the sturdiness of the frame. He turned around to see Damon holding out two of the pegs he had cut. Placing them alongside the lower crossbeam where it lay atop the door post, he nodded in acceptance. "Well done," he said. "These pegs will do nicely." Damon basked in his approval.

"Eric, could you hand me the second clarinet folders, please?"

"Yes, ma'am."

I love this kid. The quickest way to any teacher's heart is "yes, sir" or "yes, ma'am." Out of fashion though it may be, politeness has often been known to transform a C-plus into a B-minus.

Eric and I are preparing the sight-reading folders for the advanced band, which will meet next period. Already I can feel the fluttery nervousness in the pit of my stomach. In a week, this group will compete at a local music festival, and an entire year's worth of self-esteem will be on the line for me. I keep telling myself that it's not that big a deal; the principal doesn't care what rating the band makes, the other teachers at my school don't care what the band makes, the kids' parents don't care. As long as the students enjoy their musical experience, learn something about their instruments, and no major felonies are committed during class time, no one is going to give a flip about what the judges think of the band's festival performance.

Except me. Anything less than a "superior" rating from every single judge on the panel will be taken by me as an indictment of my character, my professional integrity, and my fitness to continue drawing my paycheck. Well, maybe not quite that bad. You can forget the part about the paycheck.

I hate festivals, and I love them. I hate the jitters and the pressure I put on myself. I hate the despair that threatens to overwhelm me every time I realize that the evidence of my expertise consists of a single performance by a group of hormone-addled seventh- and eighth-graders.

But I love the challenge—the chance to pull it off. I love the opportunity to measure my efforts and those of my students against a standard. I love the feeling of confident relief that comes over me when the last note is played. The simple fact is—and I can never admit this aloud, for fear that the festival gods may punish my *hubris* —I am a good teacher, a good music coach. I know how to get kids ready for a performance. I know, in my gut, that the advanced band will play better on that stage than they ever have in this band room.

Sounds a little crazy, even to me, this schizophrenic amalgam of cautious confidence and neurotic fear of failure. It's how I imagine a sales person must feel before a major presentation, or an actor before an important audition. The only way out is forward.

Maybe I'm a little more on edge than usual because my college band director is on the panel. I've heard too much of the scorn he heaps on those he considers inept practitioners of the art and science of music education. I can't accept even the most remote possibility that I might qualify for similar treatment.

"Should I do the low woodwinds now, Mrs. Thompson?" Eric asks.

"Yes, Eric. And it's 'Miz,' remember?"

"Oh, yeah," he grins. "Sorry."

Eric reminds me of the golden retriever puppy my family had when I was a kid. He has the same sandy-red hair, the same eager-to-please grin, the same big-footed clumsiness that Butch had. He's a sweet youngster, and he lives and breathes for band class. I'm sure this doesn't impress too many of his nonmusical friends, but I don't think Eric cares. Too much.

I guess I was a lot like Eric. My earliest successes came in music, and I suppose I never forgot that. I still remember the first time I played a solo at a music contest. I was petrified. My lips were so dry I wondered that I could get any sound at all out of my cornet; my palms got so slippery I didn't think I could hold my horn; and I'm sure the judge saw my knees shaking. But, by some stroke of fate, I made a First Division rating—the best. Mom was so proud.

Dad was out of town, preaching at a revival. Probably through no fault of his own, in all fairness. Music wasn't really his thing, anyway.

I had to play the cornet, you see, because both my brothers had played the cornet. And I had not only to play it, but to play it better. So I did. I remember being almost the only girl in the cornet section in my high school band. All through junior high and high school, the boys hated it when I regularly clobbered them in auditions. But it didn't matter—not the way I wanted. Try as I might, practice diligently though I did, my accomplishments were generally qualified by my gender—or so it seemed to me. I got dreadfully tired of being "that good girl cornet player at Smithfield Junior High." How desperately I longed for an endorsement that never came in exactly the model and shade I wanted.

I went to the local college, got my music education degree, and got an assistant directorship at the same high school where I had attended. After a year or two, I took the band job at one of the local junior highs.

But it didn't work for me—not there. The problem wasn't the kids, not the teaching. There simply wasn't room enough in my hometown for me and my past. I came down with an acute case of biographically induced claustrophobia. The only cure I could figure out was distance, taken in liberal doses as needed.

Besides—it had to be less stressful for Dad with me out of town, right? Less wear-and-tear on his pastoral circuitry, without having to witness an intransigent daughter dashing her pilgrim bark repeatedly against the rocks below his gospel lighthouse.

And there you have it, Eric, my lad: the story of Miz Thompson's life, in four hundred words or less. Pretty exciting stuff, huh?

Get over it, Janice. I toss the second clarinet folders on top of the stack piled in the chair of Jamal Lewis, first chair clarinetist and section leader extraordinaire. I glance at the wall clock. Ten minutes until the next period starts. Eric is finishing the last of the woodwind folders.

"Eric, did you already do the percussion and low brass folders?"

"Yes, ma'am."

I love this kid. Polite *and* efficient. I mean—what are the odds?

L inus drove the last peg into its hole, then stepped back to look at the completed door which now hung in the entry to the inn. He nodded. The work was satisfactory. Only one touch left to make. He reached for his small chisel and carved his trademark onto the upper right corner of the outermost plank.

"What is that you're carving into the door?" asked Damon, peering over the carpenter's shoulder.

"My trademark," answered Linus. "By this mark, I identify all my finished work."

"Why two birds?"

Linus stared at the mark. "I...it reminds me...of someone. Someone I once knew."

The door swung open, admitting the innkeeper.

"Look, Father!" Damon beamed.

"Linus and I finished the door, and it's not even getting dark yet!"

The innkeeper's eyes swept quickly over his son's face to the completed door, then back to the carpenter. His gaze narrowed. "How much?" he grunted.

"Two *denarii* for the two day's labor, and three more for the door itself, as we agreed," Linus replied evenly.

The innkeeper grimaced, but reached into his robe, producing a wallet. Carefully, he uncinched its top and poured five silver coins into Linus's outstretched hand. But before the carpenter could put the coins away, the innkeeper snatched one of them from his palm.

"For your bed and board tonight," he said, pocketing the coin with a half-chuckle at his own cleverness.

"I will indeed sleep here tonight," Linus replied, "but I intend to eat elsewhere. Give me back the cost of my board." He dropped his wages into his pouch, then held out a hand to the innkeeper.

After a brief staring contest, the innkeeper reached back into his wallet. He dug about for a moment, and came out with two small silver *as* pieces and three copper *lepta*. He dropped the money disdainfully into Linus's palm and turned away. The carpenter began placing his tools in his bag.

"You are not dining with us this evening?" asked Damon softly, the disappointment plain in his voice and on his face.

"I have other work to do for one of your neighbors," the carpenter explained, "and I must go there and see the shape of the job. There is daylight left which I cannot afford to waste."

Linus glanced at the innkeeper, whose back was to them, then at the lad. "I will come back before I depart Sychar," he promised. "I cannot leave without bidding farewell to such an able apprentice. Oh, and here—" he whispered, fishing in his wallet and bringing out the two silver *as* coins. "Your wages," he winked.

Damon, grinning from ear to ear, took the money, glancing over his shoulder to make sure his father didn't see.

*****

Linus eased the tool bag to the ground in front of the stone house and knocked at the door in the gate. In a moment, he heard footsteps against the stones of the courtyard inside.

"Who's there?" a loud male voice shouted in Aramaic.

Linus recognized the sound of the large man who had engaged him. "It is I," he replied in Greek, "the carpenter you saw in front of the inn."

The steps slapped toward the gate, which was flung roughly open, barely missing the end of Linus's nose. "Come in," the large man bellowed in heavily accented Greek, beckoning him toward the house. "I didn't expect you until tomorrow, but come in, nonetheless."

Linus paced across the spacious courtyard toward the wide front door of the house. The prosperity of the dwelling's owner was evident in the fine dressing of its stones, the elegant carving of the wooden fixtures. Linus knew immediately that the large, loud man was well able to afford the cost of his craftsmanship.

"This way, this way," his host blustered, leading Linus through the main portal and into a foyer which opened onto yet another courtyard, around which were ranged the various rooms of the house: the scullery, the sleeping rooms, the main room for dining and the entertainment of guests.

"Woman!" the man bellowed, making Linus wince. "Come here! Bring water! Sit there," he finished in a softer voice which was still louder than warranted, pointing Linus toward a small bench against the wall.

In a few moments, a female appeared in a doorway across the inner courtyard, her head bent low in a posture of

113

submission, bearing a water jar and a handful of linens. She entered the foyer and glanced at Linus over her veil.

It was Tabit, the woman at the well! Her eyes widened for a heartbeat as she recognized him in the same instant, then she immediately knelt, without a word, and began to remove his boots.

"When you've refreshed yourself," his host commented, "join me in the main hall. That is where the table you will build is meant to be."

Linus nodded, and the man turned to stride across the courtyard. The carpenter had quickly ascertained from Tabit's manner and the harsh way the man had summoned her that it would not be advisable speak to her as if he knew her—at least not within the man's hearing. From the slope of her shoulders and the self-effacing droop of her head, he knew that her life with the master of this house must be anything other than happy.

When he heard his host's footsteps disappear into the doorway across the courtyard, Linus said in a low voice, "I thank you for sending your husband to look at my work by the inn. As you have heard, he has engaged my services. I am grateful—"

"I said nothing to him," she interjected in a low, fearful voice, without raising her head. "He doesn't permit me to speak to him, nor to anyone else when he can prevent it. He hired you for reasons of his own. And—" she drew a long, shuddering, breath— "he isn't my husband." She placed his boots to one side and poured water over his feet.

"Then, why—" began Linus.

"As I told you," she said, "I have acquired—earned, really—a reputation. I have no one; no other family, nothing. I do what I must to keep from starving. I have few choices."

Linus could not accept that Tabit's fate was completely without alternative. "Is there no one else in Sychar who can offer you shelter?" he asked softly. "Perhaps—" his mind grasped for any straw of logic or comfort to which he could appeal— "perhaps there is someone here who shares your empathy for the Galilean. Your kinsman at the inn, maybe? Would he not take you in and rescue you from this, this...degradation?" he finished sadly.

She looked away, across the courtyard. After a few moments, she shook her head slowly. "When the Galilean came, many heard his words. Some even said they believed in him. But," she continued, glancing back at Linus, "belief dies a far easier death than habit. Life in Sychar did not change greatly after he left," she sighed. "And any alteration which did occur was shallower by half than my yearnings taught me to hope for."

"Why are you telling me all this?" he asked. "I needn't have known about your... your arrangement with this man. You could have spared yourself that humiliation, at least."

She began wiping his feet with the linen. She rubbed and rubbed, longer than she need have. Linus thought she might have decided not to answer, until he saw her shoulders trembling with suppressed sobs. She reached for his boots. Then, for the last time, she raised her face to him, challenging him with her eyes. "When the Galilean came, he taught me to stop lying to myself. Having learned that, I can no longer lie to others. That choice, at least, remains to me."

She looked down and quickly laced the thongs of his boots. Without a word, she rose, picking up her jar and soiled linens, and trod swiftly away, across the courtyard toward the scullery. She went inside without looking back.

He began to see the true dimensions of the tragedy created by the crucifixion of Jesus of Nazareth. At first, he had supposed himself the only one troubled by the needless slaughter of one who was guilty of nothing more than an unwise choice of words. But within the space of a single day in Sychar, he had met two crushed human beings whose only hope lay in the memory of their experiences with the man Linus had seen nailed to a cross atop Golgotha.

And what of the woman, Tabit? What would she do when word traveled north, as it eventually would, that the strange preacher from Galilee, the one who had proclaimed himself to be the long-awaited *Taheb*, had met his end at the hands of the masters of Jerusalem's Temple?

Linus discovered a strange, illogical rage kindling in his breast; an anger at this wandering preacher whose words spawned such cruel trust in the souls of the misbegotten, the addled, and the oppressed. Was this not the height of callousness—to teach the hopeless to believe in him, but to prove powerless as the guarantor of the very misplaced devotion he had created?

*****

The sun striped the Plain of Esdraelon with long shadows as it gently sank toward the western horizon. Today's walk had been long and thirsty, but Linus was glad to be crossing into Galilee at last. He was out of Samaria, away from the need to be on constant guard with his speech. That, at least, would be some relief.

He had been so anxious to leave Samaria that he never considered seeking lodging in her borders. Instead, he resolved to press on until nightfall, and make camp wherever darkness found him.

Several times during the day, he had reflected upon the strange chances which, within a scant day's time of his leaving Jerusalem, had brought across his path two different individuals who had met the Nazarene, Jesus.

First, the woman Tabit, whose pathetic hope struggled for a tenuous life amid her shame and helplessness. Then, the deluded Janneus, who claimed to have once been a leper.

A worrisome thought entered his consciousness: Was he a member of the same bizarre company that boasted these two misfits? Was this the reason he could not shake the Galilean prophet from the folds of his memory—because he, too, was on the way to becoming as crippled, as dazed by despair as they? What other reason but impending madness could make a man do as he had done—leaving a secure trade behind to set out upon a road with no sure destination, for no good reason he could discover?

Was this, then, the common thread binding those who followed the Nazarene—that none of them could make sense of the world as they found it? Was this why they instead chose to dance to the insane flute of this improbable prophet—a leader who proved as helpless as they before the invincible forces of reality?

No! he told himself sternly. He was not going mad! If the Galilean had indeed called to something within his heart, it was not lunacy which answered. He could not explain all the fantastic tales about the Nazarene, which seemed to spring from the ground wherever he had walked. But Linus did not intend to become dependent on such flights from reality for comfort from the world he found about him.

What, then? Was it a madman's dream that summoned the throngs lining the road from Bethany to Jerusalem, the worshiping mobs who chanted the name of the Galilean as if welcoming a returning monarch? Was it merely a fool's delusion that had silenced the indignant, accusing Pharisees and officials in the Temple? And what of that single, heart-stopping moment when he had felt the gaze of the prophet sweep over him?

For the thousandth time, Linus asked himself, "Who was this man?" And, if he should discover the truth which lay behind Jesus of Nazareth, would his own soul survive the finding?

The last time he had allowed another human being into his heart, the unwanted leave taking had ripped him forever asunder. And besides, the Nazarene was already dead—why couldn't Linus leave him in his tomb? Why couldn't he finally bury the Galilean prophet and shed his memory along with the other events in this life which had promised so much and proved so fickle?

But the slain prophet would not die. Something indefinable worried at Linus's spirit, dogged the heels of his soul, and would not be put off the scent. He could not rest until the chase wound to whatever good or ill end was ordained.

Dusk settled thickly around him. He was approaching a fork in the road. He could take the right-hand way and come, within the space of a quarter-watch, to the Galilean village of Nain. The road to Nain lay across terrain which was mainly flat and unobstructed. Though night had fallen, the light of the full moon would be more than adequate, and he might even find food and a night's lodging there.

But the left-hand path would carry him to the more distant town of Nazareth, the home village of Jesus. Nazareth lay in the hills to the northwest of Mount Tabor, and it was too far and too difficult to reach in this darkness. If he chose the left road, the way would be complicated, would lead by winding, venturesome routes to some end he could not easily foresee. If he chose the left road, he sensed all other decisions would somehow be ordered.

He led the donkey from the road and began to seek a campsite.

9

I've been staring at the screen for about an hour now, and it has been staring back, and both of us are totally blank. My mind has been flitting among ideas like a caffeinated hummingbird, but I can't force it to settle and feed. I wonder if there's such a thing as selective attention deficit disorder. I seem to be able to concentrate on everything but the task at hand.

I suddenly realize that I need to make a trip to the library. A little research is just what I need to get the creative juices flowing. A few reference works on first-century Palestine and I'll be good as new. Any harbor in a calm.

While parking outside the library, I think about the possibility that I might see Maude while I'm here. Since her unexpected outburst at my last visit, I haven't encountered her. I find myself half-hoping for the meeting and half-dreading it. I still remember the odd, embarrassed appreciation I felt at her affirmation of my quixotic literary efforts, but I also cringe at the temptation to begin to trust her. After all, what evidence do I have to justify any confidence in her? Only a weird bit of emotional outpouring that probably left her as mystified as me. Or maybe it's simply that she's a little wacko. Or I am. Or both.

Enough of this, Janice, my girl. You're here, so you might as well accomplish something. I lock my car and walk up the concrete steps to the plate-glass-and-aluminum doors.

The air inside smells sedate and bookish, like old vellum or a 1964 Sears catalog. I enjoy the feeling I get walking into a library, almost any library. The sense of calm and scholarly detachment. The sheltering orderliness of the quiet pursuit of knowledge—or of information, at least. I punch the button and wait for the elevator. I hear the car dock with the squeaky stodginess of a royal barge. I go inside and slowly ascend to the third floor.

For a weekend afternoon, the number of patrons is a bit sparse, which suits me fine. I toss my green spiral steno notebook on the nearest table and browse among the shelves until I find a book that appears to contain something useful. I take it back to my table, dig through my purse until I find a pen, and open the volume to begin reading.

I hear what sounds like a squeaking wheel on a book cart. In this setting, it's as loud as a civil defense siren. I look up, slightly annoyed, and at the same instant Maude rounds the end of a nearby bookcase. She's pushing a cart stacked high with books for reshelving.

"Well, hello, Janice!" she beams. I feel an absurd pleasure that she's gotten my name right twice in a row.

"Hi, Mrs.—I mean, Maude. How are you?" I feel absolutely effusive today, for some reason.

"Fine, thanks," she says, coming over to my table. "Doing some more research on your book?" she asks.

I nod, then grimace. "Actually, I'm hiding out from my writer's block, and coming here was a convenient excuse."

She chuckles. "Well, I imagine you'll get back on track pretty soon. I always—did…" The end of her sentence trails off uncertainly, as if she's just betrayed a secret she meant to keep.

How can I refrain from asking? "So… are you… have you Done Some Writing?" Before thinking, I verbally capitalize the last three words of my question.

"Well…" She crosses her arms in front of her and stares off to her right. Her profile is lean, aquiline. I can see the place at the bottom edge of her jawbone where her pulse taps quietly. Then she smiles faintly down at me and looks away again. "I… at one time, I wanted to write," she begins hesitantly, "but… it didn't work out for me. Not like I wanted, anyway. I guess I just didn't have the gift. Or, maybe," she murmurs, her eyes avoiding me, "maybe it wasn't worth the trouble. There weren't as many options then. So, instead," she says, gesturing around her, "I work in the place where they keep the books. Not a bad tradeoff," she asserts. Case closed, she seems to say.

My turn. "I didn't really get interested in writing until I was out of college. But I've always been a voracious reader." I grin at a sudden memory. "In fact, my dad was always getting aggravated at me because I'd hole up in the bathroom with a book and lose all track of time and other people's necessities."

She smiles, until I offhandedly add, "I guess those were just the first of many times for Dad and me."

She peers sharply at me, then covers her mouth with her hand. I am shocked to see tears brimming in her eyes.

"Maude, I'm sorry! I didn't mean—"

She shakes her head. "No, it's not you," she says in a voice husky with feeling. "It's… just… I'm remembering so many things by talking with you. Excuse me, I have to go now," she says, wheeling about and making for her book cart.

"Maude, wait! I—"

But she's gone, vanishing into the insulating mustiness of the stacked books.

Yeshua?" the old man asked, scratching his scraggly, brownish-white beard. "There have been scores of boys named 'Yeshua' living in Nazareth during my days." He peered up at Linus from the place where he squatted beside his market stall. "Why is this information so important to you, anyway?"

Linus knelt, to bring himself eye-to-eye with the grizzled, leathery-faced potter. The man's clothing was soiled with the traces of his craft, every crease in his hands and the under-side of each fingernail filled with the leavings of the clay he had, surely for all of his life, worked into the utensils which surrounded him on his straw mat. His eyes were a watery, time-stained amber and they now flickered over Linus's face with a wary, questioning look.

Linus had been in Nazareth since the last sundown. Coming today to the market to purchase food, he had noticed that almost every person paused at this potter's stall to exchange pleasantries, if not to make a purchase. It seemed that the gnarled old man with the gap-toothed smile knew everyone in Nazareth. Linus decided that he would be a logical person to ask about the prophet who had come from this place.

"I am curious, nothing more," Linus explained to the dubious artisan. "I have journeyed from Jerusalem, where this man Yeshua was… was followed by many."

The old man's eyes narrowed, but he said nothing.

"As I have walked north," Linus continued, "I have often reflected on many of the things he said—things which were strange, unlike anything I have heard before. Things which confuse the ears but beguile the heart." Nothing about the potter's posture or expression gave Linus the slightest hope that his queries would find satisfaction with this man. But he was too far advanced to halt now. "I have come here to find those who might be able to help me learn more about this man from Nazareth. Many in Judea believe he is… a prophet."

The potter's eyes widened a fraction, but the rest of his face did not so much as twitch.

"I was hoping," Linus finished weakly, "that you might be able, at least, to direct me to someone who knew—who knows him."

A long silence hobbled past on leaden feet. Just as the carpenter was about to concede defeat and rise to leave, the potter gestured toward his handiwork.

"Do you see anything here you like?" he asked Linus. "For more than three-score years, I have made my pots, urns, and pitchers; my lamps and dishes and cups. I have made them on my wheel and brought them here, to the market-place, to sell them, as did my father before me. Do you see something that pleases you?"

Linus, taken aback by the unexpected solicitation, struggled for words. "I... well, I—your work is very fine, certainly, but I am traveling—"

"Each vessel in my shop," continued the old man, as if Linus had not spoken, "is made for a specific use. For example," he said, picking up a shallow bowl, "this bowl is ideal for serving food, such as fruit or bread. But it would hardly be suitable for storing or transporting oil. For that," he went on, putting the dish back on the mat and pointing toward a large, two-handled urn at the back of the stall, "one needs something more on the order of that big one, over there. Don't you agree?" he asked, grinning at Linus.

"Yes—of course. But what—"

"So, then, I have observed this principle in my years in this trade," the potter said. "That which is perfect for one purpose may be hopelessly inadequate for another. In fact," he said, wagging the knuckle of his forefinger for emphasis, "even a flawlessly crafted vessel may be useless if put to an incorrect application."

The eyes peered brightly out of the old, chestnut-brown face, as if the potter waited for some gleam of enlightenment on Linus's face. But all the carpenter could do was shake his head in helpless bewilderment.

The aged tradesman chuckled softly at the other's befuddlement. "You don't smell like a Roman informer," the potter said finally, "so I'll venture to speak without riddles. What I am saying, man of Judea, is this: before you go about Nazareth asking questions about Yeshua bar-Yosef, you had better decide what it is you want to find. Even among those who knew him as a child; who know the family for several generations back, this fellow is a puzzlement. One even hears talk of suspicious circumstances surrounding his birth." He studied the ground between his ankles for a moment, then resumed, squinting one eye at Linus as he spoke. "You may meet those who think, like your southern friends, that he is a prophet. You will certainly find those—especially, perhaps, in Nazareth—who believe him a fool."

Thoughtfully, the aged potter ran a calloused thumb along the rim of the dish in front of him. "For myself, I couldn't blame this dish for my troubles if I were so foolish as to employ it for carrying oil. It hardly seems fair to curse the vessel for the deficiencies of the user. Of course," he sighed, "I am old and tired, so I probably don't understand everything I hear. And it has been many a long year since last I saw the oldest son of Yosef the woodcarver. But still, I say to you—" he fixed Linus with a strange, guarded stare—"that the end of the search lies, in part, within the soul of the searcher."

Linus walked slowly from the market square, nibbling thoughtfully on the *matzah* bread and parched lentils he had bought in the market, as well as the advice given him by the old potter. He allowed his feet to carry him randomly along the streets of the hillside town. Nazareth was a small place, and it didn't take Linus long to pace each of the dusty tracks between its few nondescript buildings. He turned to go back toward the place where he was staying when a chance sound, drifting along the still morning air, halted him in his tracks.

It was the steady *thok—thok—thok* of a mallet on wood.

...the eldest son of Yosef the wood-carver...

Linus cocked an ear to place the direction of the sound, and slowly worked his way to a squarish building formed of the same sun-baked clay bricks as the rest of Nazareth. From inside the open doorway, Linus could hear the familiar sounds made by a fellow tradesman. This was a carpenter's shop. Might it be...?

He peered through the doorway into the darker interior of the shop. Presently he could make out the form of a man huddled over a piece of work, trying to force some recalcitrant part of his project to fit. Linus could hear him muttering complaints under his breath as he struggled.

Stepping through the doorway, Linus gratefully inhaled the sturdy, grained scent of freshly worked wood. The occupant's back was still turned to him as he came near and laid a hand on one end of the beam the unknown carpenter was working.

"Here," Linus said softly, "let me hold this part steady for you."

The other man cocked his head about. The face regarding Linus was youthful, but with the lines of a habitual scowl etched deeply into its contours. His eyebrows knit together as he studied this stranger who had wandered uninvited into his shop. After several moments, he shrugged and turned back toward his work.

Linus could now see that it was a plow which lay across the workbench. Apparently, his taciturn host's difficulty lay in getting the handle of the implement braced at the desired angle. With Linus stabilizing the beam and the shank, the other man was soon able to peg the handle in the proper position. When the dowel was driven into place, he glanced darkly at Linus.

"Thank you," he mumbled, in a tone which added silently, "Now get out."

Linus cast about for something to say which might warm the chilly indifference of his host. He spied a saw blade, forged of iron, and hefted it appreciatively.

"Ah!" he sighed, "a saw of iron! I've been meaning to replace my old bronze blade with one of these, but I've never been able to gather enough silver to afford the iron! Tell me—does it cut as easily as I've heard tell?"

The other man stared at him for a very long time—weighing, calculating. Linus met the other man's gaze, smiling gently into the stony, closed face.

Then the silent man tossed a cubit-length of oak toward Linus and turned away, back toward the plow.

Accepting the mute invitation, Linus braced the oak against the workbench and drew the serrated blade across it several times.

"It truly is better than bronze!" he commented. "And I suspect it holds an edge far longer, also. Is this true?"

The other man nodded and went back to his work.

"Let me help you with that," Linus offered, as the Nazarene carpenter prepared to remove the plow from the workbench. The two men moved the implement to a corner of the shop. As they set the plow down, Linus noticed a half-finished bench near the wall.

"I've built a few like that one, myself," he said, pointing at the bench, "and—if you'll permit me—the piece will be much stronger if you'll cross-brace it here, and here." He drew a finger through the air to clarify his meaning.

The other man peered from the bench to Linus for several heartbeats. Then, finally, he spoke. "Show me." His face and arm-crossed posture were skeptical, yet curious.

Linus carried the bench to the worktable. He looked about until he found two pieces of wood which appeared to be about the right dimension. With forearm and fingers, he measured the space in which he meant to place them. He quickly cut them to length with the iron saw, and held them in the intended position, turning about to show the Nazarene how they fit.

As he looked at Linus's work, the man slowly began to nod. "That would make it stronger," he admitted grudgingly. "I should have thought of it myself."

"Oh, I didn't come up with this idea," said Linus quickly. "The master carpenter to whom I was apprenticed showed me this little trick. I've found it to be pretty useful, though— and not just on benches."

The other man was still studying the alteration with half-squinted eyes. Then, glancing back at Linus, he said, "I thank you for your trouble." There was another pause, as if he was coming to some sort of painful decision. "I—I am Yehudeh," he admitted finally, "known to some as Jude. How are you called?"

"Peace to you, Yehudeh of Nazareth. I am Linus, a carpenter of—well... late of Jerusalem, but on my way elsewhere."

"Jerusalem... I have people who are due back from there soon," Jude said.

"Your people—they went up for the Passover?" Linus asked.

Jude nodded.

In the silence that followed, Linus considered carefully the best way to frame his query. "While I was in Jerusalem," he began, "I heard of a man from here—a man named Yeshua, or Jesus. On my way, I thought to come through Nazareth and see—those who could tell me of him."

Jude gave a harsh bark of a laugh and turned away, busying himself with another piece of work.

Puzzled by the strange response, Linus nevertheless continued. "An old man in the marketplace told me that this Yeshua is the son of Yosef the woodcutter. You are a carpenter... surely you know this Yosef?"

After a long hush, Jude muttered a muted, despondent answer: "Yes, I know him—or knew him. I am his son."

A chill clasped Linus's heart. This was a brother of the man he had seen nailed to a cross atop Golgotha. He had come to this place hoping to find someone who knew Yeshua of Nazareth, but now... now his throat was paralyzed by the sudden enormity of his contribution to the bereavement of this Galilean family. Quietly, carefully, Linus spoke. "You said, 'knew.' Is... is your father—"

"Dead?" interrupted Jude, planing savagely on a piece of acacia wood. "Yes, he is dead. Ten seasons past."

There was a deep-rooted resentment in Jude that Linus didn't understand. Some wound, some splinter festered hot in his heart. It stained his spirit, Linus sensed, colored all the world upon which Jude gazed. That he was brother to the dead prophet Yeshua made his antipathy all the more intriguing—and unsettling.

"Tomorrow is the *Shabbat*," Linus observed, still treading gently about the perimeter of his misgivings, "and the week of Passover is ended. When will your people return?"

Jude shrugged. "My mother is old and weak. My brother James is with her, but still, their travel will be slow. Four days; five—I don't know."

His mother. The old Galilean woman, keening at the foot of the cross... Linus's vision blurred with the sudden recollection of a jagged, piercing grief.

"You have come from Jerusalem," Jude was saying. "We had word Yeshua was going there for Passover. This is why our mother compelled James to take her to Judea." Linus knew what was coming, and dreaded it. "What can you tell me of my—of Yeshua? Did you happen to see him before you left Jerusalem?"

The world swirled about Linus's head. What answer to give? How to fit the experiences of those fateful few days into words that would make any sense?

"Yes," Linus managed, finally, sitting heavily on a nearby sawhorse. "I saw him. Several times, in fact, over the last several months."

The rhythm of the planing slowed, then resumed.

"Do you know, by any chance, whether he will return this way with Mother and James?"

His voice feigned indifference, but Linus could tell that Jude had more than passing interest in the answer.

What could he say? His throat ached with indecision, his mind recoiled from the sharp, serrated edges of the truth. He had run away from this anguish once in Jerusalem and twice more in Sychar—only to find it crouched across his path yet again; here, in a carpenter's shop in Nazareth. The words burning in his throat, Linus realized the time of confession had come

"He... he is dead," Linus stammered, his temples throbbing with the effort. "Crucified."

The plane clattered to the work table. Linus could see Jude swaying, then steadying himself with a white-knuckled grip on the sides of the table. Still he had not turned to face the bearer of the tidings.

"When?"

"On the day before the Passover began."

"On whose order?"

Linus considered. Should he locate the blame on Pilate? Or should he reveal the real reason—the unquenchable enmity of the Temple establishment?

"It was... it was the High Priest who caused his death." Even his own ears rang at the treasonous sound of his words.

From Jude there was a short, sharp intake of breath; a sob he sought to stifle had suddenly escaped. He bowed his head and muttered in a flat, clenched voice, "I cannot say I am surprised. Time and again we tried to warn him, but to no avail."

Suddenly Jude wheeled about with a wild, angry look. "Do you know what Yeshua once said to us—the members of his own family? Would you like to hear the words of this—this prophet?" He did not pause for a response.

"We had begun hearing things: strange, incredible stories of crowds following him through the hills of Galilee, tales of bizarre teachings that flew in the face of accepted tradition. My brothers and I were indignant. Not only had he abandoned his family, but now he was also heaping reproach upon us by spouting insanities throughout Galilee! We decided to go and take him in hand, before he became the ruination of us all. And we would have done it, too... had not Mother insisted on going with us.

"It was not difficult at all to locate him, for as soon as we entered the town where he was, the sound of the crowd drew us toward the place where he had gathered with his— his followers. There were scores of people there! And such people! Cripples, blind, beggars... and Pharisees, wealthy women, and palace officials from Jerusalem! All were trying to crowd into the house where he was giving forth his... his teachings, if one could call them that. We could scarcely believe our own eyes—and yet there they were. Straining and shoving and circling to get at him—this one who had walked away from his own household! Only Mother seemed unsurprised.

"It was impossible to penetrate the mob, so we told one of those on the fringes of the crowd who we were, and why we were there. I will never forget the expression on that one's face when we said we were the family of Yeshua of Nazareth. It was as if we had told him we had just fallen down from the moon. I could see it all in his eyes: 'The brethren of that one!' he said to himself, and then in the next instant, as he looked us up and down, 'But they are so... so *ordinary*!' "

"To this we had come, you see! We were no longer the sons of Yosef of Nazareth, respectable tradesmen of Nazareth—no! We were the brothers of Yeshua the wonder worker—those who could only suffer by comparison! We, who stayed in our proper places, were now the lesser, the questionable ones! Is it not a great joke?

"While the messenger was working his way through the crowd into the house, I managed to elbow my way close to a window. I was standing there when the man we sent finally reached Yeshua's side, and was able to make himself heard. 'Your mother and your brothers are standing outside,' he said, 'wanting to speak to you.'

"Do you know what he said then?" Jude asked. "Do you know what my... what Yeshua said in answer?"

Linus wanted to spring up and run away. He wanted to escape the awful, vengeful grief wringing the very soul out of Jude as he spoke. But he could not. Jude's misery pinioned him fast to his place on the bench like a bird bewitched by a snake's lidless gaze.

"He said, 'Who are my mother and my brothers?'" Jude was trembling with emotion from this repugnant memory he had been zealously guarding all the days since.

"As if that were not insult enough, he gestured at those gullible fools sitting at his feet, those stinking beggars and those spittle-licking Temple functionaries, and he said to them all, 'Here are my mother and my brothers! Whoever does God's will is my brother and sister and mother!'

"I was afraid to tell them. I was so angry that I was afraid mouthing the words would make me want to kill him! But do you know what Mother said when I told her?" The answer came in a choked half-whisper. "She said, 'Then we must go. We mustn't hinder him.' And she turned and began to walk away!"

The recollection overcame him. He smashed his fists against the worktable, then fell face-forward onto his arms and wept like a lost child.

As Linus looked helplessly on, deep, wrenching sobs wracked the frame of the carpenter of Nazareth, confusion and sorrow draining from him in a dark, thick, costly flood.

After several moments, he began by degrees to gain control of his emotions. Finally, wiping his face on a dusty sleeve, he pushed himself upright. "I have often asked myself, Linus of Jerusalem, why I cannot simply put him out of my heart. It should be easy, shouldn't it? After all, here is a... a brother—who has turned his back on his family, who has preferred strangers for no better cause than their willingness to listen to his prattle, who has shown disrespect even for his own mother! Why should I not cast his memory from me, rid myself of every hateful trace of him?"

Jude looked away, drew a deep shuddering breath, and peered directly into Linus's eyes. "And yet, I tell you, that despite all this, hardly a day goes by that I do not think of his leaving with regret. I wish—" he looked away a moment, swallowing hard as he struggled again with his feelings, then back at Linus— "I wish that I could, just once more, talk with him. Or... even—" Jude's head was shaking, as if he could not believe the thoughts that came to him— "even ask for... for pardon."

Linus felt as if fists had been pummeling his chest. The nameless need of this forsaken brother, the tragic lack that could never now be filled, was sucking the marrow from his spirit. He stared ahead into darkness. And then Jude spoke a final time.

"But now, you say, it's too late for that." He turned again to his worktable, and took the plane in his hand.

10

L inus could not stay in Nazareth. Having grappled with the gaping, insoluble pain of Jude, the brother of Jesus, he could not force himself to await the coming of the prophet's mother. Before sunup he set off on the road to the towns clustered along the western shore of Lake Tiberias: Capernaum, Tabigha, Magdala, and, of course, Tiberias, the district capital.

He reflected that traveling on the Sabbath was becoming a habit for him; the last two occurrences of the Day of Rest had found him on the road. And, in both instances, he suddenly realized, he was trying to escape the spiritual discomfort engendered by confrontation with the life or death of Jesus of Nazareth. The Galilean was, it seemed, an absolute catalyst for agonies of the soul. Perhaps the relentless questioning would, after all, lead him to some end, though he had no intimation of what that end might be. The donkey snorted and tossed its head. Feeling the animal's backward tugging, he yanked impatiently on the lead rope. "Come on, you," he muttered absently.

If there was some message to be gained in this chain of events, he decided, it had better manifest itself more plainly than it had thus far. For Linus had experienced only a slowly deepening sense of despair, and the profound conviction that the riddle of life lay forever beyond his grasp, and perhaps that of all mankind.

The donkey gave a loud bray, and planted itself, legs splayed, firmly in the middle of the road. Linus was yanked backward by the sudden, recalcitrant weight at the other end of the lead rope. Provoked by the beast's sudden, unyielding stubbornness, he wheeled about, jerking with all his strength on the halter. "What's the matter with you?" he shouted at the donkey, who would not be budged. "Do you see an inn nearby, or a well? We have many leagues to cover today, and this is not the way to—"

Suddenly the road behind the donkey was occupied by four rough-looking men, conspicuously armed. Linus turned slowly about and, true to his fears, four more men blocked that way, as well. One of them, presumably the leader, stepped forward.

He strode to within an arm's length of the carpenter, then looked him carefully up and down. His eyes flickered to the pack strapped to the donkey, then back to Linus. "It appears that, like Balaam of old," he began in well-modulated Aramaic, "you would have been well served to listen sooner to your beast." An easy smile played over his face as he spoke. "Although I doubt that the outcome would have been much different. Though we are scarcely angels," he finished, as some of his men began to grin, "you would still have been hard-pressed to evade us."

Linus carefully kept silent, never allowing his eyes to stray from the chief robber's own. After a few moments, in which each man took the measure of the other, the leader of the band broke the silence. "What's in the pack?" he asked in clipped tones, his eyes losing their genial sparkle.

"Only the tools of my trade, sir," replied Linus. "I am a carpenter, traveling from Jerusalem to… to Damascus. Please allow me to pass."

"From Jerusalem? Are you, then, a son of Abraham?" the leader asked, switching smoothly to very good, albeit northern-accented, Hebrew.

Linus nodded. "I am," he replied, in the same tongue.

"Why, then, do you travel on the Sabbath?" asked the other.

Linus considered carefully, then decided he had little to lose. "One might be forgiven, sir, for asking you the same question," he responded in a voice which gave no evidence of fear, "since the excellent quality of your Hebrew—not to mention your accurate knowledge of the ancient stories of the Exodus—bespeaks your own Jewish upbringing."

The leader's eyes flashed at Linus. After several tense, heart-pounding moments, he allowed a sardonic grin to peek through the thick, dark curls of his beard. "Well and truly said, good carpenter," he admitted. "And yet, these are desperate days, and sometimes desperate men must do other than they wish—even on the Sabbath."

The leader gave a signal, and one of the others stepped forward to inspect the pack. Tugging the ropes aside and peering at the contents for a moment, he stepped back. "It's as he claims, sir," the fellow said tersely, "nothing but hatchets, saws, drills—he's a carpenter, all right."

The leader nodded. "Very well, then." Turning his eyes back toward Linus, he tapped a forefinger thoughtfully on his chin. "As you must know, carpenter, we customarily exact a small tribute—a highway tax, if you will—from those who travel the roads of Galilee."

Especially from those who travel alone, thought Linus.

"We are not common highwaymen, you must understand. We are, on the contrary, *un*common highwaymen, which is an entirely different matter!"

At this little jest, some of the men began to snicker. Very amusing, thought Linus. He was mentally calculating the amount of silver in his pouch, and how plausibly that sum could be presented to the bandits as all he owned. With any luck at all, they would take the few denarii in his wallet and not find the rest of the money, secreted in the concealed pocket at the bottom of his tool pack.

"And so, we must collect from you, carpenter, since you have the good fortune to be traveling abroad on the same Sabbath as ourselves…"

Get on with it, then, thought Linus. Name your price, or take what you will—only let me be on my way with my blood still in my veins.

"…and the further good fortune for us, as it happens, for we are needing the services of a skilled carpenter."

Linus looked quizzically at the man. "You… you need a carpenter?"

"That is correct," the other assured him. "We have a number of mattocks, axes and other, ah… implements which are badly in need of rehafting and other such refurbishment as you may be able to provide. And so, my friend, I offer you this choice: will you pay for your passage in silver or in labor?"

Linus considered for the space of several heartbeats. "I suppose you'll want to blindfold me," he observed at last.

The bandit chief nodded, and grinned. "I suppose we shall."

O, do not let the word depart,
And close thine eyes against the light.
Dear sinner, harden not your heart!
Be saved, O tonight!
O, why not tonight?
O, why not tonight?
Wilt thou be saved?
Be saved, O tonight!

Evidently, my emotional wavelengths are at a negative polarity with those of the person who selects hymns for the worship at this place. Once again, I find myself reliving a memory from my Sunday school experience that is highly detrimental to my chances of taking away anything useful from this assembly of the saints.

This song was one of my father's favorites, guaranteed to bring weeping sinners down the aisles at the end of a revival sermon. I suppose it was the dirgelike contours of the melody, the imploring quality of the lyrics that appealed to his sense of spiritual *pathos*. When I was a child, "O Why Not Tonight" seemed to have forty-seven stanzas, with the mournful chorus inserted between each. It was longer than the *1812 Overture*, and not anywhere near as interesting.

But it wasn't until I wandered into the thickly wooded morass of adolescence that the true, pernicious qualities of this hymn became manifest.

I hadn't yet made what my family termed a "salvation decision," and the pressure was beginning to mount. Nobody said anything, and that, of course, made it worse. As many adolescents will attest, absolutely nothing is required to make you feel guilty during these years. You feel guilty just for some of the things your body is doing without your permission. If acne, braces, and your first period aren't collectively the mark of Cain, it's just because they slipped God's mind at the time. Add to that the tacit, tight-lipped, forced nonchalance of a family eagerly waiting for you to hurry up and decide to save your immortal soul, and you have all the ingredients for the making of a serial killer. I couldn't even make up my mind about what blouse to wear to school on Tuesday, yet everyone expected me to walk to the front of a crowded church and announce my determination to lean on the everlasting arms? Get serious.

Well, matters had come to this pass when I found myself in attendance at one of Dad's evening revival services. I don't know why I hadn't found some excuse to be absent— no homework that night, no ball games scheduled, whatever.

I was seated on the aisle, about halfway back. Dad came to the end of his sermon and gave the invitation. The congregation leaned tiredly forward into "O Why Not Tonight."

And there my father stood, in the pulpit, staring directly at me.

By the beginning of the second verse, every eye in the sanctuary was on me, even though they were studiously peering at their hymnals—on me, the strong-willed preacher's strong-willed daughter who was still outside the fold. He might as well have been pointing at me; his eyes never left me as the woeful words tolled like funeral bells:

> *Tomorrow's sun may never rise*
> *To bless thy long-deluded sight.*
> *This is the time—O then, be wise!*
> *Be saved, O, tonight...*

The angry, embarrassed tears burned my face as I stared back at him. Why was he doing this to me in front of all these people? This was emotional, spiritual blackmail—he was trying to bully me into salvation! I remember locking my knees to keep myself in place. I remember feeling as if God and all the patriarchs were glaring at me over his shoulders, their all-seeing eyes lining both sides of the threatening road to the soul's sweet abode. I remember feeling terribly, fearfully, finally alone. And still he stared at me, daring me to step into the aisle, daring me not to.

I think it was in those awful, alienated moments, that I began to hate my father. I think it was then that our undeclared war of attrition began.

The memory floods my eyes, grapples at my throat. It rises up inside me with a constricting, twisting suddenness. I can't stay in here—I've got to get out before my past asphyxiates me.

Blindly, I stumble upward with a mumbled "Excuse me, please," and somehow get to the aisle without falling over anyone's ankles. I'm sure everyone in the sanctuary must be staring at the crazy lady bolting for the door, but I don't notice or care. I hit the church door at almost a dead run and stagger outside.

I gulp the moist night air and hear, as if from the other side of a wall, a warbling wail of grief which, I realize suddenly, is coming from me. I bend over double, hold my face in my hands, and weep uncontrollably.

And then, someone is there with me. Strong, dry hands are pulling at my shoulders, and thin, wiry arms are enfolding me. I spend my pain and confusion on a bony, comforting shoulder which smells of "Jungle Gardenia," and presently hear a voice, slightly on the brittle side, whispering over and over, "It's all right... it's all right..."

By degrees, I realize Maude has come outside to console me. I can't look her in the eye; the weight of my shame and embarrassment keeps dragging my head down. But she doesn't seem to care. I feel her hand pat, pat, patting between my shoulder blades.

"I... I'm sorry I made such a scene. I don't know—something just sort of hit me all at once." To my deep chagrin, I notice that my voice is still wobbly, off-balance.

"That's all right, honey," she assures me. "You looked like you needed some help, so I just came on out." She makes it sound like nothing more out-of-the-way than loaning a cup of sugar to a next-door neighbor. I don't believe her, but I am pathetically grateful for her graciousness.

"That song they were singing... I...it reminded me of—" The log jam of emotions constricts my throat again, and I feel Maude's arm sliding around my shoulders.

"You don't have to talk about it right now, sweetie," she soothes. "There's plenty of time for that later—whenever you're ready."

I can't disappear into the bowels of a library; I can't dash away and cower in private with my pain. The luxury of avoidance is not afforded me. I can only stand here uncam-

ouflaged in the soft, velvet night of early spring and allow
Maude to witness, to share and to solace, still unknowing, a
grief whose amplitude I had not, until now, admitted to
myself.

Through the closed doors, we can hear the congregation
arrive, with a sigh and a slump, at the end of the song. A few
precocious crickets are plinking out tentative *pizzicati* in the
cool March evening. Even through my muzziness, I can feel
the honeyed stillness, the floral-scented calm of the night. I
realize that within moments the service will be over, and the
worshipers will be leaving the church house. I don't want to
be standing here when they begin to come. I manage to find
a crumpled, slightly used tissue in my purse, and begin
daubing at my eyes.

"I guess I might as well go on home," I say, giving
Maude my best imitation of a smile. "I think they're about
finished in there, anyway."

"Yes, I expect so," she answers, without taking her eyes
off mine. "Are you going to be okay?"

"Yeah, I'm fine," I say, sniffing and wiping my eyes a
final time. "And... I really appreciate your coming out here.
It... it means a lot." To my amazement, I realize that I'm
telling the truth.

"Well, never mind about that," Maude says, giving my
arm a little squeeze. She peers at me a final time. "Maybe I'll
see you soon—down at the library?"

"More than likely."

I turn and walk toward the parking lot, just as the church
door opens for the exiting congregation.

The linen bandage was suddenly ripped from his eyes,
and Linus stood, swaying and sightless, in the harsh sunlight on the Tiberias road. He had been stumbling
blindfolded over the rough, hilly trail for half the morning,

and it took some time for his eyes to adjust to the glare of the Galilean sun.

"Yonder lies the lake," rasped the lieutenant, whose duty it was to see Linus safely on his way. The highwayman pointed east, to a flat, blue line against the horizon. "And there is Tiberias. This road will carry you into the town without further trouble. Unless, that is," he finished, his voice dropping in a warning, "you try to spy on our return route."

"I don't believe you have any worries there," Linus responded quickly, massaging his eyes. "I've been delayed long enough on my journey, thanks to your lot. No one has less desire to see the last of you than myself."

"He's a saucy one, ain't he?" muttered one of the ruffians threateningly.

"Aye," agreed the lieutenant, "but John asked us to see him safely away, and we're obligated to do so. Now off with you," he said to Linus in a rough voice. He slapped the donkey on the rump, startling the beast and sending it at a tight, stiff-legged trot down the trail, the tool sack clanking on its back. Linus ran to catch up with his animal, followed by the raucous laughter of the thiefs.

Ambling along the path which led down out of the hills toward the lake shore, Linus reflected on the time he had spent in the camp of the highwaymen. The band's redoubt was a vast cavern in the Galilean hill country. Linus remembered stumbling inside from the close, rocky defile along which they had approached, and the immediate sense of volume, a cool, opening-out sensation that told him he was in a place of some size. The cave was lit only by flickering tallow lamps and, here and there, a pitch-covered pine knot wedged into a crack in the rock wall.

The leader had approached him soon after the blindfold was removed. "Welcome to our humble home," he smiled, spreading his arms to encompass the huge, dark chamber.

"When one must hide from the legionary eagle, it is best to be underground."

"This should suit your purpose admirably, then," commented Linus drily.

"The hills of central Galilee are honeycombed with caves such as this, and we can move among them with ease. In similar places our ancient fathers hid themselves and their crops from the Midianites and Amalekites, before the days of Gideon." They had passed under one of the sputtering, hissing torches of pitch. The leader paused, glanced at Linus, and said, "I believe that I will trust you with my name. I am John of Gischala."

Linus looked at him a moment, his face a shifting ground of light and shadow where he stood beneath the torch. "And I am Linus, of Antioch in Syria," he said at last.

The two men walked on. "What placed you on the road from Nazareth to Tiberias on a Sabbath morning?" John had asked. "If you are going to Damascus, why didn't you turn west toward Nain and around the shoulder of Mount Tabor, instead of going all the way north to Nazareth?"

"I was in Nazareth because... because I was curious about a man from there named Yeshua—Jesus, the Greeks style him."

"Ah! That one!" John muttered, shaking his head.

"You know of him?"

"I have heard him speak, but who in Galilee has not? He had gathered quite a following, before he estranged himself with his words." There was a long, reflective pause. "He is either a soft-headed fool, or a dangerous deluder of good men; I can't say which."

"What do you mean?" Linus asked.

Instead of answering, John of Gischala pulled aside his cloak and unsheathed a Roman short sword concealed beneath his clothing. As the weapon glittered in the torchlight, Linus wondered how a Galilean robber-captain had obtained a weapon of the legionaries.

"This," John asserted in a clenched voice "is the instrument God will use to liberate the kingdom of David and Solomon. The Sadducees may counsel caution, and the Essenes may pray for the intervention of the angels, but there are those of us who remember what the Almighty did in the days of Judas the Maccabean—what was accomplished by a few men who trusted in God and weren't afraid to strike blows for freedom."

A moment more he glowered at Linus; then, sheathing the weapon, his voice lost some of its heated, angry edge. "I knew a man of Bethsaida—Simon by name, known as Peter to many—who once felt as I do. He was a strong man, a man who knew how to use his knife and his fists. And he would have made a fine lieutenant when the time came." John paused, looking away.

"Whatever happened to him?" Linus asked.

John cut a sidelong glance at the carpenter. "He fell in with the Nazarene, Jesus."

One of the dozen or so rough-looking disciples...

"I remember one time, at a place not so very far from here. . .this Jesus was getting quite a reputation, you see. He was saying things that made sense to many people—and the word was he could heal the sick and infirm. Rumors were running throughout Galilee that he might be the risen Elijah who was to prepare for the coming Messiah. Some said he might even be Messiah, himself. So, I went out to see and hear for myself.

"We were on the other side of the lake, at a place removed from any nearby towns. There must have been two, three thousand men gathered—that was the kind of excitement that was in the air. I remember thinking, 'Could this be the day we've been waiting for? Could this man be the one God will use to forge us into a single, unified, holy army?'

"As we gathered, several of us voiced regrets at not having brought provisions. There was—there was food, though. I remember that, although I still don't know who brought it, or from where."

John strode to a nearby table—which badly needed bracing, Linus noticed—and scooped a handful of dried dates from a baked-clay bowl. He offered them to Linus, who declined. Absently munching one of the pieces of fruit, the bandit leader continued. "When the Nazarene talked, I could feel the words on my face, feel them stirring against my spirit, striving with it. But when he was gone, I could not see where the words had come from, nor their destination." He glanced at Linus, and shook his head. "Besides, I've never been much on words. I've always preferred action to rhetoric.

"Many of those gathered there thought we should raise the banner—force him to announce himself. For myself, I thought that anyone who could summon such a multitude to the wilderness could surely inspire an army to march on Jerusalem.

"But when we went to find him, he wasn't there! He simply wasn't to be found! And then, someone caught up with him a day or two later—on the other side of the lake." John scowled, crossing his arms on his chest.

"What happened?" Linus asked, sensing there was more to the story that John rued to tell.

"More words!" the highwayman scoffed. "And such words, as I heard tell... They said he talked about his flesh being the meat of those who would follow him, his blood being their drink—mad stuff such as that! The last thing we need is for able-bodied men to waste themselves at the bidding of a muddle-headed imbecile! When I heard these reports, I cursed myself for putting such hope in him as I had. But Peter..." John of Gischala shook his head in dismay. "I never would have believed that Simon Peter could be taken in by such moonshine."

The road was leveling; Linus could smell the flat, slightly oily scent of Lake Tiberias, carried to him on the freshening breeze. And ahead, the outline dancing in the heat rising from the ground, he could see the town of Tiberias. Quite bold of the zealot band, he thought, to locate their base so near the capital of Herod Antipas's tetrarchy. Though the day was hot and sweat stung his eyes, Linus lengthened his paces. It would be good to be in a place where a cool breeze and more than a single inn might be found. And perhaps traveling companions, as well, he hoped. The next bandits along the road might not be so kindly disposed as those he had just left.

The main road into Tiberias ran along the lake shore. As Linus drew nearer to the city, the air grew thick with the cries of gulls, the smell of fish, the rough, loud voices of the fishermen. Large numbers of boats were drawn up on the beach, their sun-blackened crews squatting beside them as they gutted the catch or mended nets. Still more boats rocked in untidy ranks on the swells just offshore, as the fishermen cast out and drew in their nets, tirelessly seining the shallower waters of the lake for the gleaming, wriggling take they could sell on the streets of Tiberias or Capernaum or Magdala.

How many of these work-hardened men, Linus wondered, had been in the throng with John of Gischala? How many of them had gathered in the wilderness across the lake to hear the Nazarene's words blow like the winds of heaven across their spirits? How many of them had been quickened by him, had longed to draw their concealed blades and march, with him leading the horde, on Jerusalem?

And why had Jesus abdicated the role? Linus reflected on the times he had witnessed the prophet's careful avoidance of the mantle the zealots were eager to thrust upon him. The way he had used the death of the rebels in the tower of Siloam as an object lesson, not of zealous devotion to the restoration of David's throne but of the consequences of sin.

Give to Caesar what is Caesar's, and to God what is God's...

The man, seemingly by accident, commanded the sort of enthusiasm from the masses that a military commander might wish from his troops on the eve of battle, yet he shunned their ardor as if it were dangerous to him.

This, too, played a part in his death. Linus remembered the way the dagger-man in the *Lithostratum* had shouted for Bar-Abbas. Had Jesus of Nazareth grasped the scepter the zealots would have thrust toward him that day on the lake's eastern shore, he might, at least, have made his death a memorable one.

In the town, Linus found an inn which faced the lake, and through its doorway a pleasant, cooling breeze wafted almost constantly. And, as if by design of his will, a band of merchants was there who intended to journey across Herod Philip's tetrarchy to Damascus.

That evening around the board, the companionship was jovial and the wine plentiful. The master of this house was almost the precise opposite of the dour, stingy innkeeper of Sychar. This man genuinely delighted in the comfort and cheer of his patrons. As the talk drifted easily from politics to trade to food to travel and back, the innkeeper was constantly leaping from the tableside to bring another ewer of wine, another loaf of freshly baked bread, another bowl of succulent olives.

By the time the last lamp had guttered out, Linus was well filled, and the excellent wine had produced a merry, ringing sensation between his ears which promised but a short wait for a sound slumber. He had no more than laid his head on the bundle he made of his outer cloak when the silent, satiny shroud of sleep fell comfortably about him. On his last night in Galilee, Linus slept like a well-contented child.

11

L inus blew away the sawdust and inspected his work. He tilted the small wooden cask this way and that, looking for a faulty joint, a place where the finish was not smooth. Nothing. He opened and shut the lid several times, observing the fit along the line of closure. Perfect. Picking up a rag, he wiped off any remaining dust, then poured a half-palmful of oil onto the rag and began rubbing the oil into the green-tinged olive wood.

This job had cost him a bit more than his ordinary work; the hinges and the tacks holding them in place were of iron and had to be obtained from a smith. Still, the patron who had ordered the cask was able to amply compensate Linus for the additional expense and effort.

He was about to rub oil onto the bottom of the cask when he suddenly realized he had not imprinted the work with his mark. Should he take the trouble? After all, the cask was finished. To chisel the emblem into its base might damage the meticulous work he had done. Why not simply let it go this time?

But he knew the true reason behind his reluctance had nothing to do with the cask. He could no longer look at his two-birds trademark without thinking of the blood-stained cross which bore the same legend. Knowing that the symbol of his skill had once been affixed to an instrument of avarice and power-lust, he was increasingly loath to use it. The one source of pride remaining to him—his commitment to crafts-manship—had been sullied. Now each time he carved the emblem, the memory of the pollution was renewed within him. Quickly he rubbed oil on the base of the cask and set it aside.

He had been in Damascus for just over two full cycles of the moon. Damascus was a large city and finding work had not been difficult. The weight of the silver in his purse was three- or four-fold what it had been when he arrived with the caravan of merchants from Galilee. Each day he went to the agora where he had rented a tiny stall, and set out a few small items to attract the attention of passers-by. At the worst, he would sell a child's pull-toy or a footstool he had cobbled together in his spare time. At best, someone needing a skilled carpenter, seeing the things he had built and the tools of his trade, would commission him for a more exten-sive project. And each night he would return to the small rooftop room he leased from the tanner who, with his family, lived and worked in the house below.

Linus suspected that the tanner had no little difficulty in letting this room, given the evil odors produced by his craft. Still, he was a good man and, as it happened, a Jew who had been living in Damascus for almost two-and-a-half score years. He was a burly, jovial bear of a man and his name was Tullius.

Now Linus heard the slap of sandals on the stairs which ascended the outside wall of the house to the roof. A shadow fell across his doorway, and a familiar, hearty voice bellowed a greeting.

"Good morning, Linus! See what Naomi has baked for you! I have told that wife of mine time and again that our agreement does not call for feeding you, only letting this room to you—but she is a hard woman and pays me no heed."

As the tanner shook his head sadly, Linus grinned and reached eagerly for the steaming loaf of *chametz*-bread, a dollop of rich goat-cheese melting down its sides. He tore off a hunk and stuffed it quickly in his mouth. "Please, Tullius," he urged around the mouthful, "sit down and enjoy with me the fruit of your wife's disgraceful liberality!"

The tanner laughed—a deep, belly-shaking laugh—and grabbed the loaf from Linus's hand before he had finished speaking. From somewhere, Tullius produced a ewer of clear, cold water, and the two men nimbly set about the swift destruction of the large loaf.

Tullius eyed the just-completed cask. Wiping his fingertips on the front of his clothing, he carefully picked up the small box, turning it this way and that, opening and closing the lid. His lips pursed appreciatively, he nodded as he set it gently back in place.

"You do good work, boy. I haven't seen too many woodcarvers who are your equal, nor recollect any who are your betters."

Linus bowed his head in gratitude.

"Now, give me another chunk of that bread," Tullius growled.

"I see that your sincerity is exceeded only by your appetite," Linus laughed.

"Correct," admitted Tullius, cramming another huge wad into his mouth.

The two men ate together in silence a few moments more. As Linus halved the last portion of the cake, passing a piece to Tullius and keeping one for himself, he asked, "When is your son due back from Jerusalem?" As was traditional among some Jews of the Diaspora, the oldest son of the tanner had taken his own eldest, Tullius's oldest grandson, to the Temple to receive his *bar-mitzvah* there during the

Shabuoth — the Feast of Weeks—the festival, commencing fifty days after Passover, that commemorated the giving of the Law to Moses on Sinai.

Tullius squinted upward in calculation. "He should be in...today sometime, I reckon. By sunset it will have been...what? A sabbath and six days since Pentecost?"

Linus nodded, reaching for the water jar.

"Then he and Timon ought to be in before sunset. By the way, Linus, I presume you will accompany us to the synagogue this evening—not that I give a fig one way or another. But Naomi wants to know."

"I would be honored; after all, I would scarcely dare offend the woman who baked this cake—even if her husband is an ungracious oaf who eats food intended for his guests."

The tanner roared with mirth, aiming a back-handed swat at the dodging carpenter.

The synagogue Tullius and his family attended was known as the House of Zion, and was one of the older synagogues in Damascus. In the generation or so since its founding, the House of Zion had grown far beyond the *minyan* of ten men required for its establishment. Some twenty families—many of which, like that of Tullius, comprised grown sons and daughters with children of their own—now gathered each Sabbath in a simple, sturdy structure located at the end of Straight Street, near the southern bank of the Abana River. Faithfully they came to listen to the reading and exposition of the *Torah*, to hear and recite the prayers and songs of Israel.

> *"Shema, Israel:*
> *Adonai elohenu, Adonai echad—*
>
> Hear, O Israel:
> The Lord our God, the Lord is One..."

As the rabbi intoned the ancient Hebrew invocation that opened each service of every synagogue throughout the world, the congregation stood, all heads bowed in reverence. They would remain standing until the traditional benedictions had been given and the Ten Commandments recited. As the rabbi reached the end of the benedictions and began the recitation of the Decalogue, he switched from Hebrew to Greek, reading from the Translation of the Seventy which had made the venerable teachings of Moses accessible to the multitudes of Jews who, living far beyond the borders of Judah, had never learned the tongue of their forefathers.

"You shall have no other gods before Me...

"You shall not make for yourselves an idol...

"You shall not misuse the Name of the Lord your God...

"Remember the Sabbath day by keeping it holy...

"Honor your father and your mother...

"You shall not murder...

"You shall not commit adultery...

"You shall not steal...

"You shall not give false testimony...

"You shall not covet your neighbor's house. You shall not covet your neighbor's wife, or his manservant or maidservant, his ox or donkey, or anything that belongs to your neighbor," the rabbi read.

"Amen," responded the congregation in unison.

"In the future," the rabbi continued, when your son asks you, 'What is the meaning of the stipulations, decrees and laws the Lord our God has commanded you, tell him—" He paused, looking out at them expectantly.

The congregation responded in unison:

"We were slaves of Pharaoh in Egypt, but the Lord brought us out of Egypt with a mighty hand. The Lord commanded us to obey all these decrees and to fear the Lord our God, so that we might always prosper and be kept alive, as is the case today. And if we are careful to obey all this law before the Lord our God, as He has commanded us, that will be our righteousness."

From the front ranks of the congregation, a man's strong, clear voice sang the first line of a psalm, and the assembly joined together in raising David's ancient hymn of praise for the *Torah*.

> *The law of the Lord is perfect,*
>   *reviving the soul.*
> *The statutes of the Lord are trustworthy,*
>   *making wise the simple.*
> *The precepts of the Lord are right,*
>   *giving joy to the heart...*

"Amen," finished the rabbi, as the last line of the melody wavered gracefully to a close.

"Amen," answered the congregation. There was a momentary rustle as the worshipers seated themselves on the straw mats that littered the floor of the synagogue. The rabbi rolled up the scroll of the *Torah*, covered it with its vellum sheath, and kissed it. He replaced it in the ark at the front of the synagogue and took out another scroll. He reached the lectern, unrolled the book and searched with his index finger for the place to begin. Finding it, he glanced up at the gathering.

"From the scroll of the Census of Israel," he announced, signalling the beginning of the first exposition of scripture. "'They traveled from Mount Hor along the route to the Sea of Reeds, to go around Edom. But the people grew impatient on the way...'"

As the rabbi's voice droned on, Linus allowed his eyes to wander among the seated worshipers. These were good, honest faces; the faces of hardworking people. In the time he had spent in Damascus, he had grown more and more attached to Tullius and his household. Lately he had begun thinking of settling here for a time. Wasn't this as good a place as any to allow his wandering feet to rest?

" '...they spoke against God and against Moses, and said, "Why have you brought us up out of Egypt to die in the desert? There is no bread! There is no water! And we detest this miserable food!' "

Linus's glance swept over the sons and oldest grandson of Tullius, seated with the rest of the men. The boy Timon sat very straight and tried to look quite serious; this was his first occasion to sit on the men's side. Then Linus noticed the expression on the face of Jason, his father. Tullius's oldest son appeared deeply troubled; his eyebrows were knit severely together, and he nervously chewed at his bottom lip as the rabbi continued reading the day's first scripture lesson.

"...then the Lord sent venomous snakes among them; they bit the people and many Israelites died. The people came to Moses and said, 'We sinned when we spoke against the Lord and against you. Pray that the Lord will take the snakes away from us.' So Moses prayed for the people..."

What could be causing such a disturbance within the normally placid Jason? Linus wondered. He should be beaming with pride to have his son seated beside him. Instead, he looked like one who wrestled with an evil spirit.

"The Lord said to Moses, 'Make a snake and put it up on a pole; anyone who is bitten can look at it and live.' So Moses made a bronze snake and put it up on a pole. Then when anyone was bitten by a snake and looked at the bronze snake, he lived." The rabbi nodded thoughtfully as he slowly rolled up the scroll, then raised his eyes to the congregation and began to speak.

"In this passage, brethren, we see illustrated the gracious provision the Eternal makes for His people Israel. Though they had wronged His glory, though they had doubted His steadfast love, and though death was all about them, still He caused Moses to raise up for them a very symbol of that scourge which was in the camp, that through it He might cause their lives to be saved..."

As the rabbi said these words, Jason's mouth hung open in an expression between fear and awe—as if in the rabbi's simple discourse on a familiar story he read some portent of momentous implication.

"...and just so, even to us, my children, has the Almighty demonstrated His grace. For even in these days, when death and destruction hang in the air about our heads, Adonai has given us His holy *Torah*, that we may look to it and be saved."

> *God is our refuge and strength,*
>   *an ever-present help in trouble.*
> *Therefore we will not fear, though*
>   *the earth give way*
> *and the mountains fall into the heart*
>   *of the sea...*

As the last strains of the hymn faded into silence, Linus could see Jason, with a mighty effort striving to gain control of himself. His nostrils flared as he took deep draughts of air. His eyes were closed, as though he were willing himself back toward calm.

"And now, I have asked Jason, son of Tullius, to come and give us the second lesson, from the prophets," the rabbi was saying. "He and his son Timon are just arrived back from Jerusalem, where Timon received the *bar-mitzvah* at the Temple during the feast of the Pentecost."

Tullius beamed proudly at his grandson, who blushed and ducked his head.

"And now, Jason... will you come?" the rabbi invited, inclining his head toward the place where Jason sat.

Slowly Jason levered himself to his feet and walked to the front of the synagogue. He selected a scroll from the ark and spread it carefully on the lectern.

"From the scroll of the prophet Isaiah," he began in a tenuous voice.

"'Who has believed our message, and to whom has the arm of the Lord been revealed? 'He grew up before him like a tender shoot, and like a root out of dry ground,'" Jason read, his voice growing stronger with each phrase:

He had no beauty or majesty to attract us to him,
nothing in his appearance that we should desire him.
He was despised and rejected by men,
a man of sorrows and familiar with suffering.
Like one from whom men hide their faces
he was despised, and we esteemed him not.
Surely he took up our infirmities
and carried our sorrows,
Yet we considered him stricken by God,
smitten by him, and afflicted.
But he was pierced for our transgressions,
he was crushed for our iniquities;
the punishment that brought us peace was upon him,
and by his wounds we are healed.
We all, like sheep, have gone astray,
each of us has turned to his own way;
and the LORD has laid on him
the iniquity of us all…

By the time Jason reached the end of Isaiah's portrait of the enigmatic Suffering Servant, he was fairly singing. But on the last phrase, Jason's voice broke, and tears could be discerned on his face. With a tremendous effort, Jason again gathered himself. Much, thought Linus, like a man about to dive headfirst into a frigid stream of unknown depth.

"Brethren, at the feast of the Pentecost just past, I learned—" he took several deep breaths—" I learned of the fulfillment of these words from the Prophet Isaiah." He stared around the room for a long moment. "And I heard of the one whose coming brings them to completion—in our day."

All eyes shifted to the rabbi, seated at the front. His was the immediate authority in matters of interpretation, and clearly Jason had stepped into uncertain territory with this strange analysis of the shadowy, much-debated words of Isaiah.

The rabbi, discomfited as much, perhaps, by the abnormality of the proceedings as by the implications of Jason's remarks, cleared his throat. "By the fact that you refer to 'the one who comes,' I presume that you place yourself in the camp of those who see in Isaiah's Servant of the Lord the Messiah whose coming we await—is this correct?"

"No, teacher, that is not exactly what I meant to say."

The rabbi cocked his head quizzically. "How so?"

Jason stared at the open scroll before him. Then, locking eyes with the rabbi, he announced in an even-toned voice, "I am saying that Messiah has already come."

In the hush that followed in the synagogue, Linus felt the cold pinpoints of premonition on his cheeks and the back of his neck. He knew whose name would fall from Jason's lips when the inevitable question came—which it did, now, from the rabbi.

"And who and where is this—this one of whom you speak?" he asked, in genuine puzzlement.

Jason's answer was immediate and forceful, as if during the entire journey back from Jerusalem he had anticipated this moment. "He is Jesus of Nazareth, a man whom God approved by signs and wonders. Through the wickedness of unjust men he was given up to the Romans, and crucified—"

A confused murmur swelled from the gathering. What madness was this? Linus wondered. How could Jason or anyone else believe in a Messiah—a prince of the line of David—who was nailed to a Roman cross? Of what use was such a deliverer? How could a dead king offer salvation to Israel? Even though Jason had not—unlike Linus—seen the squalid, futile circumstances of Jesus' death, how could he place such exalted confidence in one who had failed to deliver even himself from the clutches of Annas and his son-in-law?

Then came Jason's next words, delivered in a voice loud enough to ride down the waves of aghast bewilderment that slapped against his knees —"but after three days, God raised him from the dead. And now he is seated in the heavenly places with the Lord, and has sent the Spirit of the Lord to dwell in the hearts of men, as the prophets foretold."

The dubious muttering ceased abruptly, as Jason's words went from madness to greater madness. Silence was the only response possible for such incredible phantasms. If Jason was daunted by the wall of mute disbelief which faced him, he gave no sign. Instead, he lurched onward, flinging yet more fevered words into the fray.

"The resurrection of Jesus was witnessed by those who followed him, for he appeared alive to them and to hundreds of people in Judea and Galilee. And on the first day of the feast in Jerusalem, his chief disciples affirmed these things, accompanied by signs and wonders—"

"He has lost his mind!" shouted a man at the back of the room, unable to listen any longer. "I, too, was in Jerusalem for the Feast of Pentecost, as were perhaps two hundred thousand other Jews from all parts of the world! I saw and heard nothing of this—this weird business of which Jason speaks! This talk of resurrection...a condemned criminal ascending to the right hand of the Holy One...heresy! Blasphemy!"

Tullius leapt to his feet and wheeled to face the man who had just spoken. "Jonas, you may say anything about me you like, but you make a dangerous error when you call my son a blasphemer! I don't pretend to understand what my son is saying, and maybe I don't agree with all of it. But I know his heart." The tanner's eyes searched the room, then returned to the face of his son. "I think we ought to hear him out." He stood a moment more, willing them all to agree with him, then seated himself.

Jason looked gratefully at his father. "Jesus the Messiah promises everlasting life to those who repent and follow his teachings. Just as he was raised from the dead, so too shall we all rise on the Day of the Lord, in bodies that cannot be corrupted, to live forever!" His face blazed with fervor, his voice rang like a call to arms.

Again the rabbi raised his voice. "Jason, you speak of this. . . this Jesus of Nazareth as the Servant of the Lord—yet you admit he was hung on a Roman cross. Remember the condemnation found in the Scroll of the Law, which says, 'anyone who is hung on a tree is under God's curse.' How, then, can this man also be the Messiah, on whom the favor of the Lord dwells in unlimited measure?" Still, the teacher's voice carried no overtones of anger or malice—only a confused plea for a suitable explanation.

Again, Jason's answer was quick to hand. "It is just as you taught earlier, Rabbi Ananias, in the lesson from the Pentateuch. Moses raised up for Israel a symbol of death which became, instead, a symbol of life to those who obeyed..."

Linus gasped softly as a memory surfaced, unbidden. A memory of a group of Grecians in the Temple courtyard with the Nazarene. An unexplained peal of thunder, and a battle waged and won across the visage of the doomed prophet. And these words—

But I, when I am lifted up, will draw all men unto myself...

"In just this way," Jason was saying, "the Eternal has caused the Messiah to be raised up, that Israel, in beholding his shame, might know the full disgrace of her own sins. As the prophet Isaiah says, 'by his stripes we are healed...'"

The service concluded, the congregation of the House of Zion exited the synagogue far quieter than usual. As the worshipers made their way through the darkening streets of Damascus, scores of muted, worried discussions took place.

"Risen from the dead! How could such a thing be..."

"But Jason said hundreds of people witnessed the thing..."

"Jonas was there, and he says he saw nothing like what Jason related..."

"When Jason read from Isaiah, my heart stirred within me..."

"How can a man ascend to the right hand of the Majesty? And how can we worship him? Doesn't the Shema teach us, "the Lord is One"?

"Risen from the dead? Could such a thing truly be?"

Walking dazed among them, Linus neither shared nor heard any of these anxious exchanges. Instead, his mind was a melee of conflicting thoughts and contradictory emotions. Once more, he thought. Once more, the Nazarene has found me.

One by one, recollections rose up before him; some to accuse, some to beseech, some to chasten or to deride.

When you have lifted up the Son of Man, then you will know who I am and that I do nothing on my own...
I have questioned this man, and have found no basis for accusation against him...
I will draw all men unto myself...
Crucify him! Crucify him!
Give to Caesar what is Caesar's, and to God what is God's...
If he truly saved others, let him use his power on himself, now!
Whoever drinks the water I give him will never thirst...
Rabbi Yeshua, Rabbi Yeshua! Have mercy on us!
Neither will I tell you by what authority I am doing these things...
He talked about his flesh being the meat of those who would follow him...

Whoever does God's will is my brother and sister and mother...

The voices and images followed each other in a soundless, deafening cascade of faith and despair, of peace poured out with rage. A part of Linus longed to believe in Jason's tale of the impossible, and a part of him rebelled.

Could it be that the force that ruled the universe was not, as Linus had often felt, completely aloof from the cares and troubles of mankind? Could it be true that the mighty acts of the Eternal were not confined to the ancient, half-mythical past? That He still genuinely cared enough for the plight of His hapless people to break His silence, to openly declare Himself, to drive such an overt stake as resurrection into the heart of a hostile cosmos?

How Linus yearned to believe that death was not the final rude insult that it seemed! For a tiny, unguarded instant, he allowed himself to remember the face of Heracleia; allowed himself to cherish the fleeting thought that perhaps a senseless, brutish expiration was not the end.

But, ah! the cost of such a faith! How could he afford it? How could he again open himself to the possibility of hope, without at the same time offering occasion to its loathsome twin, despair? Wasn't it safer to expect nothing? Those blind from birth could not rue the loss of a flower's beauty; deafness pained most keenly those who had once heard the laughter of children, the song of a lark. And if he huddled insensate beneath the blows and random cruelties of the universe, might he not be granted, at least, the scant comfort of the numbness he sought?

But, a tiny voice whispered, wasn't such a void of feeling a form of suffering in itself? And wouldn't it be more desirable to have seen but a single bloom, heard but a single trilling bird song, than be forever self-damned to painless oblivion?

Like a condemned man going to his place of execution, Linus trudged up the stairs to his rooftop room, staggered through the door, and slumped against the wall. Helpless before the bewildering barrage of questions assaulting his soul, he crouched in a corner and wept.

I'm sitting in the band room, staring vacantly out the large windows in the back wall as I listen to Billy Evers attempt his chromatic scale audition. School is out for the day. It's April, and the school year has passed the Point of No Return. It's the time of year when spring has decided, once and for all, to quit bluffing. Everybody on the campus knows that summer is coming, but they also know that we still have a good eight weeks of school left. It's difficult to say whom this knowledge affects most—the teachers or the kids.

Boy, is this fun. Billy, the unfortunate cornet player seated nervously before me, must perform this rudiment, like all the other intermediate band students, for a grade. In Billy's case, this is likely to be an unpleasant experience. In my case, that's a given. Billy is a nice kid, and he has a reasonably good attitude. Doubtless he'll go on to become a productive and upstanding member of society. But he is not, by any stretch, destined for musical greatness. When he plays, his embouchure, despite my best remedial efforts, looks like a strangulated prune. Imagining Billy Evers in first chair is like imagining Frosty the Snowman as mayor of Gila Bend, Arizona.

"No, Billy. You started on second-line G. You have to start on low F-sharp, remember?"

"Oh, uhhh… yeah. I was thinkin' of that other scale we had to play last week. Sorry."

"All right, then. Go ahead." That other scale. Billy, Billy, Billy… that's the oldest trick in the bag, son.

As Billy's labored tones inch agonizingly up the two-octave scale, I allow my gaze to escape out the windows to the open sky beyond. There is a light pole just behind the band room's back wall, and I notice a downy woodpecker tapping diligently on the creosote-treated spar, just below the metal beam of the mercury lamp.

Coming to school in the early mornings, I've occasionally heard his raucous, cry, but this is the first time I've seen him. He aims a half-dozen rapid pecks at the splintery pole, then cocks his head to listen for the movements of the grubs and insects that aren't there. But he doesn't know that. His instinct tells him that an exposed piece of wood with no leaves has to be dead, and dead wood is where bugs and worms are. He sidles around and around the pole, looking for lunch in all the wrong places. If he's disappointed, I can't tell it by his efforts. There can be no sustenance for a wood-pecker in a light pole, but this guy is determined to find out the hard way.

And suddenly, I realize I'm on the pole beside him, that I've been there for—how long? How long have I been vainly circling my own creosote pole, tapping for nourishment that wasn't there? For how many years have I labored, wonder-ing why I wasn't being filled, wondering why the discontent wouldn't go away, hoping no one would notice as I quietly starved to death; circling, circling, circling—and maybe the whole time a banquet was waiting for me in the trees across the street?

My breakdown at the church service a few nights ago has unlocked something in me, or jarred it loose. I never real-ized, until these last few days, that my ambivalence—no, Janice, call it what it is—my hatred for my father is like the cork in a bottle I hoped I'd never have to open. But now the cork is loose, and the contents are spewing around inside me, and I'm not sure what may happen. But something will.

Billy is looking at me strangely. I realize that he has been finished with his chromatic scale for several silent moments now. With what I hope is a convincingly professorial nod, I make a notation in my grade book.

"All right, Billy. That's fine. You can go now."

Billy has his horn in the case and is striding quickly toward the instrument storage closet, presumably elated to have passed with such unexpected ease this musical gauntlet.

I think I'll visit the library soon. Maybe Maude will be there.

12

Not surprisingly, Maude's house is done in Early Grandmother. It all has a wistfully familiar feel: the crocheted doilies atop the Chippendale side tables, the striped afghan laid oh-so-casually across the arm of the overstuffed chair, the pleasantly cluttered appearance of the small sitting room, the faint scent of cedar and mothballs. The only thing lacking is a Victrola, with Rudy Vallee scratchily singing "Your Time Is My Time."

"Come on in to the kitchen," she beams, needlessly indicating the way to the room plainly visible through the arched doorway. "I've got a fresh pot of tea brewed."

I'm vaguely disappointed that Maude uses an automatic drip coffee maker to brew her tea. After seeing the sitting room, I'm more prepared for a whistling copper kettle and a tray laid with china, linen napkins, and dainty wafers. Instead, Maude pours tea from the coffee maker's Pyrex pot into two large ceramic mugs. I deeply inhale the orange-and-spice aroma. "This smells good. Just what I need to get my heart started."

She smiles at the compliment and slides into a chair across the small, thickly grained oak table. I run a hand across the dented, time-stained surface. "This is a neat table. Antique?"

She nods. "Yes. It belonged to my parents."

A long pause, as we both carefully sip at our tea. Putting hers down first, she turns her head and gazes out the window above the sink. Involuntarily, my eyes follow hers. The window is a primary-colored stampede of suncatchers in various forms: birds, butterflies, flowers—their bright shapes stuck to the glass panes with clear acrylic suction cups. My gaze wanders over Maude's shoulder to the small white refrigerator, a-flutter with clippings and notes. Centered at eye level is a small plaque, done in counted cross-stitch, which reads, "Old librarians never die; they just check out."

"Wouldn't it be nice," she says finally, breaking the silence, "if everything we inherited from our parents was as useful as this table?"

My eyes snap to attention, and she is looking right at me. I make a false start toward my mouth with my mug, then set it abruptly in front of me. Again she turns to look out the window. This time my eyes stay on her.

"I've been thinking a lot about what you've told me," she says. "The stuff about your dad, and what you remember from your childhood." She turns to look at me, then glances down to sip her tea. "I guess that's why I wanted you to come over here this morning. Maybe something good can—" Her voice stops abruptly, as if it's collided with an immovable object in her throat. She picks up her mug and goes to stand over the sink, staring outside through the gaps between the suncatchers.

"Of course, it was a different time," she says after a long silence. "There wasn't much expectation, in those days, for parents to provide—what's the term that's so popular now?—*nurturing*, that's it. Not much about that. If you fed them, clothed them, disciplined them, and took them to church, you'd done about all that was needful.

"And, my goodness! The notion of a *father* nurturing his children..." She emits a short, dry little laugh. "Why, of course, that would never have done at all. Papa was... he was the head of the household. The final authority. The stern captain of the family ship."

Is it my imagination, or do I hear a note of pained sarcasm creeping into Maude's voice?

"So of course he couldn't be troubled with any of that silly, coddling, feminine nonsense." She raises her mug, takes a sip, then another. "I learned early that Papa wasn't too interested in my drawings, didn't have time to listen to the little nonsense songs I made up for my dolls. 'Go on, now, Maudie,' he'd say. 'I've got things to do.'

"He always had things to do. He was a busy man, Papa was. Of course, everyone was busy in those days. There was a Depression on, and you had to stay busy if you wanted to eat. And everybody in town knew Papa and Mama, so they got lots of calls. And they answered most of them. Most... but not all." She puts down her mug and grips her elbows, hugging herself tightly, as if against a sudden chill. "I remember his back best of all. His back and his hands. His back was what I saw when he was home... sitting in his chair, buried in the newspaper or a book, listening to the radio. His hands, when he spanked me for being in the way, or for prattling while he was trying to read, or for..." She draws a shuddering breath slowly in, then allows it to leak just as slowly out. "Do you know... I can remember the spankings, but I can't remember a single hug." She turns toward me, a small, apologetic smile quivering on her lips. "I don't mean to run on."

"No, it's okay," I assure her quickly. "I... it helps to know... to hear—"

"— that you're not the only one?" she finishes for me.

"Yeah... Something like that." To break the long hush which follows, I take a couple of sips from my mug.

"Well, there's one thing I've learned, Janice," she says finally. "And that's this: you're never the only one. But sometimes, that admission is the hardest step of all."

This is getting a little too close to the bone for my taste. "So... when did you get interested in writing?" I ask. There. Parry and counter-stroke.

She returns to the table, staring thoughtfully at the air above my head. "Oh," she sighs, remembering, "I guess from about the time I was old enough to begin reading really well by myself. I'd make up conversations with the characters in the books I read at the library. We lived in a small town with one of the Carnegie libraries, you see. So I was very fortunate in having access to a variety of books that most children of my generation—in that part of the country, at least—didn't have. Oh, goodness!" she smiles, flushing pleasurably at the memory, "I had such talks with Peter Rabbit and Alice and the Five Little Peppers! By the time I was ten years old, I'd filled both sides of several tablets. After all," she says, peering into the ruby-orange depths of her mug, "a child has to tell her dreams to someone. And Alice didn't think I was silly. Peter Rabbit always had time to listen to me..."

"When did you stop?" I ask quietly.

She shifts the mug in a small, uneasy circle. She looks up at me, then away. Her voice, when it comes, is an ashamed half-whisper. "When Papa finally convinced me to stop dreaming."

I want to cry, or something. I want to give her a hug, offer some comfort. Instead, I adopt a pensive expression, nod a few times, and take another slow sip of tea.

The morning was clear and almost painfully bright. Over his left shoulder, Linus could see white-capped Mount Hermon, its majestic form distance-shrouded in royal purple. The road wound along easily beside the Abana River through the valley between the Lebanon and Anti-Lebanon mountain ranges. The party had been traveling since just before daybreak, making its way along the road which led north to Heliopolis and, just beyond that city, to the highway of the Orontes which would take them into Antioch.

Linus traveled with a group of about thirty merchants, peddlers, tradesmen, and other assorted wayfarers. He had caught on to the entourage only by means of a chance remark made by the stonemason who occupied the stall adjacent to his in the marketplace in Damascus. This fellow, Armitius by name, said he would be traveling to Antioch with the next caravan because of a recent spate of Imperial building activity. He hoped to improve his prospects and wondered aloud whether a carpenter who, after all, was a native of the provincial capital, might not stand an even better chance of adding to his fortune.

This proved the only encouragement Linus needed. He was present in the marketplace the next morning, after bidding a fond farewell to Tullius and his family. In the predawn grayness, the caravan gradually took form: a number of heavily laden donkeys, men bent beneath bulging backpacks or hitched to creaky pullcarts, a few of the wealthier types mounted on horseback with pack animals behind, even a curtained, ox-drawn wain escorted by four mounted, well-armed outriders—a welcomed addition to the entourage, since they would be traveling many days across isolated stretches of country controlled by the Nabatean Arab king, Aretas. Aretas frequently turned a blind eye to bandit raids on parties making their way through his domain, and those who traveled these lonely marches were well-advised to look to their own defense.

Just before dawn the city's gates swung open, and the travelers pushed forward, west along the river road.

Now the sun was high enough to be flashing intermittently upon them through the crags and peaks of the Anti-Lebanon range. The air still held much of the coolness of the night, but before long the summer heat would be almost unbearable. Even now, the good-natured bantering and easy conversation of the early morning had given way to a quiet punctuated only by the grunts of human and animal effort, the squeaks of the rigging, the rumbling of the oxcart's wheels. When the sun was well up, fatigue became the primary enemy. It was best now to save strength for the task of forging ahead.

As they crossed the rocky washout made by a seasonal freshet, a low, grinding roar, swiftly followed by a loud cry, went up from the rear of the convoy. Linus wheeled about to see what caused the commotion.

As he neared the wain, now surrounded by a number of the traveling party, he could see that one of the wheels had sheared through the pin holding it on the axle and now lay on the ground, several paces behind the wain. The end of the axle had been dragged heavily across the rocky terrain by the unheeding team. The other thing Linus noticed as he drew closer was the heady, sweetish-sharp scent of spices. This, presumably, was the reason for the heavy guard traveling with the wain—it was loaded with a large quantity of precious myrrh, aloes, cloves, and other expensive condiments.

Immediately, Linus saw what needed to be done. The axle, though damaged, was still sound. All that was required was to cut another pin to fit the hole in the axle, then to remount the wheel, securing it with the new pin. He stepped through the circle of onlookers and was about to speak with one of the outriders, when the curtain twitched back. A woman's voice came in a low, concerned tone. "Marcus, what is the extent of the damage?" she asked in excellent Greek.

"I'm not sure, lady," the guard replied, "but I think it best that you stay—"

"All that is needed," Linus interrupted, "is a new pin. I am a carpenter by trade, and I would be happy to repair the axle. We should be on our way again within the time it takes the sun to rise above those peaks."

As the outrider studied Linus's face, the curtain opened a fraction more. Linus's eye fell upon the shadowed face of the wain's occupant, and grew wide in astounded recognition.

It was Phoebe, the Greek woman he had seen at the Temple during the last Passover!

He needed only to see her eyes—lustrous, dark, shimmering with an irrepressible vitality. Again, as in the courtyard of the *Goyim*, he was arrested, entranced, tangled in these eyes.

But now no veil obscured the rest of her features. Her hair was a midnight-dark cascade of tight, shining curls, her nose, finely wrought and delicate. Her lips were full and flushed, and a fine, strong chin led the eye irresistibly to her long, graceful neck. Her skin was smooth, flawless; in its perfection it seemed as thin as fine parchment. And yet a strength, a self-possession emanated from her which permitted no notion of frailty. This very paradox, he sensed, was a part of the spell she cast on him. Linus realized that she was speaking to him.

"—repair the pin?" He knew she had said more, but these words were all his addled senses heard.

"I must ask your pardon, lady," he stammered when his tongue came unglued, "but could you repeat your question?"

"I asked, sir, whether you are the one who says he can repair the pin?" she added with a coy smile.

"I am," he said, hoping wildly that she could not hear the hammering of his heart against his ribs. Still he could not tear himself away from her eyes.

She cocked her head curiously, peering at him through a half-squint of attempted recollection. "Have I seen you before, sir?" she asked, confusion wrinkling the bridge of her nose—a heartrending, perfect dimple that, having seen once, a man might gladly endure great hardship to witness again.

"I... I know not, lady," he managed at last, "whether you have seen me... but it is certain as sunrise that I have seen you." Suddenly abashed at his impudence, he tore himself away. "I will go and look in my kit. Perhaps I have a scrap of wood that will serve." Striving mightily to keep himself from trotting, he strode toward his donkey.

As he went, Phoebe stared at his retreating back. She shook her head and smiled faintly, then let the curtain of the wain fall back into place.

The train camped that night in a draw created by one of the myriad seasonal streams that meandered down from the Anti-Lebanon toward the Abana. As darkness fell, the travelers gathered into impromptu groups about one of the handful of cooking fires to prepare and share food and offer companionship. Within moments, jugs and flasks were passing from hand to hand and low, easy laughter could be heard above the crisp crackling of the flames.

"A good day's walking, eh, Linus?" chattered Armitius good-naturedly, squatting beside the carpenter. "By the braided beard of Zeus, I don't know when my poor feet have hurt so. But of course, you're accustomed to traveling, aren't you? For myself, I've been in Damascus long enough to appreciate a soft pallet and a good drink of wine at day's end, but there'll be plenty of that available in Heliopolis, by my reckoning. One of the—oh, thanks!" Armitius tilted his head back, taking several long, noisy pulls at a flask handed to him by one of the other travelers. "Ahh! That's good!" he sighed appreciatively, wiping his mouth with the back of his hand. "Anyway, like I was saying, one of the other fellows was telling me that we should make Heliopolis by nightfall tomorrow, if we have another good day, and no more bad luck like that ruckus with the wain."

The stonemason's prattle wound about Linus's head like the smoke from the fire, and went just as unheeded. For in the eyes of his mind, he was contemplating luxuriant, coal-black curls and eyes that glistened with dark, humid fire. And then something was jostling at his elbow.

"—want any of this?" Armitius was saying, poking at him insistently with the neck of a flask.

"What's that?" he said, like a man suddenly roused from sleep. "What did you say?"

Armitius peered at him curiously. "Have you heard a word I've been saying?"

Linus glanced nervously about him, then back at the stonemason. "I... ah... no, I suppose not." Abashed, he took the flask from Armitius, tossed down a perfunctory swallow, and passed it back.

Armitius gave him a long, askance look. "Are you taking sick? You have an odd, green-gilled look about you like you swallowed a piece of spoiled mutton—"

"No, I'm fine," Linus assured him with a heartiness that sounded false even in his own ears. "Really. All I need is... is just..." His eyes were pulled, as irresistibly as the course of the moon and stars, toward the most distant fire in the camp, the one kindled on the ground beside the wain. The aroma of cloves rose like clouds of incense within his mind.

Armitius eyed him a moment more, then leaned toward the man seated on the ground beside him. "Better keep a watch on this one," he muttered, jerking a thumb toward Linus. "He don't act right, somehow..."

Fool! Put her out of your mind! Linus shouted silently at himself. She's Greek! You're a Jew! She's rich—a wealthy purveyor of spices with four menservants! You're no more than a rough, dirty carpenter! You're addle-headed to even consider it! And then he recalled that delicate dimple of uncertainty across the bridge of her nose, remembered the silky, translucent perfection of her skin, imagined how her cheek would feel against his hand...

A hand fell on his shoulder, and he sprang up like a scalded cat.

"Whoa, there!" cried a man in surprise, as Linus's unexpected reflex knocked him backwards onto the ground.

Linus stood, staring wide-eyed and panting at the hapless fellow, who now gathered himself from the dust and, keeping a wary eye on Linus, began brushing himself off.

"I...I'm sorry," Linus stammered. "I didn't know you were—"

"That's all right," the other man assured him, none too convincingly. "I assumed you heard me coming."

Armitius glanced sideways at the traveler beside him, and the two men nodded knowingly.

Linus realized that the man who had startled him was one of the outriders from the wain. "I came to invite you to our fire," the man said at last, gesturing toward the wain. "My mistress wishes to thank you for repairing the wheel so quickly and well, and to give you payment for your work."

Linus was breathing flame, his heart battered his breastbone like a caged beast. He stood for several moments, unable to force his tongue to form the words that would carry him to the fire where waited the impossible object of his reverie, the new-found treasure he could never claim. At last, he nodded.

"Come, then," the outrider said, wheeling and striding away toward the wain. Linus followed him, as if wandering unguarded into a dream.

"The heat's done him, sure," murmured Armitius, shaking his head sadly.

Approaching the fire, Linus could see several figures silhouetted against the flickering blaze, hunched busily over the victuals they held in their hands. Phoebe was seated beside the wain, leaning her back against a wheel. She was fully lit by the mellowing glow, and Linus felt his breath catch in his throat—half in admiration and half in self-conscious embarrassment—as he beheld her, head uncovered, laughing easily with the men as she gnawed with honest appetite the bread she held in her hand. Sternly reminding himself that they were no longer in the Temple courts, that different customs ruled here and in the woman's native

Achaia, he neared the place where they sat. Linus could hear one of the attendants directing a question toward her.

"Mistress, I don't understand. Why should an immortal god care a fig whether I steal a loaf of bread from a stranger? If I'm hungry, and Lady Tyché places food in my path, what difference does it make that I filch it from someone to whom I owe no obligation in the first place?"

"I fear, Praxos," Phoebe countered, "that you are confusing your luck goddess's voice with the rumblings in your belly."

The others chuckled quietly at this gentle barb. Phoebe continued.

"What would you do if some poor, starving wanderer came upon the food store in this wain and helped himself to our provisions?"

Praxos answered without hesitation. "I'd beat the lout black and blue and send him on his way," he asserted.

"And yet, you have just said that Luck might place food belonging to others in your path," Phoebe countered, "and that you might justifiably eat that food."

"True enough," shrugged Praxos. "Obviously, if Tyché intended this straggler to have our provisions, she wouldn't allow me to catch him in the act."

Another appreciative chuckle from the others. Phoebe smiled ruefully, popped a handful of dried fruit in her mouth, and resumed her tack into the wind of Praxos's obstinacy.

"But, Praxos, is not the bread you would steal as valuable to its owner as our provisions are to us?"

"Perhaps so," mused the servant, "but I owe a stranger nothing. You are my mistress, and I cannot permit a beggar, or anyone else for that matter, to steal from you."

"I thank you for your loyalty, Praxos, but you fail to see—" She broke off, glancing upward as Linus and his guide neared the fire. "Oh! The carpenter!" she beamed, and the others swiveled to look.

Before the silence could become awkward, Phoebe gestured to the servant on her left. "Lysander, bring me the bag of silver." As the attendant got to his feet and went behind the wain, she smiled up at Linus. "Won't you sit down? There is plenty of food, as you can see."

Linus sat down in his very tracks, his pulse hammering in his ears. Someone placed a bowl of food in his hands.

Lysander returned with a small bag and gave it to Phoebe. She weighed out several silver coins, which she held toward Linus. "My servants and I benefitted greatly from your skill this morning, and I am not willing that such timely assistance go unrewarded. Please, take this as payment, my good—oh!" she interrupted herself, peering curiously at Linus. "I only just realized—I don't know your name!"

After several false starts, Linus managed to croak out his name.

His hostess regarded him oddly for a moment, then brightened. "Well, I am indebted to you, good Linus. And I am called—"

"Phoebe," Linus blurted, immediately blushing with shame. "Your name is Phoebe," he mumbled, mortified.

No one spoke for several moments. If her gaze was curious before, she now appeared positively dumbfounded. "That is... that is correct, but how could you—"

"Your man mentioned it when he brought your invitation," Linus lied, his eyes fixed studiously on his food bowl as he wished desperately to back out of the trap he had sprung on himself.

Phoebe's eyes found those of the servant who had summoned Linus. Silently the man shook his head. With a look more befuddled than ever, Phoebe sighed. "Well, in any case, good Linus, I want you to take this silver as a token of my gratitude for your work." Again she stretched her hand toward him.

Linus looked shyly at Phoebe, then away, shaking his head. "Thank you," he said quietly, "but I require no payment for rendering aid to a fellow traveler."

"Nevertheless," she persisted, jingling the coins assertively in her fist, "I would have you take this money. I will not have it said that I show no appreciation to those who do me good."

So many words, so many thoughts crowded into Linus's mind that he feared his skull might split open. Go on, fool! he ordered himself, Find your tongue! Say something!

"You are most kind," he managed finally, "but sharing your fire and your food is all the payment I ask." That, and..." Again, a shackle of timidity clenched his tongue. With furrowed brow, he groped busily in the bowl he held in his lap, taking several bites of the bread he found there.

"Yes?" Phoebe urged. "Something else...?"

Swallowing a morsel of food that felt as large in his throat as an Egyptian melon, he shook his head quickly. "No, nothing else," he muttered, refilling his mouth as quickly as he could with dried fruit and salted meat.

"Well, then," Phoebe said at last, ceding a slight shrug of disappointment, "very well. I suppose I can't force you to take the money," she sighed, slipping the coins back into the purse. "But... you will stay a while," she asked demurely, "won't you?"

Linus stopped chewing a moment as his eyes were dragged captive toward hers. He nodded, and dove immediately back into the protective concealment of his food.

I'm sitting in a faculty meeting, wishing desperately to be somewhere else. Actually, that's not quite true. My mind is so deeply mired in apathy, I'm not sure I'm capable of wishing desperately for anything. Even a good faculty meeting is less stimulating than televised chess, and this one is several levels below good. I feel as if I'm receiving a slow, gradual frontal lobotomy.

Some luckless functionary from the district computer office is valiantly explaining the new digitized grade sheets. A thin-lipped, mouse-faced lady who takes her assignment far too seriously, she tilts vainly against the massive windmill of my indifference, stressing again and again how wonderfully easy the new system is, how much work it will save me in figuring grades, how fortunate we all are to work for a school district with the bold vision to adopt this state-of-the-art computerized system.

My nostrils flare and stretch as I stifle a yawn. Lord, if You'll just let me out of here, I'll go all over the world proclaiming the glories of digital scanning technology. Mr. Ho, the building principal, is seated at the front of the library, just behind the computer lady, facing the rest of the faculty. His arms are folded in front of him, and he has a very serious, businesslike expression on his face—but then, I've never seen Mr. Ho without a serious, businesslike expression. I suspect he probably sleeps that way.

As I stare at the little-used card files, my mind wanders gratefully away from the discussion at hand. I reflect on Maude Barton, and on the odd, limping process by which the two of us seem to be drawing closer together. If I believed in such things, I'd say that we were being joined by a kind Providence. Since I'm not too sure I buy that, however, I have no good explanation for the staggering coincidence of our meeting, and the discovery of our mutual spiritual handicap.

Something Maude said that morning in her kitchen floats to the top of my mind. "You know, Janice," she said, "it's not that our folks meant to do anything bad. They weren't trying to hurt us. It just never occurred to them to help us. They'd been swimming upstream all their lives; they didn't have time to notice we were drowning."

Why didn't they notice? And why, even if he thought I was making my way upstream behind him, did my dad insist on tossing me an anchor?

And then I'm remembering something else Maude said. "Maybe, in a way, we're being unfair, Janice. Had you ever thought about that?"

I must have looked really puzzled. I felt that way.

"What we're asking them to do," she'd said, hugging herself in that chilled, vulnerable way, "is to fix us. To make us all better. To heal us. Aren't we?"

"Well... I don't guess I'd ever—"

"Think about it," she'd continued, her thoughts gathering momentum as she took another quick sip of tea. "Isn't that why you hate your father—because he didn't nourish you the way he should have?"

It sounded so brutal and self-serving, phrased like that. I felt the inner fences going up, felt myself backing away from an unpleasant confrontation with something dark inside me.

And then, those bespectacled green eyes had come straight at me. In a voice as uncomfortable as truth, Maude had said, "And asking another human to do it, or being hurt and angry because they can't, isn't going to help either of us in the long run."

Thinking about Maude's pronouncement, I get flustered all over again. Didn't she understand anything? God *was* my problem—couldn't she see that? God sat on Dad's shoulder, whispering instructions in his ear, keeping him away from home, keeping him busy with things other than me. God was there that night at the revival meeting when my father undressed me in front of a church full of people. God was unblemished perfection and searing, accusing light, the eagle-eyed Referee Who never missed a call. When I got too close to God, all I got was hurt. Maybe Maude was right, maybe I did need healing—I'd come to suspect as much, anyway. But God as the cure? Hold on a minute. Let's not get carried away here.

Yet... what if she's right? What if the discontent I feel at the center of myself is a void put there on purpose, a created discomfort that can be assuaged only by a Creator? What if all my rebellion, all my griefs, all my wounded pride—what if all of it is really just a patchwork quilt of threadbare pretexts, the sad posturing of a beggar who insists she's a queen? What if I've been using my father's guilt as an excuse for my own? What if I've been judging God by Dad's shortcomings?

I feel a nudge at my elbow; the meeting is breaking up. Good. A little motion and activity might be just what I need.

Nan Colyer—eighth-grade social studies and reading— leans over to pick up her folders. She looks across the table at me, then toward the computer lady at the front of the room, and rolls her eyes. I give her a sad little smile of agreement. "Brother," she moans in relief, "am I glad that's over!"

"Yeah, me, too."

But is it really over? Or just beginning?

13

O nce more, Linus inspected the line that tethered the donkey to the back of the wain. Not that the line required it; he had tied and retied the tether at least five times already, and secured the pack on the beast's back at least as often. No, it was he who needed the inspecting, his hands that needed some task, however meaningless, to occupy them.

He had stayed at the fire beside the wain, listening to the conversations between Phoebe and her men, until only a handful of embers remained. He had observed carefully as Phoebe attempted the reformation of the recalcitrant Praxos. Linus was awed by the depth and accuracy of Phoebe's knowledge of the Mosaic law and the teachings of the prophets. He had known, from the brief encounter in the Temple, that she was associated with some Greek synagogue as a "God-fearer," but he was in no way prepared for her astonishing fluency in the Hebrew scriptures. Again and again, she appealed to the Law as she tried to convince Praxos of the disparity between his sense of ethics and that evoked in the Decalogue.

But not only to Moses and the prophets did she appeal. The thought of Aristotle and Epicurus was known to her as well, and the further refinements of Plato found a place in her argument.

But despite Linus's absorption in the dialogue, and despite all Phoebe's attempts to enlist his opinions and comments, he kept a close tongue in his head. He was afraid that his lack of erudition would make him an object of ridicule among this learned household, where even the servants could discuss philosophy and the brilliance of their mistress blazed like a diamond. He also feared greatly what betrayals his tongue might commit, were he to loose it from its short rein and allow it to run where it willed. He could not so much as steal a glance at her without feeling rhapsodies of impossible longing spinning along every nerve and sinew. And so he made do with as few words as courtesy would permit.

Then, as the fire had died low and the servants, each in turn, had hidden yawns behind their hands and begged permission from their mistress to find their beds, she had turned to him. "Good sir, I find I am most perplexed in your case."

Uncertainty peered out at her from his eyes.

"I have invited you to take bread, I have offered payment for your labor, which has been refused—albeit most politely—I have had you as my guest during my attempts to further the education of my household servants, and I still find I do not know the source of the nagging memory of you. You said earlier that we had met—indeed, you called my name before I could give it to you. My man denies that he told you my identity." She gave him a long, appraising look. Under her gaze, Linus felt himself squirming inwardly, though he strove mightily to give no sign. "What answer have you for my quandary?" she insisted at last.

He swallowed several times, or made the attempt. "I... I believe—that is, we... we haven't exactly *met*, you understand..."

She silently refused to pick up the awkward thread which he offered with his imploring look. After a long, uncomfortable silence, Linus said, "In the Temple. In Jerusalem, at Passovertide. I saw you there—with men of your country."

Her eyes widened momentarily, as a sudden memory flashed across her mind. "You! The one in the crowd—who stared at me!"

His face stinging with shame, Linus hung his head in a silent admission of guilt.

"You were among those who gathered about the Galilean, Jesus!" she said, more to herself than to him. "And... and you were at the place where they killed him!" she said, amazement at the recollection quickening her voice. "I saw you there—atop the hill outside the walls!"

"My lady," he began slowly, "I am sorry. I never intended to give offence—"

"Then you must know what has happened!" she breathed excitedly, as if she hadn't heard his words. "Do you? Were you there? Did you see it?" she queried, her words a tangled, exhilarated rush.

Unsure of her meaning, Linus could only stare in confusion.

"His resurrection! Did you see Him alive again?" The color rose in her cheek as she spoke. "I was in Jerusalem during the last feast—Pentecost, isn't that it?—and I heard some people in the synagogue talking about it. A number of them received the ceremonial bath in his name, they said. I wondered if I should have..." And then her eyes leapt again to his, a feverish gleam glistening from her countenance. "He really was—is—the *Kristos*, the *Mashiach* , isn't he? Since his coming, things will be different, won't they? What do you know? You are from Jerusalem, and you must know everything, must have heard more! Please tell me everything you've heard, won't you?" She begged him with the insistence of a child, her eyes wide with fervor.

The memory of the startling speech of the tanner's son in the Damascene synagogue unfurled again within Linus's mind.

Like one from whom men hide their faces
   he was despised, and we esteemed him not...
After three days, God raised him from the dead. And now
   he is seated in the heavenly places with the Lord...
And I, if I be lifted up...

Again Linus felt himself thrashing about in his own confusion, wanting to believe, yet afraid to do so. Wanting to
confess to Phoebe his blood-stained emblem on the cross of
the Nazarene, yet fearful of revealing his secret shame—for,
if her belief was true, was he not accessory to the greatest
crime the world had ever spawned? A part of him longed to
confirm her fervent belief in the impossible, yet the rest of
him was frightened by the vulnerability such an endorsement might create for the protective shell of fatalism in
which he sought refuge.

At last, Linus shook his head helplessly. "I... I was not
there, lady. I left Jerusalem on the day... on the day of his
death. I know nothing about the things you mention." The
words burned his tongue almost as badly as a lie.

A crestfallen, wounded look replaced the eager one of
moments before. "Oh," she said in a flat, disappointed voice.
"I see."

The coals popped once, then again, punctuating the stillness of the night. Linus could hear the sounds of snoring in
the darkness about the wain. "The... the hour grows late,
lady," Linus said apologetically. "I should be going—"

"Will you walk with me tomorrow?" she asked suddenly. "You are... there are things I would like to ask
you—that is, if you don't mind. You could tie your beast to
the back of the wain."

Linus stood and stared in the direction of his pack. His
mouth opened several times before he could force a sound
from it. "I... very well," he said at last. "I will... I will do as
you ask."

Now, following a restless night, Linus stood beside the wain, searching his mind for something to say to this entrancing, forbidden woman of Achaia—something that would not betray the things he must conceal from her.

He was frightened by the insistency, the intensity of the sudden longing he felt in her presence—had felt from the very first time he laid eyes on her. Though reared in cosmopolitan Antioch, he was still Jewish enough to be instinctively disturbed by the thought of intimacy with a woman who did not share his heritage. He had known Jews who married outside the nation of Israel—but woefully few happy ones. And so a battle raged across the convoluted terrain of Linus's spirit: how to avoid rudeness toward this woman—who, after all, had shown him nothing but respect and kindness—without feeding the fond fantasies that threatened to overrule his judgment during every moment he spent in her presence?

The column was forming for the day's travel, the wain's outriders tugging and tying the last of their equipment into place on the backs of their mounts. One of the horses stretched its neck toward the donkey, standing as if half-asleep behind the wain. The horse's nostrils flared, scenting the beast, and it nickered softly, as if to gently waken the donkey for the beginning of the march. The donkey made no reply, other than the single twitch of a drooping ear.

The curtain of the wain parted a hand's width, and Linus heard Phoebe's voice, wafted to him on the rich scent of commingled spices. "Linus?" she called softly. "Are you there?"

Nervously he cleared his throat. "I am, lady."

"Please. If we are to be traveling companions, you must be less formal. My name will do much better."

"Very well, then…" he responded, after a longish pause, "…Phoebe," he said at last, touching her name to his lips as if it were a live coal.

The train moved out, stringing along the rut-marked track. A full day's journeying would bring them across the valley into Heliopolis, a city of no great size, but large enough to afford them the provisions that would carry them on to Emesa, the next stop along the way to Antioch.

The rising sun was still a mere, brightening rumor, lost far down below the shoulders of the Anti-Lebanon range, and the lingering night-chill of the highland country made the travelers' close-wrapped cloaks of great comfort. Stumbling now and again as his stiff limbs began to limber, Linus kept pace beside the lumbering, creaking wheels of the heavily loaded wain. When they had been traveling for perhaps two leagues, the curtain of the wain twitched back.

"Linus," Phoebe asked, "have you always lived in Jerusalem?"

"No, only for about the past eight years," he replied, without looking up from the ground in front of his feet.

"Where did you live before?" she asked.

"Antioch. That's why I'm going back—I have people there."

"Your... your family?" she asked, carefully studying the seam of the wain's rough-woven curtain.

He took perhaps fifteen paces before replying. "No— well, yes, I suppose. Yes—my family. My kin, at least."

"Why did you go to Jerusalem?"

Another long silence. "I thought I might... I went seeking something... something I had lost."

His tone bespoke raw emotions lying just below the surface of his words and warned her not to probe too deeply. And yet, she could not resist asking, "And did you find it?"

"No," he said immediately, with a force which surprised even himself. "I didn't. That's why I left."

"And you," he said, his curiosity beginning to overcome his reticence, "how is it that you came to the spice trade?"

"By being my father's daughter," Phoebe answered. "That, and having no brothers or uncles to whom my father's enterprise might pass. I was the last resort."

"Forgive me... Phoebe," he observed, "but it is more than a little unusual to see a woman traveling these parts alone—especially with such an expensive cargo."

"I don't travel alone. My servants are well-trained fighters, and besides that, I know how to use this," she said, yanking back the curtain's edge to show the jeweled haft of a Legionary-styled short sword. "Anyone who thinks this wain an easy prize will pay dearly for the assumption," she announced, her eyes flashing.

Linus, mildly chastened, huddled into his cloak like a turtle retreating into its shell. The nearest outrider tried, with little success, to hide his amused chuckle in a contrived coughing fit.

They traveled in silence a short distance before Phoebe said in Hebrew, "I assume you are a son of Israel."

"Yes," said Linus, "but why are we suddenly speaking Hebrew?"

"As you may have noticed," Phoebe replied, arching an eyebrow toward the outrider who had laughed, "other ears attend our words. Those things we wish to keep between ourselves are best said in Hebrew."

Linus nodded, smiling briefly. "I have few doubts of your comprehension after hearing your exposition of the Torah last night around the fire." He glanced toward her quickly, then away. "I have heard rabbis who could not manage as well."

"Thank you," Phoebe said quietly. "I hoped I was not mangling your sacred texts too badly."

"When did you have the time to learn Hebrew?"

"I persuaded the rabbi of the synagogue in Cenchrea, the city of my birth, to give me instruction." She reflected a moment, then added, "To reach the bedouins of Arabia and their supplies of myrrh, one must travel often through

Palestine. I have found that those of popular influence in Jerusalem and its environs respond more favorably to requests couched in the language of Abraham and Isaac. I felt it was important enough to take the time and effort required."

"Strictly for reasons of commerce, then?" said the carpenter.

She looked down, toying distractedly with the hilt of the short sword. After several moments, she gave him an unsteady glance. "No, I suppose not. I... I have long been a devotee of your religion. I suppose I felt I might learn more in Hebrew than I could in Greek." She blushed slightly, than asked quietly, "Do you think me foolish?"

"Certainly not!" Linus rejoined. "Why would you fancy so?"

"Oh, I'm not sure," she said, staring into the distance as she sat in the swaying wain. "I have often thought it futile for a Greek mind to attempt the complexities of your law. Some things in Moses and the prophets lie, I fear, forever beyond my grasp."

"Indeed, lady, some things in Moses and the prophets are too hard for those who have spent a lifetime in the pursuit," Linus assured her. "Why else do you think the graybeards in the Temple courts do nothing all day long but sit and debate the scriptures? Since the time of Nehemiah and the rebuilding of the wall, some seven generations now, they have done this—and are perhaps no closer to answers now than when the business first started. But I think it is perhaps the pursuit of truth, rather than its discovery, which most intrigues many of them."

Phoebe looked at him in amused surprise. "Why, my dear sir!" she enthused, "these are the most words you have uttered in a single burst since I have made your acquaintance!"

Linus glanced at her, grinned sheepishly, and shrugged.

"The pursuit of truth…" she mused presently. "That is a chase my people, too, have followed for long ages. Aristotle, Zeno, Epicurus, Socrates, Plato… Many are the great minds that have coursed after that elusive quarry, many the hiding places they have searched, widely varied the terrain over which they have hunted. But somehow…somehow, for me, at least, a lack exists—a void, even in the teachings of the great thinkers of past years, which has always disquieted my soul."

"And yet," Linus observed after a thoughtful pause, "the teachings of the philosophers—what little I remember from my meager education, you understand—seem far superior to the capricious, hither-and-thither beckonings of myth."

"Like Praxos's worship of Lady Luck, for instance?" smiled Phoebe.

"Exactly."

"That is true," she admitted. "Those who are truly devoted to the ethical systems taught by the philosophers come far nearer to living unified lives than most adherents of the mysteries. But still…in the voice of the God of Abraham and Isaac, I hear the ring of an unassailable verity, trace the outlines of a Principle which cannot be reduced to any component parts. I feel," she said, catching and holding Linus's eye with an expression of absolute conviction, "that somehow, the end of the philosopher's quest must be found in the will of the One your prophets call 'El Shaddai.' "

Her eloquent conviction turned Linus's eyes inward, wafted the stinging scent of reproach through the passages of his heart. That she, a gentile, could see the beauty of the Covenant more ably than he…

"And I also think," she finished, "that this Jesus, called the Christ, is an irreplaceable part of the final answer."

There was a long silence, punctuated only by the squeaking of the wain's rigging, the crunching of the path beneath hoof and boot.

"And so," Linus observed at last, "that's how you came to know Hebrew so well."

"That's how," she agreed quietly.

Linus mused a moment. "How odd. In the years I spent in Jerusalem, I learned to yearn for the Greek I heard as a boy in Antioch. And you, born to Greek, discovered a longing for Hebrew." He looked at her strangely. "A peculiar, circular journey we two have made, is it not?"

She tilted her head quizzically, then gave him a crooked smile. "Could it be that a philosopher lives inside the dusty garments of the tradesman?" she asked.

Linus blushed deeply. Quite some time passed before either of them spoke again.

It's Saturday morning. I'm lying on the couch in my nightshirt having a nutritious breakfast of Twinkies and Dr. Pepper—sugar-free, of course—while stimulating my mind with Garfield cartoons. If this goes well, I may go take a shower and change into more formal attire. If not, I may go back to bed for some leveling work. I'm keeping my options open.

I know I should be at the word processor, but for some reason Linus won't tell me what happens next in the story. I suppose I could dictate to him, make him do something arbitrary, but as a responsible creator, I can't permit myself to act contrary to my nature. Isn't that what the philosophers say— that the one thing God is incapable of is contradicting His own essence? I seem to remember hearing or reading that somewhere. Or maybe I just now thought it up. In that case, it's Garfield and Twinkies every weekend from now on. If only profundity were that simple.

Licking the marshmallow creme from my fingers, it occurs to me that junk food is an interesting metaphor for my life. A quick burst of energy, a round of frantic activity, but no real nourishment, no lasting effect. Tastes good during the act of consumption, provides temporary satisfaction, but your body is a little bit the worse after the digestive process is concluded. Still, in a perverse way, it seems to fit. Perhaps Twinkies and Sugar-Free D.P. are, after all, the perfect communion elements, the Body and the Blood for a generation that gets its ethics from Madison Avenue and its philosophy from MTV.

The phone rings. Wiping my hand on my nightshirt, I lean over to reach the cordless while stabbing at the "mute" button on my TV remote control.

"Hello?"

"Janice, this is Maude."

"Oh, good morning, Maude. How's it going?"

"Well... all right, I guess." Her tone gives her away.

"What's wrong, Maude? Are you okay?"

"Yes, honey, I'm fine, really. I just... there's something I have to do today, and I'm not sure I'm quite able..." Her unspoken request screams at me, impossible to graciously ignore. When my mom used to manipulate me this way, it drove me crazy. But I feel sort of responsible for Maude, and I can't let her down.

"Do you want me to come over, Maude?"

"Would you mind?"

"No, not at all. I'm not doing anything anyway. I'm not dressed yet, so give me—" I look at the clock on the bookshelf, —"say, forty-five minutes? Are you at home?"

"Yes, honey. That would be... I'd just appreciate it so much—"

"Forget it, Maude. I'll see you in a little while, okay?"

"All right, honey. And thanks again."

"No problem. Bye."

Driving across town to Maude's house, I turn on the FM radio in my car, resuming my American pop culture binge. There's an oxymoron for you: "pop culture." I wonder if I've been stricken with a case of aesthetic bulimia. Perhaps, after awhile, I'll stick my finger down my throat and purge my sensibilities of all the swill I've ingested this morning.

Maude is waiting on the front steps of her house. I pull over to the curb and she steps quickly to the passenger-side door just as I jab the "power" button on the car stereo player. "Thank you so much for coming," she says, with a smile hurriedly pasted over the worry-wrinkles on her face. "Let me get something from inside, and we'll go."

Go where? I wonder as I watch her half-jogging back toward the house, disappearing inside. Seconds later, she reemerges, locking the door behind her and coming toward the car, carrying one of those overdone, Victorian-looking wicker baskets with the big, circular handles. When she reaches the car, I can see that the basket is full of oranges, apples, bananas—and a box of dominoes, double-six variety. I don't have time to ask her anything. As soon as she ducks inside, she says, pointing, "Go straight on the way you're headed. We need to get on Center Oak Parkway and go west."

I shrug and put the car in gear. As we're pulling away from the curb, I ask, "By the way… where are we going?"

She gives me a guilty glance, then looks down. Buckling her seat belt around her, she says quietly, "To visit my father." The belt clicks shut with a sound like the locking of a gate, and she stares out the window on her side, unwilling or unable to meet my eyes.

"Maude! I had no idea your dad was still alive. I… I guess I assumed—"

"Of course you did," she interjects, without looking at me. "He's eighty-five years old, but I always think and speak of him in the past tense. When we get there… you'll see why." She says nothing else for the duration of the drive, except to give terse, monosyllabic directions.

Eventually, we pull up in front of a red brick building, liberally frosted with white trim finished in every imaginable Colonial-style molding and curlicue. "Shadybrook

Convalescent Center," the sign in front proclaims euphemistically. "Where We Care <u>About</u> You, Not Just <u>For</u> You," it adds beneath.

Maude still hasn't looked at me. "I don't know exactly what's come over me, Janice," she says, fussing with her seat belt, "but... This is never easy, you understand, but this week—I don't know. I guess I've been thinking too much, maybe..." Finally, reluctantly, she peeks over at me. "Anyway... I'm so grateful you came."

"Sure, Maude," I reply with a cheeriness as inadequate as the painted assurances on the sign. "I'm glad to help out. Ready?"

A deep sigh. "No, not really," she says, reaching for the door handle. "But let's go anyway." Walking toward the front door, she grabs my hand convulsively. I give her what I hope is a bolstering squeeze. And then we're inside.

Like many nursing homes, this building is organized into four long, straight halls, lined with rooms for the residents. The four halls converge on a central nursing station, located behind a chest-high, circular counter lined on the inside with intercom switches, telephones, and monitors of various types. A small foyer leads from the door we've just entered to this central control area. The foyer is furnished innocuously, as if to appeal to the least common denominator of its patrons. There is the inevitable television set, with the inevitable soap opera or gardening show playing to no one in particular. Along one wall, a large bulletin board is covered with a bright, mawkish mural, executed in construction-paper cutouts of green grass, two-dimensional trees, and symmetrically puffy clouds drifting past a beaming Mister Sun. "It's May!" the board gushes in red block letters, "and time to say 'Happy Birthday' to..." Snapshots of the month's dozen-or-so celebrants are tacked to the board, each mounted on a yellow square of construction paper, with the name and attained age stenciled below in bold black print.

A number of the residents are parked in wheelchairs in the spaces between the furniture and along the walls, and a few are seated on the couches and chairs, their walkers or four-legged canes close to hand. I am determinedly, brazenly cheerful, smiling broadly and nodding toward anyone who will maintain the slightest eye contact. Beside me, Maude grins defensively, walking as if on eggshells toward the central nurse's station.

The smell is a vaguely unpleasant yet familiar amalgam of disinfectant, institutional food, and stale lilac potpourri. It is subtly different from the odor of a hospital because of the faint reek of decay. Or perhaps it is the quiet stench of fear— a silent, motionless panic in the face of debilitating, invincible old age.

It occurs to me that these people—these sunken-cheeked, slack-jawed ones with the flesh hanging in useless folds from the backs of their arms—were children once. Once they ran and laughed and leapt with abandon from the top rails of fences, once they coddled dolls and played at hide-and-seek or leap-frog. Once they gazed upward into the loving or admonishing or scolding face of a mother, a father. Once they played hookey from school, held hands, carved initialed hearts into the bark of trees.

I am saddened to think of all that is fading with them, of all the memories that are locked inside, which they will take irretrievably to their graves. Perhaps even now that gnarled old man, his frame bent nearly double with arthritis, sits on the couch gazing vacantly at the wall above the television and recalls a day when the air was purer, when the sun—not a construction-paper caricature—shone with fierce jollity down upon him as he raced, kite in tow, across a jonquil-studded meadow. Perhaps that old woman, pushing herself with her one remaining leg, backwards down the hall in her wheelchair, is reminiscing about the very first time she was called upon to recite in school—the butterflies dancing in her stomach as she stood straight and tall beside her desk, smoothing back her pinafore and beginning in a careful, studious voice:

Listen, my children, and you shall hear
of the midnight ride of Paul Revere...

But all those stories, all those memories are dissolving in the slow, sure acid of time. And at this moment, I feel cheated by the loss.

"Hello, Miss Barton," says one of the nurses behind the counter, smiling brightly at Maude. Her eyes glide smoothly across toward me, and I nod.

"Hello, Ruth," Maude replies, extending the basket toward the young black woman. "I brought you all some fresh fruit, if you'd like it."

"Oh, bless your heart!" says Ruth, selecting an apple from the basket. "You're so sweet to remember us!"

"Well...here, take some more. There's plenty," Maude urges. Ruth passes several pieces of fruit to her co-workers at the station.

"Mornin', Maude," calls an older nurse who has just returned to the nurse's desk. "He's ready for you. In his wheelchair, all brushed and dressed and ready to go."

"Thanks, Grace," says Maude, her voice dropping several tones in pitch. "Don't you want some fruit?" she inquires after a pause, as if to stall a moment she is dreading.

"Oh, no, thanks just the same," answers Grace, giving Maude a quick, apologetic smile. "Gives me gas."

"Well, then..." Maude looks down the hall, as if staring down the bore of a loaded cannon. "I guess we'd better get down there, Janice," she finishes, with a joviality about as authentic as antlers on a duck. We walk down the corridor until we come to a room numbered "12-E" and labelled with nameplates reading, "Ernest Walker" and "Jonas Barton." Maude pushes open the door. "Hello, Papa," she says, "it's me—Maudie."

I'm surprised at Mr. Barton's appearance. From the few comments Maude has made, I realize that my mind has constructed the image of a tall, rawboned, craggy-faced man, with perhaps an unruly shock of white hair. But as she bends solicitously over her father, I see, instead, where Maude got her fine features, her thin fingers and slender build. She is the female representation of her father. Jonas Barton is a slight, bald man who sits bunched in his wheelchair, bending crookedly over the table in front of him as he peers raptly at a pile of assorted coins. Now and again, his trembling, feeble hand reaches slowly out to remove a nickel, a penny, a quarter, and place it carefully on the stacks of similar coins he has begun on the table's perimeter. I notice that his fingers never uncurl—not quite. His skin is chalky-white, in contrast to the brownish liver-spots splotched across his complexion. He is wearing a shirt of some nondescript plaid and khaki trousers. I can see perhaps an inch of the pasty skin of his calf above his drooping socks, his feet passively inside bedroom slippers which appear to have received no wear at all. Although the temperature outside is in the high seventies, Mr. Barton has a gray wool cardigan sweater slipped over his shoulders, like a shawl. He stares fixedly at the pile of coins as if it holds the key to his future.

"Hello, Mister Walker," Maude calls, greeting her father's roommate. The other occupant, a huge, fleshy black man whose bulk is wedged impossibly tightly into the confines of his wheelchair, smiles and nods at Maude. "Good to see you, honey," he says in a voice surprisingly soft for such a large frame. His hair is close-cropped and white as freshly laundered wool.

"How's he doing?" Maude asks, nodding toward her father.

Mr. Walker looks at his roommate a moment, then back at Maude. He shakes his head. "Pretty much the same," he says, giving a sad little smile. "He sits there and plays with his coins, or whatever else someone brings him to fiddle with. Won't talk, won't read, won't watch TV—just sits there," Mr. Walker finishes tiredly, "just like that."

"Would you like an apple, Papa?" Maude asks, raising her voice and trying vainly to get her face between her father's and the coins in which he is absorbed. "I brought you some fresh fruit—I'll slice some for you, if you like," she offers without, I sense, much hope that she will be acknowledged, much less answered.

The shaking, half-closed fingers reach out, plucking a quarter from the pile, placing it gently on a stack of its mates. The eyes never waver from the object of their fascination.

"Well, all right, then," Maude says presently, just as if her father had politely declined, "you don't have to eat any, if you don't want it. But I'll bet Mr. Walker would like an apple or a banana." Her eyes lift hopefully toward the roommate.

Mr. Walker looks at the fruit, then at Maude. Something very much like pity shimmers from his eyes, and the line of his mouth blurs between a smile and a sob. "Sure, honey, I'd really like one of those apples, if you've got a spare."

"Why, of course!" says Maude in a pert, relieved voice, selecting the biggest apple she can find. "I've got a knife in here somewhere, Mr. Walker, and I'll slice that for you," she says, digging in her purse.

"That's all right, sugar," he says softly, leaning over to take the apple from her hand, "I don't need it sliced. That's one thing that's left to me, at least—I still got most of my teeth." He chuckles softly, taking a bite. Only after he has chewed and swallowed, leaning to his right to place the apple on the night stand beside him, do I notice that he has another half-eaten apple in his lap, which he now shields from Maude's vision with the magazine he had been reading before we came in. He glances at me and realizes I have seen the other apple. His eyes flicker from me to Maude, who has turned her attention again toward her father. Mr. Walker's eyes lock with mine as he shakes his head, almost imperceptibly.

Maude looks up at me. "Janice, I'm going to go visit with Papa's dietician for just a minute. Do you mind waiting here while I go?"

"No, Maude, of course not."

"All right, then. Papa, I'll be right back," she says brightly, and leaves the room.

My eyes shift back to Mr. Walker. He gives me a conspiratorial wink and a grin. "Glad I caught your eye there," he says.

I smile at him, beginning to like him immensely. "That was a really nice thing you did for Maude," I say, stepping around Mr. Barton's wheelchair to sit on one of the beds.

Mr. Walker shrugs. "She needed to give me that apple. So, I needed to receive it. That's all there was to it."

A coin clatters to the table in front of Mr. Barton. Our eyes shift to him as he fumbles with frantic slowness to hem the dropped nickel between his thumbnail and forefinger. Even the pads of his fingers are wilted with age, and time has deadened his fingertips so that the nickel scoots this way and that, defeating his best efforts to retrieve it.

"How long have you and Maude's dad been room-mates?" I ask after a moment.

Mr. Walker ponders a moment. "'Bout five years, best I can figure."

"Was he always like this?" I ask, inclining my head toward Mr. Barton.

"No, not really," says Mr. Walker sadly, studying his roommate's almost motionless profile. "At first, he could talk to you, carry on a little bit of conversation. Never laughed much nor smiled, but at least it was somebody to talk to." His voice tolled with regret. I can hear the breath hushing in and out of Mr. Barton's nostrils, coming in faster and faster bursts. Mr. Walker nods toward him. "Why don't you help him out a little, there? He's startin' to get upset."

I lean across and trap the recalcitrant nickel allowing Mr. Barton to clasp it in his fingers. Without the slightest sign of thanks, as if the nickel had leapt spontaneously into his grasp, he places it on the nickel stack and resumes sorting through the coins.

"But even when he could talk, or would," Mr. Walker continues, "he'd hardly give Maude the time of day." He shakes his head. "I felt real bad about the way he did her."

"How about you?" I ask. "You seem… well, umm…" Suddenly my question doesn't seem like such a good idea.

"Out of place?" he finishes for me, a tiny, playful smile tickling his cheek. "Too alert to be in here with all these wore-out old people?"

I'm squirming inside by now, and he knows it. "Well… yeah, sort of," I manage weakly.

He chuckles softly. "Don't worry, honey. I ask myself that, all the time. It's my back. I hurt it real bad a long time ago, and it's just got worse and worse as the years go by. It's so weak now I cain't even get out of this chair by myself. Even if I could, the pain'd be so bad it'd likely kill me. And besides all that, I ain't no spring chicken myself. There's some here that's older than me, but there's a sight of 'em younger, too."

"What about your family?"

He shakes his head. "Wife died five years ago, and my kids are scattered to the four winds. Got a boy on one coast and two girls on the other. It's pretty hard for them to get out here very much."

The sadness and loss in his voice make me want to cry.

"But," he says a couple of seconds later, "my disability pension pretty much pays my keep here, and the folks in this place are real nice to me." He picks up Maude's apple, studies it a moment, and takes another large bite. "I cain't complain too much," he says, between noisy chomps.

I hear Mr. Barton's fingernails scrabbling along the table top. He has managed to seize the last coin remaining in the pile—a penny. Deliberately, he places it atop the penny stack. Then, his task finished, he stares blankly at the place where the coin pile had been.

He sits frozen in this attitude for perhaps two full minutes. Doubtfully, I look at Mr. Walker. "Should I...will he get upset with nothing to do? Does he want to start over?"

Mr. Walker shook his head. "No, starting him over won't do no good. Once he's done with a project, that's all she wrote. You can mix it up again and put it in front of him, but he'll just sit there, glassy-eyed like, until you take it away and bring him something different. He's been through coins, decks of cards, poker chips, colored toothpicks—"

"Dominoes," I mutter, making the connection.

"Do what?" says Mr. Walker.

"Dominoes. Maude brought him a set of dominoes today. Double sixes."

"Well, is that a fact?" says Mr. Walker, showing real interest. "Say... when Jonas there gets done with them bones, maybe I could find someone around here who knows how to play dominoes or forty-two!"

"Tell you what, Mr. Walker," I say, "if he's finished with them the next time I come with Maude, I'll play you a few games!"

He gives me a broad, warm, ivory-lined smile that seems to last for an hour, that wraps around me like a hug. "I'll tell *you* what, sugar," he says finally, "why don't you call me 'Shake?' That's what my friends call me."

"All right, Shake. You've got a deal."

14

The walls of Heliopolis rose up from the grassy Syrian plains, shimmering in the heat of the summer afternoon. The sight was a glad one for the travelers, who were anxious for the beds and warm food the town would afford.

Shading his eyes with his hand, Linus peered ahead; they should be able to reach the town's gates by dark, he decided. It would be good to have a roof overhead once again. Traveling with this large train added much to the safety of the journey, but the carpenter always slept better when surrounded with sturdy walls.

"Linus," Phoebe called from within the wain, "what arrangements will you make for lodging when we reach the town?"

"I suppose I will find an inn and take a bed there—I hadn't thought much of—"

"I have a kinsman in Heliopolis," she interjected. "In fact, he is an agent for me. I must make delivery of some of this shipment to him, and he will lodge me and my servants in his house." She paused long before speaking again. "Will you—would you consider taking a bed there? It might be considered... payment for the repair of the wheel."

"Lady, I have already said—" he began, protesting.

"Yes, yes, I know. Fellow travelers and all that. But the fact is"—the curtain twitched aside, and she peered pointedly out at him. "I would count it a personal favor if you would accept."

What was he to do? This Grecian damsel was twisting him into knots that would surely defeat even the legendary Samson! She was touching chords within him that had not vibrated since... Sternly he commanded himself to refuse. It was unthinkable, indecent! How could he allow himself to consider—

"Very well, lady," he heard his traitorous lips say. So ashamed was he of his weakness of character, he could not look her direction as he spoke. "I will come to the house of your kinsman."

Phoebe let the curtain fall and leaned back against a bale of aloes, smiling.

At sunset they reached the gates of Heliopolis. The travelers went their separate ways, agreeing to meet by the north gate at first light. Armitius looked hurt when Linus refused his offer of sharing the cost of board at a nearby inn, but when he saw the carpenter preparing to leave in the company of the spice wain and its party, his eyes widened in surprise and comprehension. He sidled up to Linus and nudged the carpenter conspiratorially in the ribs. "Now I get it, lad, now I get it," he grinned and winked. "You just go on and have a good time, and don't worry an instant about old Armitius. I always did admire a man with an eye for an opportunity."

Linus glared angrily at the stonemason, then wheeled and stalked off, following the wain.

Armitius turned shrugging to the man next to him. "What did I say?" he asked, befuddled.

They entered the house of Phoebe's kinsman through a wide, well-guarded stone gate, which opened onto a courtyard at least twenty paces wide and as many deep, and fairly ablaze with sconced torches. To one side were the stables, to the other the servant's quarters and sculleries. A hewn cistern sat in the middle of the yard, from which servants had drawn draughts of sweet, cool water they now offered to each of the members of the just-arrived traveling party. Other servants came to unharness and lead away the animals toward the stables. Still others set about the business of unloading the wain under the keen oversight of Praxos, who stood glaring this way and that, watching like a hawk to see that his terse, tight-lipped commands were carefully obeyed.

Standing perplexed amid the bustle, Linus realized that everyone except him was carrying out a task that had been assigned and performed before. In the businesslike, to-and-fro scurrying of the servants, the practiced supervision of Phoebe's men, the obvious preparation and planning that had taken place before their arrival, he traced the signs of a highly organized and well-practiced routine. He looked about him in amazement.

On the other side of the cistern, directly facing the gate through which they had entered, stood the house proper. It was of dressed stone, and the light from oil lamps—surely hundreds!—blazed from each of the score of windows visible on the front of the two-story structure. And now, from the front portal—framed by two fluted columns of alabaster crowned by ornate Corinthian finials—a tall, meticulously groomed, silk-robed man came down the front steps, his arms wide in greeting. At the same moment, Phoebe stepped out from the wain, walking with a wide smile toward this man. "Cousin!" Linus heard him call. "Be thrice welcomed!" They embraced.

Linus was awestruck. This man was merely an agent! How would the house of Phoebe appear by comparison? From the richness of her cargo and the presence of four mounted servants, Linus had deduced some notion of Phoebe's wealth. But this! The horde of servants swarming about, the huge courtyard, lit almost as if in daylight, the spacious mansion—the casual display of such opulence made Linus dizzy, made him know himself to be truly mad for the ridiculous things he had imagined as he walked beside Phoebe's wain.

There were times during the long walk when he had actually imagined that she enjoyed his company—that she derived, for whatever unfathomable reason, genuine happiness from his society. There were even periods during their conversation on this or that subject when he forgot his reticence, when he heard himself voicing thoughts he had not, until the moment of their utterance, known he had words enough to articulate. Indeed, he fancied it was the enchantment of Phoebe's presence that called such unrehearsed words forth, summoned them from some place within him where they had lain dormant against this very day.

But these foolish maunderings were swept away by his sudden remembrance of the vast gulf stretching between his world and hers. Regardless of how much she might profess a love for Moses and the prophets, Linus knew with a heartsinking certainty that her walk of life was so completely foreign to his as to be beyond comprehension. That a gentile woman—and a person of such manifestly vast resources—could take any interest in a plain, backward fellow such as himself. . . the notion would have been ludicrous if not for the tiny barb of pain digging into the tender flesh of his heart. Now, as he watched, she walked toward the house, arm-in-arm with the master of the mansion. Even as he told himself he should have expected nothing else, his throat ached with the sudden pain of loss.

"A bath is prepared for you, sir, by order of the master," said a soft male voice in Linus's ear. He glanced around to see a young manservant, standing patiently with eyes politely averted, gesturing toward the house. Linus nodded and allowed the page to lead him toward the Corinthian columns and the door they framed.

Feeling a hand on his shoulder, Linus flinched and started awake. He had fallen asleep in the warm, scented bath. A manservant knelt beside him on the clay-tiled floor surrounding the sunken stone vat the carpenter reclined in. Linus peered a question at him.

"My apologies, good sir," the man began softly, "but I am instructed to bring you to the board. My master wishes you to be present for the feast he has prepared."

Linus levered himself to his feet, then stared about in confusion: while he was asleep, someone had stolen his clothes!

"Forgive me, sir," the servant intoned, as if reading his thoughts, "but I have taken the liberty of supposing these garments might be appropriate." The slave gestured toward a backless chair, over which were draped a finely woven white linen tunic, a belt of braided white velvet, and a light-weight woolen outer robe of rich crimson hue. Eyes wide with impressed surprise, Linus padded wetly toward the clothing, gingerly fingering the fine fabrics. "But," he asked warily, "what has become of my clothing?"

"It is being washed," the servant replied, "and will be returned to you on the morrow... if you wish."

Linus detected the faint note of sarcasm in the slave's last words, but chose to ignore them. "Very well," he said at last. "These will do, I suppose." The manservant began to rub his body with a soft, absorbent cloth.

The slave led him through a corridor paved, like the rest of the lower floor of the house, with clay tiles. The walls were covered to the height of a man's shoulder with smaller, glazed tiles composed into a mosaic depicting the wine-god Dionysius presiding over a revel attended by nymphs and satyrs. The corridor opened onto a spacious, well-lit hall, dominated by the large, heavy-laden board at its center. According to the Roman style, three couches were placed about the board. On the couch at the head of the table reclined the master of the house. The couch to his left was empty. And on his right—Phoebe.

At the sight of her, Linus faltered a half-step. Like himself, she had bathed and changed her garments. No longer did she wear the simple linen traveling tunic; now she wore a billowing drape of sheer, purple silk belted at the waist with a thin silver chain, over an ankle-length under-shift of flawlessly white linen. Her raven-colored locks tumbled in glad profusion over her shoulders, and her eyes sparkled like black stars in the flickering light of the sur-rounding lamps.

He willed himself to give no sign, forced his face to remain impassive, focused his vision somewhere else, any-where else but upon Phoebe. His host gestured needlessly toward the vacant couch, and Linus, feeling unaccustomed awkwardness, took his place.

The table was loaded with foodstuffs: several different kinds of cheeses, olives both green and black, silver bowls full of almonds, dates, figs, and rare pistachio nuts from faraway Cappadocia. There were ewers of wine beside decanters of water for mixing, and steaming platters of meat, freshly roasted with herbs and leeks. There were slices of melon and hot yeast-bread. Linus had never in his life seen so much food spread for only three people. Even the festive meals of his childhood *seders* dimmed in his memory beside the profusion he now gazed upon.

The host reached for a ewer of wine, but Phoebe halted him with a word. "Wait, Demetrius! Remember what I told you..."

"Oh... yes, my mistake," the cousin apologized. He smiled at Linus. "It is my cousin's wish that you pronounce a blessing on this meal. A traditional blessing of your people, if you please."

Linus stared from Phoebe to her cousin. Was this a mockery? Did she seek to patronize this rude Jew who had plodded all the day long beside her spice wain? But, no. Looking at her gentle face, her warm, expectant eyes, he knew she intended him no harm. Raising himself to a sitting position, he raised his hands to heaven and closed his eyes.

"Barukh atah Adonai eloheynu melekh ha 'olam borey pri hagafen... Blessed art Thou, O Lord our God, Ruler of the Universe, Who creates the fruit of the vine," he prayed in Hebrew, "and blessed art Thou, Who creates the fruit of the earth. Amen."

"Amen," responded Phoebe softly.

When Linus opened his eyes, Demetrius was peering curiously at them both. "Now?" he asked.

"Now!" Phoebe laughed, and each of them reached for the ewer of wine in front them.

"Tell me, then, Demetrius" she said, as she added water to the wine she had poured, "what is the latest news of the wide world? We spent but a single night in Damascus, and it is over a week since we left Jerusalem. What have you heard?"

Demetrius shrugged as a slave materialized silently behind him, picking up his master's mahogany bowl and filling it with food from the various platters on the table. "I haven't heard much in a week or so," he began, taking a sip of wine, "but I suppose the big news from Rome is that Caesar has exiled all the Jews from the capital—" he broke off, staring at Linus. "Oh, I'm sorry, friend! I didn't mean to—"

"Think nothing of it," said Linus placatingly. "The affairs of Jews in Rome affect me little at all... That is, unless Caesar has placed a bounty on the heads of the whole nation!"

"No, no, nothing of that sort," laughed Demetrius, relieved. "What happened is just this: it seems that four Jewish fellows, somewhat less than honest as it chances, conspired together to dupe a noblewoman of the city who had embraced your religion. They solicited from her gold and purple fabrics, purportedly for the upkeep of your temple in Jerusalem. But when they had procured the goods, they used them instead for the maintenance of their own comfort. Fulvia—that is the woman's name—upon getting wind of the hoax, reported the matter to her husband, a knight named Something-or-Other Saturninus. When Tiberius heard the matter, he responded by banishing all the Jews living within the imperial city."

"And so a multitude of innocent people suffer because of the greed of four scoundrels," observed Phoebe, taking a bite out of a fig.

"This will not be the first, nor perhaps the last time that such a circumstance befalls my people," said Linus, absently toying with the pistachios in his bowl. "It seems that the many are forever suffering for the sins of a few."

"But," interjected Phoebe, searching Linus with her gaze, "might it not also be true that sometimes, the suffering of the innocent produces good for the many?"

Linus held her stare for three breaths, four. Then his eyes fell, and he busied himself with the food in his bowl.

Demetrius, oblivious to the undercurrents rippling across the table, continued his tale. "I don't know about all that, but I also heard that Caesar conscripted four thousand Jewish youths to the isle of Sardinia to put down a rebellion of some sort. Whole trains of Jews are beginning to show up in cities across the Empire. I saw a poor, bedraggled group of them arrive in Heliopolis just today." He popped a large morsel of meat into his mouth, and signalled for his finger bowl. "The pitiful louts. Looked like they'd trekked the whole length and breadth of the world, so shabby was their appearance."

"Demetrius!" warned Phoebe, aiming a pointed glance toward the silent Linus.

"Oh, dear!" apologized Demetrius with a distressed expression, "again I've said the wrong thing!"

Linus looked up at his host, a sad half-smile brushing his lips. "That's all right—really. I can agree somewhat with what you've said. Indeed, sometimes I think my nation is bent on self-exile—for we don't seem to quite fit anywhere in the world." Without volition, he felt his gaze drawn toward Phoebe, lingering long and without hope in the dark orbs of her eyes. Tearing himself away at last, he fell again to toying with the sweetmeats in his bowl. "No, your words are not without merit, Demetrius. I fear that instead, you have just uttered a prophecy."

Phoebe peered across at him, her eyes brimming with compassion. She longed to understand the complex pain of this quiet man, to comprehend the nameless burden that seemed to ever halt him at the threshold of happiness. In moments like this, Linus put her in mind of a famished beast tied on a rope a hand's breadth shorter than the distance to its food. Or a dog who once knew a kind master but has become feral; who sniffs at the scent of the town and its distant memories of warmth and shelter, but who turns at last to the bleak comfort of its freedom, haltered forever by its own wariness.

Demetrius peered in puzzlement from his cousin to the morose stranger she had brought into his house. Then, with a cheeriness he didn't precisely feel, he said, "Well, then! We haven't had any bread, have we?" He clapped his hands briskly, and a slave was at his elbow, bending to take up the tray holding the yeast-cake. "Here, everyone!" the host urged, "tear off some of this excellent bread. Clopas, here, baked it, and he'll be ever so put out if it isn't eaten!" Demetrius chuckled at his little jest, and his guests smiled—politely, nothing more.

I get up from the word processor and walk around the room a few times, squinting and rubbing my eyes with my fingertips. I've been writing for a couple of hours now, and the screen has started to swell and contract, the letters have begun to look like a jumble of pica-sized break-dancers. I take a drink of the room-temperature soda left in the can I opened an hour ago.

It's Sunday night, normally the most depressing time of a teacher's week. But this Sunday night is different, because there's only one more week until school is out for the summer. I glance over at the stack of video cassettes I've secured to while away the last five class days of the term. These tapes are very important to me—they are my lesson plan for the week.The last concert has been played, the music passed in and sorted, the horns checked in. Along with the kids, I'm powering down into summer mode.

I hope the librarian at school hasn't misplaced my reservation for the monitor and VCR. Trying to reserve a VCR or a movie projector during the last week of school would be a joke. The equipment has all been spoken for since the middle of April. I'm not the only one who'll be teaching Modern Cinema and Television the last five days of school—not by a long shot. I only hope I'm not showing them the same stuff they saw last year.

I reflect back on the term, and all in all, it's been pretty decent. The advanced band did well at the festival, and a number of kids in each of the bands made a lot of improvement from September to May. I think about the ninth graders who will be going on to senior high school, and I'm a little sad. Even though I've only had them a single year, I got to know and appreciate many of them—except for the few clowns and ne'er-do-wells in the percussion and cornet sections I wouldn't mind shipping off to Pluto. But mostly, they were good kids.

And then I think about the seventh- and eighth-graders who will be coming up, and I'm consoled. And I wonder about the kids who'll be coming in from the sixth grade, the ones I haven't even met. Will there be a young genius among their ranks whose blossoming I may be privileged to foster? Will there be a renegade for whom music may hold the key to reclamation? Will I finally get a kid who can learn to play the bassoon?

I can afford to be philosophical about such matters now. The long, green stretch of summer gives me distance, affords me objectivity. By the time August rolls around, the threatening, impending whir of Labor Day's wings will have driven all such esoteric considerations from my head. It'll be back to the struggle from Point A to Point B, with blessed little time to raise my head above the lip of the trench.

I went to church this morning, at Maude's invitation. Strange to tell, I didn't mind it. I should say I did mind it, for a change. Something happened there that engaged my mind, stuck with me. Brought me... comfort, now that I think of it. For a couple of minutes, I connected—apparently for reasons entirely beyond my control.

It wasn't the sermon, which was nice and well-intentioned, but mostly wasted on me. It was—I should have known it—a song. One that I sang a thousand times as a kid, and that I've heard sung at least a thousand times since:

> Just as I am, without one plea
> But that Thy blood was shed for me;
> And that Thou bid'st me come to Thee—
> O Lamb of God, I come! I come!

But that wasn't exactly it. either. No, it was another verse—this one:

> Just as I am, though tossed about
> With many a conflict, many a doubt;
> Fightings within and fears without,
> O Lamb of God, I come! I come!

Listening to the words—listening, because I still haven't brought myself to sing aloud yet—something clicked into place in my mind. I looked at Maude, dutifully belting out the alto line beside me, and I thought about the weird, convoluted tangles in my own mind, and it hit me: Maude just sang about the two of us. *Fightings within... Many a conflict, many a doubt...* The old sixties bromide came to mind: "I have met the enemy, and he is us!"

By the time we got back to her house from the nursing home that day, Maude was sobbing uncontrollably. I was really scared. I thought she might be going to the bottom of the blender, and if there's anyone less qualified than myself to perform emotional CPR, I'd hate to meet her. After all, I've had plenty of reasons to question my own grip on reality. Talk about the blind leading the blind!

I couldn't just leave her alone like that, so I walked her inside. I sat beside her on the overstuffed couch, just sort of holding her hand and patting it, and getting up every couple of minutes to get more tissues, and feeling really awkward and embarrassed, but not knowing what else to do.

"I was afraid this was going to happen today," she said finally, between sobs and after several false starts. "I felt it coming, and building, and I tried to hold it back, but I just couldn't." More sniffles and sobs, more tissue, more patting of hands, and me still not knowing what to say.

"I want to get past it," she said after a couple of minutes, "I want to absolve myself and him of all the missed opportunities, all the emotional deprivation...

"I want to yell at him!" she shrieked suddenly, scaring the daylights out of me. "I want to make him sorry, and make him pay, and make him admit he was wrong, all those years, all those cheerless years." She cupped her face in her hands, and poured out her grief as if she were vomiting an endless flood.

By degrees, the catharsis burned itself out. Maude began to surface from the abyss of her sorrow, wiping her face with her hands, with her forearms, with the hem of her dress, grabbing wads of tissues at a time. When she could almost hold her lips steady, she looked at me. "I'm sorry, Janice. I guess I'm not a very good example today."

I shrug. "It's okay, Maude. Nobody can be strong all the time." Such advice I can give! If Maude only knew. What a laugh!

She turns to me again. "You saw how he was, Janice. You saw how he's shrivelled—what little of him is left."

I nodded. "Yeah, I guess..."

"Well, then. Can't you see my dilemma?" Her voice is almost matter-of-fact, with just a slight tremor left.

"Don't think I haven't thought of things I'd like to say to him," she said, a chill wind of bitterness in her voice. "Oh, I've thought and I've thought and I've thought! 'Why didn't you ever encourage me in a single thing that was important to *me* ? Why didn't you exhibit to me a little bit of the compassion you spread around on all your out-of-work friends? Why didn't you ever—" Her voice broke, and she grabbed at her mouth, reminding me of someone who felt a sudden twinge in the back. " 'Why didn't you ever read me a story? Or tell me one?' Oh, Janice," she said, shaking her head with resentful assurance, "I could tell him so many things! But now—he's retreated behind the barrier of senility. He's cheated me again, don't you see? I know I should forgive him, should ask God to take away the pain, the hurting, but…" She stared for several moments into a void whose dimensions I couldn't guess. "By the time I realized what I needed to say to him," she said finally, "he's gone where I can't touch him. And seeing the husk of him that's left just makes it worse—just reminds me of who he was, and who he helped me become."

And then she said something that froze my heart.

"Janice," she said, her lips quivering anew, "you still have a chance to confront your demons. Mine are out of reach."

And then, less than a week later, sitting in church beside her, singing that song, I realized how well its words described us. And for an instant, for a scant half-second, a window opened for me—a little. Maybe, just maybe, that was why we were there, in that cramped little sanctuary and its crowded pew, singing a rusty, unadorned, true old song. We were there, Maude and I, just as we were. Despite all the ragged and torn places, all the holes in our lives, with our conflicts and our doubts, we were attending a come-as-you-are party. Helpless, and looking for a cure. Not giving in, not quite yet. Doing the best we knew how. *O Lamb of God, I come...*

Maybe.

The sun had made twelve passages over the caravan from the time it left Damascus, and at last the travelers had arrived in Syrian Antioch. Here, in the capital of the Imperial province of Syria, some would stay. Others would linger a few days, perhaps a month, taking on provisions or making trades, and then would travel on to another opportunity. Still others would tarry but a night or two.

Entering the city, Linus trudged along beside the wain, striving gamely to ignore the saddening weight that dragged at his spirit like a sea anchor. He told himself he should be happy, should be eagerly anticipating the renewal of ties with the many friends and relations he had left here eight years past. Matthias, though not a young man when Linus had left, would be busy at his trade, turning out the best woodcraft in Antioch. And Anna, his wife—how would the years have changed her? Miriam, their daughter, must surely be married by now, perhaps have children of her own. And then there was Caius, their son, who had visited him in Jerusalem during this past Sukkoth-tide. It would be good to see them, to embrace them once again.

It was no use. The knowledge of Phoebe's imminent departure was far more telling than all the pleasant anticipation. She was leaving to continue on her way to Achaia, and he would probably never see her again. Despite his efforts to prevent it, this knowledge weighed him down, sapped the joy he should have felt in this homecoming.

At last, they came to the street where he must turn aside to go to the houses of his kin. Phoebe, seeing his eyes stray toward the branching way, signaled to the servant walking beside the oxen. The man hauled backward on the line attached to the nose ring of the off ox, gradually bringing the phlegmatic beasts to a lumbering halt. Phoebe stepped down from the wain and stood beside Linus as he untied the donkey from the back of the wain.

"You will leave us here?" she asked needlessly.

Linus nodded, unwilling to meet her eyes. The wain and its attendants formed a small island in the busy flow of the street. All about them the babble of commerce continued unabated, but the noise was no more than an echo in Linus's ears. Confusion and loss pounded in his head, the war raging in his breast drowned out all external sound—save Phoebe's voice.

"You could go with us, you know," she said in a flat, hopeless tone. "What will I do if another mishap occurs with the wain?" she laughed, but the sound quickly died in her throat. They were trapped within two different worlds, it seemed. Though she longed to break through the barrier of his desolation, she did not know the way, could not find the key to unlock his acceptance.

Linus felt caught inside a whirlwind, spinning helplessly round and round, buffeted by the whirling debris of his past. Go with her! he screamed at himself. Follow your heart! She will be gone, taking with her perhaps your last chance for happiness! Why continue to torture yourself with a past you cannot change, with laws you cannot keep?

"I have kin in this place," he heard his traitorous lips saying, "and I should go to them. I... I think it best so," he lied, stabbing a blade into the protesting throat of his feelings.

They stood together for perhaps thirty heartbeats, Phoebe's eyes locked on his face, his roving here, there—anywhere but toward the dark, sweet prison of her gaze.

At last her voice broke the silence. "Well then... I suppose we should be finding an inn. The animals will need fodder and—" she glanced at the sky— "the day draws down toward night." A sigh blew raggedly through her tightening throat. "I have enjoyed our talks, Linus, carpenter of—Antioch," she said, willing her chin to remain steady. "The spice trade often brings me this way, and perhaps on another time…" She allowed the offer to hang in the air unspoken, praying that he might pick up the thread she held tenuously out toward him.

He opened his mouth, then closed it. He felt her eyes on him, and though he knew he should avoid doing so at all costs, he turned to face her. He looked into her eyes and felt as if he were falling, falling, forever falling into their intoxicating depths. He knew if he did not turn away this instant, he would never be able to do so. "I want… I wish…" he began, in a voice like a drowning man's.

A question wrinkled her forehead.

"Goodbye," he husked, and spun about. "Come on, you," he growled at the donkey as he strode off, almost trotting down the street. She watched him go until the crowd swallowed him from sight. With an iron act of will, she composed her features. She turned slowly and stepped into the wain. She looked at the nearest rider, whose face was discreetly averted. "Let's be on our way," she said, in a voice somewhat less steady than she might have wished. The ox driver flicked the off ox's flank with the rod he carried. The wain rumbled slowly into motion, creaking as it rolled down the street.

Moments later Linus was dodging back along the way he had gone, cursing the donkey for its slowness. "Come on, stupid beast," he grunted, jerking uselessly on the lead rope. He arrived at the head of the street.

But the wain was gone. Faceless crowds now hurried past where, moments before, her feet had stood. For an instant, he imagined he scented the exotic, sweetish aroma of cloves and myrrh. But then the spell was broken. He turned and trudged lifelessly back down the street, toward the house of Matthias, his kinsman.

PART III

THE HOMECOMING

15

Forcing a swallow past the despair lodged in his throat, Linus made his way up the Street of Horses, the thoroughfare that led toward Matthias's home. As he walked, he forced his eyes outward, commanded himself to look about, to remember the familiar and remark the new, the changed. Anything to occupy his vision and drown the accusing, harrying voices that derided his folly in allowing Phoebe to leave alone.

In the newer precincts of Antioch, Linus had heard, streets were built according to the Roman plan, being wider and straighter, many paved with stones and crushed gravel. But since the Street of Horses was in an older section of Antioch, it was narrow and unpaved, hemmed close on either side by houses and shops, booths and stalls. It twisted and turned this way and that, following no plan other than the random, changing demands of those who trod it during the decades of its haphazard growth. Such streets could not be said to have been built; they simply came into being.

Here was a butcher's stall which Linus remembered. As he recalled, the fellow who ran the place had an arrangement with a nearby temple of Cybele whereby he might purchase any meat offered to the goddess. Since the temples often received choice selections from the truly devoted or the truly desperate, this butcher could sometimes provide delicacies to the public that they might not easily find elsewhere. Linus looked at the pork haunches, the carcasses of lambs and goats and fowl that were all about the stall. He smelled the flat, dusty odor of dried blood and heard the droning of the flies, which contested with the butcher's patrons for the enjoyment of his wares.

As Linus weaved back and forth among the crowds clotting the street, he heard a cry that tickled something in his memory: "Games of chance! Come and try! Guess the place where your tetradrachmon hides and take one of mine! Come and try! See if you can take money from a half-blind old cripple! Games of chance! Come and try!"

He located the direction of the hawker and worked his way through the crowds toward him. He remembered this fellow—indeed, Linus could not recall a time when he had not been working the streets of Antioch. Now Linus could see the shabbily clad hawker squatted against a wall, his weathered crutch close to hand. He wore a dirty linen patch over one eye. His right hand was missing completely, and on the left he retained but his thumb and the last two fingers. Linus remembered that the man's disfigurement had been attributed to an unfortunate encounter with an axe—wielded, the tale ran, by a furious victim.

"All right, then, Digitus!" said a big, swaggering man who stepped between Linus and the hawker. The gambler sat behind a small wooden board, polished glassy-smooth by decades of use, on which sat three palm-sized clay cups, turned upside-down. The big man squatted down and slapped a tetradrachmon coin to the board. "I've been watching you closely, you old fraud," he bellowed, "and I think I've got your system figured out. Let's play."

Digitus gave his mark a brown-toothed smile, and fished in his tattered robe for a similar coin. Placing it to the side, he pinched the man's coin between his thumb and little finger, deftly catching the middle cup between the stump of his right wrist and the heel of his left hand. The coin disappeared beneath the cup, and Digitus began plying his trade.

Linus watched, fascinated as he had been in his youth by the dexterity with which Digitus slid the cups about on the board, using his stump and mangled hand. His forearms were a blur as he swapped positions with the cups, and he kept up a tireless patter, worn as smooth as the gaming board with usage:

"We move them 'round, we move them back. Watch close now, or it's money you'll lack. It could be here, it might be there; we know it's got to be somewhere. If you can guess the proper cup, you'll keep your own and pick mine up."

After a final flurry of movement, Digitus sat back on his haunches, his faded brown eyes glittering as he silently invited the player to make his choice.

The big man's smile now looked frozen in place, and slightly wilted at the corners. Linus hid a smile behind his hand. He had seen this expression on the faces of Digitus's patrons many times—he had worn it more than once, himself. Digitus used his appearance to good advantage. Looking at him, one could never imagine being bested at sleight-of-hand by this half-handed, one-eyed beggar. And yet, as the big man hesitated still over his choice, it became plain that the years of Linus's absence had taken nothing from Digitus's skill.

"There," the man said finally, stabbing a finger at the middle cup.

Digitus smiled—a bad sign for the player, Linus knew—and flipped over the cup with his thumb. Nothing.

"By the beard of Jupiter!" the man swore, "you tricked me! I followed the cup without blinking once, and you—you lifted the coin, somehow!" The man raked a forearm across the game board, scattering the cups and exposing his coin, which had been resting beneath the right-hand cup. He was about to grab it, when a blade appeared at his throat, its point dimpling the skin above his Adam's apple.

"I beat you," Digitus said, in the same emotionless voice he used in his patter, "and that coin now belongs to me. Reach for it only if your neck means nothing to you."

The hawker's face was as flat and remorseless as a serpent's. Linus shuddered, yet knew that Digitus had no choice: his game was only profitable if his marks respected his rules. Until a player came along who was faster, keener-eyed, or bolder than this one, Digitus would keep his winnings.

Linus continued down the street. As darkness thickened, the crowds began to thin. He peered nervously about him, beginning to have doubts about whether he had chosen the right way. This street seemed familiar, but...It had been eight years or more since he had walked the avenues of Antioch. Could he have mistaken the turning?

And then a child rushed past him, a brown-haired girl of perhaps five seasons, clutching a spray of wildflowers. Looking at her, Linus started to call out "Miriam!" for she was the very image of Matthias's and Anna's oldest daughter. But then he realized this could not be Miriam, for she had been more than twice the age of this girl when he had left for Jerusalem.

"Child!" he shouted instead. "You, there—the girl with the flowers! Hold a moment, if you please!"

The girl halted, spun about to face him and eyed him dubiously as he hurried toward her, dragging the recalcitrant donkey behind him. She put a finger in her mouth, betraying her instinctive mistrust of the stranger who now approached.

"Child," he said, when he was within five paces of her, "are you, by any chance, the daughter of Miriam, daughter of Anna and Matthias, the wood-worker?"

The girl's eyes opened wide in surprise, but the finger remained in place. She nodded.

"And do you have an uncle named Caius?"

Now her mouth dropped open, and the hand she held to her lips fell in amazement to her side. She nodded again.

"Good! Very good, indeed!" grinned Linus. He reached into his robe, producing his wallet. He fished out a silver

denarius and held it out toward the girl. "I am an old friend of
your mother and uncle—and your grandparents, too. This
denarius is yours if you will take me to them."

A troubled look clouded her brow as she stared from the
coin to Linus. Clearly she wanted the silver, but something
held her back.

"Please, child," Linus coaxed, "it's quite all right. You
don't know me, because I left before you were born—but I
used to work with your grandfather in his shop, and I want
very much to see him again."

The wrinkles became deeper on her forehead, but she continued to eye the denarius.

Linus had a sudden idea. "You see, little one, Matthias is
my cousin. Doesn't your uncle Caius have any children?"

She shook her head solemnly.

"Oh, well…" Linus searched for another tack. "Well, if
Caius were married and had little children, they would be
your cousins, correct?"

The girl calculated a moment, then nodded.

"And if you had little cousins, wouldn't you love them?"

Another nod.

"Well, then!" he beamed, "you see how it is! Won't you
please take me to Matthias and Anna—and your mother and
uncle as well? And won't you please take this coin from
Linus, a friend of yours you've only just met?"

He smiled gently, slowly squatting to put himself on eye
level with the girl. Warily, hesitantly, her little hand reached
out. Never taking her eyes completely from his, she plucked
the coin from his outstretched hand, clutched it tightly in her
fist, and spun away.

"Thith way!" she lisped, dashing off in the direction she
had been going when he first saw her.

"Wait, child!" Linus begged, yanking at the donkey's lead
rope. "Come on, you!" he growled at the beast, craning his
neck to keep the little girl in view. As quickly as he could, he
followed after.

It's ten in the morning—do you know where your protagonists are? One good thing about the summer is that I've got an almost unlimited amount of time to write. That's also one bad thing about summer. I don't have any other duties to distract me from the agonizingly slow pace of my word count.

I glance at the kitchen counter, and the query letter sealed, along with three sample chapters, within its envelope, stamped and addressed to yet another publisher who probably doesn't read unsolicited manuscripts.

Why am I doing this to myself? Why do I think that anyone is going to read this stuff? And why do I continue to slave away at a project as difficult, as consuming, as decidedly off the beaten track as writing a book? Why can't I just be one of the millions of people who are going to write a book someday? Why am I cursed with this insane determination to finish what I've started? And why *this* book? I mean, with my background and experiences, you wouldn't normally expect a work with such overtly religious overtones, would you? A thousand times since I started this thing, I've asked myself this question. Why a New Testament setting? Why Linus the fictitious carpenter, Linus the Not-Exactly-Lion-Hearted?

And yet, staring at the blinking cursor at the end of the last line of text on the screen, I can't imagine not finishing this story, not seeing it through to its end—wherever that is. I've come to realize that this book represents something on the order of an exorcism for me—or a blessing. There is something that this project is supposed to teach me, maybe about myself, maybe about life, liberty, and the pursuit of happiness, maybe about...I don't know. But I've got to finish. I know that for reasons which are maddeningly obscure. The work is becoming its own justification. I have to write it because it's there, and it won't go away until I do. If then.

I glance at the desk calendar. It's only the first week of June, and already I'm worrying about whether to go to Mom and Dad's for the Fourth of July. It's one of those dilemmas that has no painless answer. Either way I go on this one, I get jabbed. Which is the least taxing—guilt or frustration? If I beg off, I get the guilt. If I go, I get the other.

I could have enrolled for a graduate course. The college only allows a single day for the holiday, and I could always plead "too much course work—not enough time to make the trip—too tired—got a paper to write." Come to think of it, I ought to get started on my master's anyway.

This is neurotic, Janice. Entering graduate school to get out of going to your parents' house? Call the guys in the white coats.

I suppose I really ought to go. Filial duty and all that jazz. Honor thy father and thy mother. Which makes me wonder...what would have happened to a Hebrew kid with a dysfunctional parent? Or was it so difficult just to survive in those times that they couldn't afford the luxury of fussing with technicalities like self-esteem or the lack thereof? If you're worrying about raising enough food to last until the next harvest and how to keep from being wiped out by the neighboring tribes, maybe consideration of such esoterica gets put on the back burner. Or maybe one generation's dysfunction is another's norm—different times calling for different solutions. Could it be that society invents its own pathologies, as well as its own cures? Perhaps the late twentieth century should seek a second opinion. Its own diagnosis doesn't seem to be working out too well.

So, are you going to Mom and Dad's or not? I long to avoid the high potential for confrontation, but Maude's words keep ringing through my head: *my demons are out of reach...*

Again I see her father sitting beside his bed, his existence boiled all the way down to the pathetic, miniscule kernel left to him—to sort through the odds and ends that are left, to categorize and rank the minutiae which no one else cares about. And I see again, sense again Maude's frustration with his retreat. Does he know, can he form a concept for the helpless devotion Maude would pay to him if he could receive it? Does it matter to him that she offers him apples he cannot taste, sheds tears he cannot see, knows pain he caused—but cannot imagine? Would he own his responsibility if someone could penetrate the armor of his senility?

And—I dodge the thought, but it's quicker than me, cuts off my retreat, looms large in my face—am I headed for the same helplessness, the same lifelong incompleteness, that afflicts Maude? Is she what I am becoming?

"God, why can't I just get on with my life?" To my shock and embarrassment, I realize I'm talking out loud—no, better yet, praying out loud! Yes, folks, it's true: it's gotten so bad, she's finally started gibbering to herself.

Or am I? Could someone be listening to my semi-coherent psychobabble? Is there actually a person on the other end of the line? "Are you really there?" I continue, feeling a little dumb, but—feeling something else, too...something good. I keep on talking, just saying any weird thing that trots through my mind.

"I'll admit, there are lots of times when I thought you weren't there—or wished you weren't. But...I don't know what to do about Dad. I always thought you were on his side, not mine. I always thought I couldn't do the right things—couldn't measure up. I always thought you only helped those who helped themselves, and I wasn't sure I wanted your help, anyway.

"But I'm running out of ideas. I can't seem to get away from my feelings about Dad. They're like a roadblock, halting me whichever direction I try to go—forward, backwards, sideways, whatever. So, I guess what I'm asking is..." I grope about inside my inadequacies, looking for words to frame thoughts I never knew I could have, hadn't suspected until this moment...."is for you to help me." Help me. Those are the words, the key. A strange, unexpected sense of relief begins to trickle into my consciousness as I repeat them. "Help me. Help me know what to do, what to say. Help me to—to get past the past, somehow. Please...help me."

I sit dumbfounded for several minutes, scarcely believing what I've just heard myself do and say, not sure whether I'm losing my mind...or gaining it.

The image of Shake Walker pops into my head. I feel a sudden urge for a deep, gentle voice, and a game of dominoes. Maybe this afternoon...

———————————

Hurrying after the child, Linus saw her pause by a certain door, glance back toward him, then dash inside. The sweating carpenter glanced about him: the house his diminutive guide had vanished into was not situated as he remembered Matthias's abode. Could it be that he had been tricked, hoodwinked by a clever street urchin quick enough to see his bewilderment and reckon a way to capitalize on it? But now a man stepped from the door the child had gone through. He peered in puzzlement down the street, then back in Linus's direction. Catching sight of Linus, he seemed to recognize someone who had been recently described to him. He stepped toward Linus, friendly curiosity wrinkling his face in a crosswise, uncertain smile.

"Greetings, friend!" he called. "My daughter told me that a man with a donkey was following her, and had given her money to bring him to her house. Might you be this mysterious benefactor?"

Linus smiled ruefully. "Aye—but I fear she may have misunderstood my desired destination." Linus's eyes flickered over the clothing and open, friendly face of the man he addressed. His features were Greek and his face was clean-shaven, after the manner of the Romans. Linus could see the clay etched into the fissures of his tough, work-hardened palms, and could see the curled, singed hair on his forearms. "I am Linus, a carpenter, late of Judea, but now returned to— my home." He held out his hand toward the stranger.

"And I am Trochaion, a brick-maker," the man replied, gripping Linus's hand briefly. "Tell me, now: how has my daughter misled you?"

"Ah! When she passed me in the street, she appeared to me as the perfect likeness of a girl I used to know when I lived here before...but, that's no matter." He smiled at the brickmason. "I would gladly have given her the denarius just to see the beauty of her face."

"I thank you for your kind words," answered Trochaion forthrightly, "but I cannot permit her—"

"No, no!" Linus said hurriedly. "I asked her a question she probably could not understand. She is not to be faulted for taking a denarius which was freely offered."

"Still," the other man mused, "a denarius! Not a sum to be sniffed at! Come, then, tell me where you wish to go, and perhaps I may provide the aid you requested from my daughter."

"Perhaps," agreed Linus. "But, I would have sworn," he continued to himself, shaking his head, "that I had seen in her the rebirth of Miriam—"

"Miriam, you say?" interrupted the brickmason. "Did you say Miriam?"

Linus looked up at him, puzzled. "Well…yes, I suppose—"

"Miriam is the name of my wife! And more than one person has exclaimed at our daughter's likeness to her mother. Could it be that—"

At that moment, a woman stepped out of the house and called out, "Trochaion! Is anything the matter?"

He spun about, pointing to her. "There!" he said to Linus. "Is this the person you seek?"

Linus stared open-mouthed at the confused woman in the doorway. It might be…she looked very familiar. "Miriam?"

And now it was she who stared. "Are you…? Cousin Linus!" she cried, racing from the doorway and throwing herself into his arms. Linus caught a glimpse of the shyly curious face of the daughter, peering from behind the door frame at the unexpected scene playing in front of her house.

Linus held Miriam away from him, grinning for all he was worth. "Miriam! You are truly beautiful, as you were when I left. But then it was the beauty of a bud's promise; my eyes now behold the loveliness of the opened flower!" She smiled demurely, tossing an involuntary glance at her husband, who stood, beaming, close by.

Linus turned to Trochaion. For an instant, he was troubled by the thought that Miriam was a Jewish woman, married to a man who gave every evidence of being Greek. But then he put it from his mind. He made his choices, and Miriam had made hers. This was not Judea. It was not his affair. "You are to be envied, my friend," he said to the proud husband. "If you didn't know before, I tell you at this moment: this wife of yours is a treasure without price."

The young brickmason beamed in tacit, abashed agreement with Linus's assessment.

"Come, cousin!" Miriam urged, tugging at Linus's arm. "Come inside! Someone is here who will be overjoyed to see you!"

"I'll see to the beast," Trochaion said, taking the lead rope from Linus' hand as Miriam pulled him toward the doorway.

"Who might be so anxious to see a dusty old carpenter?" Linus asked. "The tiny maiden I gave the denarius to, perhaps? You must tell her," he said, laughing, "that I am a poor man, and cannot continue to give away silver—"

He looked through the doorway and there, sitting in the yellow pool of light from an oil lamp, was Anna. Her eyes rose to meet his, and her hand went quickly to her mouth, covering a gasp. He held out his arms, smiling.

"Linus!" She pushed herself heavily to her feet, dropping the bouquet of wildflowers she had been admiring, and half-stumbled to meet him. As they embraced, Linus heard her sobs, felt the trembling of her back.

"My dear, dear kinswoman!" he said, patting her affectionately, "why the weeping? Am I grown so gaunt in my years away that my appearance summons such instant sorrow?"

"Oh, Linus," the older woman sobbed, "how often in these last days have I begged the Eternal to send you back here to us! How many times have I besought him to summon you to our need—and now, like an answer to my prayers, you are come!"

"Softly, softly, my good woman," Linus soothed, holding her at arm's length. "Surely the provincial government is not in such desperate straits that my coming is its only remedy!"

Through her tears, Anna chuckled at Linus's witticism. "No, no—the Syrian Legions are well intact and Proconsul Quirinius is firmly in command; you need not fear on their behalf. No," she continued, looking intently into his eyes, "what I mean is that with Matthias gone—"

"What talk is this?" Linus demanded, staring in consternation from Anna to Miriam. "Matthias...gone?"

Anna's eyes lanced toward her daughter's. "You didn't tell him?"

Miriam shook her head helplessly. "Mother, there wasn't time."

Anna's gaze was a wounded blend of grief and compassion as she regarded Linus. She laid a hand on his arm and said gently, "Linus...your kinsman—my husband—is dead."

Linus's vision was aimed straight ahead, but he saw nothing except the blank gray shroud of another unexpected loss. "How long?" he whispered at last.

"He died during Passover," moaned Anna, tears seeping afresh from the corners of her eyes. "A fever took him. There was...I tried everything," she mourned.

*There will always be a place in my shop for a good carpenter...*It was the remaining thread, the tenuous tether that had drawn him back here, when all other destinations had failed of their promise. And now, Matthias was dead. Matthias, who had taught him his trade from the ground up. He heard a tiny corner of his mind scoffing bitterly at the dark propriety of such a homecoming as this. Why should he have expected any better?

He felt a tiny hand touch his own, felt something pliant and slender pressed into his palm. He looked down. The child who had led him here stood timidly by his side. In his hand he held a stalk of wildflowers.

"For you," she muttered quietly in her lisping voice, averting her face. "Grandmother Anna can share."

16

The dominoes click and swish about, face-down on the formica top of the bedside table, as Shake's dark mahogany-hued hands shuffle them this way and that, stirring them into a random jumble for the next hand of the game. Again I look down at the scorecard. I have a meager fifteen points to Shake's thirty. "The way you thrashed me last time," I say as we each begin drawing our seven dominoes, "I'm not sure I want to play again."

Shake chuckles deep down in his chest, shaking his head in amused disdain. "Now, now! Listen at you, talkin' that trash! The last game's over, but this one ain't even started yet, sugar. Don't be givin' up this quick," he admonishes. I give him a wry grin as I select the last of my tiles and push the rest to one side, forming the boneyard.

"I guess I'll open," I say, finding the double six in my hand and shoving it, face up, to the center of the table.

"All right, let's see...that makes fifteen for me," Shake announces smugly, playing the six-three onto my double.

"Now, Shake! Here you go again!" I complain, writing his score on the pad.

Again the jolly, *basso profundo* chuckle. "I can't help it, honey! It's just the luck of the draw!"

"I wish we could find two more people, so we could play 'forty-two,' " I gripe, knowing Shake loves every minute of it.

"Maybe with a partner, I'd stand a chance against you." I play a six-two on the other side of the opening double. "There. That gives me five, at least."

"There you go, sugar," Shake encourages, "there you go. Now you catchin' on!"

I hear the squishy sound of crepe-soled footsteps coming through the open door behind me. I look over my shoulder to see a nurse entering the room.

"Hello, everybody!" she bellows cheerily. "How are we doing in here?"

"Howdy, Cora," replies Shake. "We doin' just fine. How are you today?"

"Oh, fine, Mr. Walker, fine, thank you. And how's Mr. Barton getting along?" she says, bending to look at the unmoving figure in the wheelchair.

With nothing to sort, Jonas Barton sits in his chair, staring catatonically at the wall ahead of him. Cora peers into his face. "Good afternoon, Mr. Barton!" she says in a voice that must surely carry all the way to the nurse's station. "How are you feeling?" She lays a hand on his shoulder, shaking him gently.

No response. Not even a blink. Cora pulls back a blanket draped across Mr. Barton's lap, checking the catheter bag. "Everything looks just fine," she announces to no one in particular, resettling the blanket and giving Maude's father a final, proprietary pat on the shoulder. "Anything else I can do for anybody?" she says in what I assume to be her customary half-shout.

"You don't know how to play forty-two, do you?" Shake asks, giving me a surreptitious wink.

"Beg your pardon?" she asks, thrown off stride by the unexpected query.

"Never mind," Shake says, waving a hand. "We doin' all right. Thank you for askin'."

"Well…all right, then." Cora spins and flounces outside, en route to deliver her next ray of sunshine.

"Does she talk that loud all the time?" I ask when she is safely out of earshot.

Shake grins and nods. "Um-hmm, sure does. Somewhere along the line, she got the idea that anybody who lived in a nursin' home was hard of hearin'. She got so used to hollerin' that now she cain't talk no other way, I reckon." He plays a two-four—no points, I note with satisfaction. "I think Jonas there hears her all right," Shake continues, scowling, "but he's afraid to answer, 'cause Cora might strike up a conversation with him."

I laugh, and Shake breaks into a mischievous grin. It feels so good, this spontaneous burst of uncomplicated joy, like rainbow crystals shaken loose inside my chest. I play a three-one. "That's five more for me," I say.

"Now, watch out!" Shake warns, shaking an admonitory finger at me. "You gettin' too good too quick!"

"Just the luck of the draw, Shake. Don't give up; the game just started."

He nods, laughing. "All right. You got me that time."

A quiet moment stretches comfortably between us. We both make some plays. Then I'm stymied; I have no dominoes that will play on the end tiles, so I must draw from the boneyard.

"Shake, tell me something," I ask as I reach for a tile. "What's your secret?"

"Do what?" he asks, giving me an askance look as he studies the formation. "What secret you talkin' about?"

"Well…you're a happy person," I begin, a little embarrassed by my own question, but not enough to dim my curiosity. "You make other people happy, just by being around you. But you can't get out of that chair."

"Um-hmm, that's right," he nods. He winces, unable to make a play. He reaches for the boneyard. "But I still don't get—"

"You told me you hardly ever get to see your family, and yet you take the time to notice Maude when she's here—to try and give her the encouragement she can't get from her own father."

Shake looks thoughtful as he places a tile on the end. Without his saying anything, I note the ten points he has just earned, jotting it on the scorecard. "So...what I'm asking is—how do you do it? Most people in your position would be more interested in what other folks could give them. But you're a giver, yourself. How do you manage? I'd really like to know." Much more than the satisfaction of curiosity is riding on Shake's answer. I realize, too late, that by making this inquiry I have made myself vulnerable.

"Well, sugar...I don't rightly know about no secret." Shake scratches the fine, white wool on his scalp. "I guess I just always thought that I only had so much time in this life, and they wasn't no use to makin' it miserable, for one thing. And then..." he toys with a domino, flipping it over and over in his palm as he considers his next words. "Come to think of it, maybe I do have a secret, after all. What is it the apostle Paul says in—I believe it's in Philippians, ain't it?—where he says, I have learned, in whatsoever state I am, therewith to be content. I can do all things through Christ which strength-eneth me.' "

Quoting the words from Paul's epistle, Shake's voice sounds different; without getting any louder, it takes on an added resonance, an intonation of quiet authority which is its own validation. I may choose to ignore the implicit conclusions Shake has drawn—but I lack the strength to contradict them.

We play in silence for perhaps a minute and a half, while Shake's words reverberate through my soul like silken thunder. I remember hearing my father quote words like those Shake has just recited, but on his lips they bore scant resemblance to what I've just heard. I imagine the use to which Dad might put these words of Paul: he would pin them to the far wall as a target I might aim at if I dared, a standard of holiness to be strained toward rather than a source of comfort and deliverance to be received with gratitude. In

Shake's usage the words have become a trusted staff to lean upon; for my father they would be more like a yardstick.

"Learning to be content…that's one I'd like to get in on," I remark, wistfully. I make a play—a double five. "That's fifteen for me, isn't it?"

"Sure is," Shake smiles, as I scribble the numbers on the score sheet. "Honey," he then asks, peering carefully at me, "you got a load on your mind that's about to wear you smooth—ain't you?"

I keep my eyes on my dominoes, but I can feel the full force of his faded amber gaze. Even though I opened the gate into this pen with my earlier question, I'm suddenly unwilling to face the truth that awaits me there. Stubbornly, I keep my face down. "It's your play, isn't it?" I ask, an annoyed tone leaching through the facade of my nonchalance.

I can feel Shake appraising me thoughtfully. "Yes, I reckon it is," he answers, after a moment. I hear the cushions of his wheelchair squeak as his weight shifts, feel his meaty, warm hand touching the skin of my forearm. I look up, and he's leaning across the small table top, peering into my eyes with an expression as tender and vulnerable as the face of a hurt child. "Why don't you tell old Shake what's botherin' you, sugar? You want to, don't you? That's why you come to see me today, isn't it? It won't go no farther than this room, if you don't want it to." I feel him patting gently on my arm. "I ain't real smart, but I got ears," he says, "and it seems to me like that's what you mostly need right now."

Still I cannot bring myself to utter the words that are yearning to be released. I cannot bear the exposure of my insecurity, the abdication of my long-cherished misery.

"Come on, honey," Shake urges softly, "let it go. You keep it all inside, you wind up like that, someday." His finger points past me, to the silent, crumpled form of Jonas Barton.

I feel my resistance crumbling. I feel myself slipping past the threshold of my habitual caution into the warm enfolding of Shake's genuineness. Even as I warn myself of the danger, I've already gone over. This time I will throw caution to the winds. This time I will trust. This time something will happen. Something good.

———————————

Linus scratched his beard as he studied the sketch he had made on the parchment scrap. He looked up from the sketch, mentally calculating the amount of wood and time needed to build the cart wanted by the miller who stood nearby.

Adding a bit to his estimate to be certain of his profit, he turned to the miller. "I can have it ready for you in five days."

"Really?" the tradesman sighed, pleasantly surprised. "I would not have thought—but," he asked, tethering his enthusiasm to his caution, "how much will it cost me?"

"Twelve denarii," Linus replied without hesitation.

"Twelve…how much is that in tetradrachmae?"

Rolling his eyes upward, Linus figured the ratio. "Forty-eight tetradrachmae, or thereabout. We can begin work this afternoon, and," he finished, reading the hesitation in the miller's posture, "if the cart is not finished properly in five days, you may reduce the fee by one-third."

Arching his eyebrows, the miller pondered a moment. "Forty-eight tetradrachmae…that is a fair amount of money."

Linus waited silently, allowing the miller to talk himself into the bargain.

"Still, I need that cart soon. Very well," he said, turning to Linus, "let's strike hands." They signified their mutual consent to the arrangements, and the miller strode out into the street.

Caius, who had witnessed the entire negotiation, shook his head in admiration. "I am still amazed, cousin. You can strike an agreement in the time it would take me to properly understand what the customer wants!"

Linus shrugged. "No more than experience, Caius. One day, you will set the price for your labor with the familiarity of a master. It's a matter of learning, that's all."

"Still, I am grateful you came back to Antioch," the younger man said. "When Father died, I knew I could not fill his place. I did my best, but—"

"No matter," said Linus, making notations on the sketch with a piece of sharpened charcoal. "We need to buy lumber. If we don't get the miller's cart built in the next five days, there'll be less bread in the house than otherwise. Come along, and I'll show you a few things your father taught me about selecting the proper wood for a job like this—and paying the proper price. Mind the shop, Chrestus," Linus called to Caius's manservant as they strode out the doorway.

Walking beside Caius toward the timber market, Linus reflected on the past few months since his return to Antioch.

Matthias's unexpected death had thrown his well-established trade into disarray. Caius, though becoming skilled in the actual work of the shop, had no knowledge of other critical areas of the business. Customers who might have provided profitable work turned away because of Caius's hesitancy. Materials cost more than they should have. Work was not finished when promised.

Linus's arrival provided a steady, veteran hand at the helm, and it was not long before the traffic in and out of the shop began to grow, the activity to return to the steady bustle it had known during Matthias's lifetime. It worried Linus deeply to know how perilously close Anna and her son had come to financial ruin. Anna and Caius knew it, too, and never failed to thank the Eternal for Linus's timely return to Antioch.

But for Linus, the praise was a bittersweet affair. He could not think of his return to the city of his birth without also thinking of her in whose company he had traveled from Damascus. In the darkness, when he lay on his pallet in Anna's house, he often fancied the scent of myrrh and aloes blowing through the window grille on the warm, bewitching breezes of the night. From time to time as he walked the streets of the city, he would catch sight of a shock of glistening black curls, and his breath would stall in his chest—until he watched long enough to realize it was not she, but some other. Phoebe was a phantom who went with him wherever he roamed, whose memory played upon his mind as a bard's fingers strum the chords of a harp. Though he strove to restrain them, thoughts of what might have been afflicted him with a constant, sweetly sad torture.

Not that he lacked for opportunities. Those who were close to him noticed his long, silent moods, interpreting them, as friends will do, as symptoms of an illness that might be cured by a dose of matchmaking. When he had been in Antioch a few weeks, Anna had taken him aside. "Linus, you are too young to be alone for the rest of your life. You have mourned Heracleia and the child long enough," she stated matter-of-factly. "Now, then...I know several young women who..."

Even in the synagogue where the family gathered, he could not fail to notice the shy glances of the maidens and the not-so-shy glances of their mothers. It was clear to him that he had been marked as a prime target by every family with an eligible daughter, and the position made him acutely uncomfortable.

As if partially sensing his thoughts, Caius, walking beside him, said, "Linus—do you know what I heard in the synagogue last Sabbath?"

"No, what was that?"

"I heard that Trochaion's brother Nicolas will be returning soon from Jerusalem."

"From Jerusalem, you say?" Linus's curiosity was mildly tweaked by mention of the city he had abandoned. "What took him there?"

"He was there for the last feast of Pentecost—he is a proselyte, you know—and for some reason, he stayed all this time after the feast was concluded. I don't know why."

"A proselyte?"

"Yes," Caius nodded. "He and Trochaion have been associated with our synagogue for several years, but only Nicolas was willing to undergo the rite of *b'rit-milah.*"

"Circumcision is no small affair for those not of our people," Linus observed. "The Greeks don't see it in the same light as you and I, you know."

"True," Caius agreed. "I've had more than one gentile friend ask me why we insist upon mutilating our menfolk. I've decided it's no use trying to explain."

Linus nodded.

"Still, Trochaion is a good man," Caius continued, "and as faithful to the Law as an uncircumcised man can possibly be. He's good to my sister. Perhaps, one day…"

"But what of this brother, this Nicolas?"

"Oh, yes. Well, I don't know much else, except that he managed to send ahead word that he would be back in Antioch soon, and that he had some very important tidings to share with all of us."

*Jerusalem…Pentecost…Important tidings…*Linus felt a stirring of familiar, unsummoned restiveness.

As they entered the timber market, the two men stared about in confusion. Usually, the large, fenced square outside the city walls was a beehive of activity. With the constant stream of building projects decreed by the legate of Syria—not to mention the normal needs of the private citizens of a large city like Antioch—wood for construction was constantly in demand. The din of cart wheels coming and going, the shouts of workers and patrons haggling over purchases, the back-and-forth drone of saws and the dull whacking of axe blades cutting the raw timber into planks and beams—normally, all these could be heard many paces before one reached the compound. What could explain the unnatural quiet that cloaked the place today?

At last, the overseer of the market peered out at Linus and Caius from the shed where he kept his headquarters. Linus could never remember having seen the man actually inside the rough structure—he was always running here and there about the market, shouting at laborers or dickering with buyers and sellers. Slowly, dispiritedly, the man came toward them.

"Greetings, Strato," called Linus. The man returned the salutation with a weak wave. "What is the reason," Linus continued, "for the unnatural stillness of this place today?"

"Are you the only ones in Antioch who haven't heard?" the manager asked in a defeated voice. "Proconsul Sulpicius Quirinius has departed for Rome, just after he called a halt to every building project he had commissioned in the last two months."

"Why is the legate leaving the province?" asked Caius in amazement. "Has he fallen from favor with the emperor?"

"No, nothing like that," responded Strato. "It seems there is some sort of financial crisis in the capital—something to do with land values and rates of usury. I don't understand it, except that the wealthy families appear to be caught in a vise. I suppose the legate is going there to salvage his affairs as best he can. But, meanwhile—" Strato gestured hopelessly toward the stack of timber— "how in the name of all the gods am I to move this merchandise?"

Walking back home, Caius commented in a voice of respect, "Never would I have believed lumber could be bought so cheaply."

Linus smiled. "Strato was glad enough of our small trade to be somewhat more generous than usual, to be sure."

"Still, I would have agreed to his first price," Caius insisted, "but you pressed him for a concession."

"When the planks and beams are delivered," Linus replied, "we must inspect them carefully before giving Strato the rest of the money. It may be that he will regret the bargain he has made so much that he will seek to make up for it in poor quality."

"True enough," Caius admitted. "Nevertheless—it was a very good price."

Linus made no reply other than his customary shrug. They walked awhile in silence.

"Cousin," said Caius presently, a troubled expression crumpling his brow, "do you—do you think it wrong for

Miriam to marry a gentile—even a God-fearer, such as Trochaion?"

They took perhaps a score of paces before Linus replied. "What I think," he said slowly, "scarcely matters, it seems to me. You have said Trochaion treats his family well. Is that not sufficient?"

"Perhaps...I don't know—"

Linus suspected the true source of Caius's discomfort. "What is it, boy? What troubles you?"

It was some time before Caius could force himself to speak. "There is...there is a woman," he managed finally.

"There are always women," Linus remarked, drily. "I fail to see why that should present such a difficulty for a young, strapping fellow such as yourself."

"You don't understand, Linus, not at all...She's...she's a gentile. But I love her."

Had Caius planned for days, he could not have concocted a more forceful blow to his kinsman than these words. Linus struggled to halt the avalanche of emotion breaking loose within him. Not understand? he shrieked silently at himself. Not understand! Of course I understand—more intimately than he will ever guess!

"I was brought up to respect Moses and the prophets," Caius continued in a worried voice, "and I don't wish to affront the covenant of our forefathers. But..."

Linus knew, could sense the tension troubling his young cousin. Had he not felt within himself that same tugging as his heart was pulled one way and his mind another? How well he knew the perplexing warfare which now raged between Caius's heritage and his longings!

For the moment, Linus sidestepped the question. "What is her name?" he asked gently.

"Agrippina," the boy replied, uttering her name like an incantation.

"How did you meet her?" More dodging, Linus knew; but what answer could he give without lying to the lad—or to his own heart?

"Her father is a blacksmith my father often bought nails and other iron goods from. I frequently went with him to her—that is, his shop. I've known her for years—since we were children, I suppose. But now," Caius concluded, his voice congealed with barely suppressed feeling, "we are much beyond being children.

"Mother knows, I think, although I have never openly mentioned the matter. And, having seen the way she is with Trochaion, I am not much encouraged. Even though Trochaion has taken responsibility for her upkeep and treats her like his own mother, she holds something back from him—and from Miriam for marrying him. It's as if she can't quite permit herself to approve. I don't relish the prospect of what she might say to me."

"Indeed," remarked Linus, not knowing what else to say. They were almost back to the shop. Linus's mind reeled with the irony of his dilemma: silently hating himself for having cast Phoebe aside, he must now advise Caius on how to proceed with his beloved gentile maiden. He would have laughed aloud but for the jagged splinter of loss festering in his chest. He halted just outside the doorway of the shop and peered as intently as he could into the earnest, confused face of his younger cousin.

"Caius, my lad," he said quietly, "I fear you've asked the wrong man to advise you on this matter. I have—I have known those who entertained thoughts of love with gentiles," Linus continued, looking away as he trod dangerously near the precipice of his own emotions, "but—for me, at least—the answer is...is anything but obvious. I will say, however—"

Their eyes again locked, as Caius awaited Linus's next words.

"—that the same God who gave Moses the Law also created the human heart. And...in these days...who knows what He may do?"

Caius stared at Linus in confusion for some moments, then stepped through the dark doorway into the shop. After standing with his eyes closed for several heartbeats, Linus followed.

On the following Sabbath, the congregation of the synagogue known as the House of the Covenant gathered in its smallish one-room structure. After the singing of the psalms and the day's lesson from the Law and the prophets, the rabbi gestured toward a man seated with Trochaion and his family.

"Our brother Nicolas has returned to us," the rabbi smiled. "He has asked permission to address the congregation. Nicolas," the cleric beckoned, "will you come?"

The brother of Trochaion—older, Linus guessed, by his appearance—stood and walked to the lectern. He smiled over the crowd, and began to speak.

"I bring you greetings from the Synagogue of the Freedmen, in Jerusalem!" he began in a firm, round voice. "And—I bring you good news, beyond anything you could have ever imagined!"

Of all those present, only Linus had an inkling of what would follow. The carpenter took a deep breath and sought to quiet the hammering in his chest.

"God has done a thing in our day, the like of which will never be repeated while the world stands!" Nicolas proclaimed boldly. "He has sent His only begotten Son, the *Kristos*, that we might believe in Him and have life which never ends!"

As he knew they would, the people seated about Linus stared at Nicolas without moving, as if they were uncertain whether they were looking at a prophet or a lunatic.

"Jesus of Galilee was born of a virgin, who conceived him not in the embrace of an earthly husband but by the power of God's Holy Spirit. He performed signs and wonders—healing the sick and lame, restoring sight to the blind, cleansing lepers—"

The face of Janneus of Ginaea materialized in Linus's mind. *I was called unclean, outcast...leper...*

"—and even raising the dead! Then, by the hands of wicked men, he was killed—"

Why not say 'crucified'? Linus thought. Compared to what you're about to announce, that should be easy enough for them to swallow.

"—but God Himself raised Jesus from the dead," Nicolas proclaimed in a voice that rang with triumph, "and he now sits at the right hand of the Presence. He calls all men to repent, to be washed clean in his name, and to walk in righteousness before God and man!"

By now, a worried murmur could be heard throughout the assembly. Nicolas, if he heard, gave no sign. His voice blazed on like a beacon on a dark night.

"And in these days, God has poured out His Holy Spirit on those who gladly receive the tidings of the *Kristos*. He has done this to confirm what He prophesied through the prophet Joel:

> *'I will pour out my Spirit on all people.*
> *Your sons and daughters will prophesy,*
> *Your young men will see visions,*
> *Your old men will dream dreams.*
> *Even on my servants, both men and women,*
> *I will pour out my Spirit in those days…'*

"And I, with my own eyes, have seen these things of which the prophet spoke so long ago," asserted Nicolas. "I have seen uneducated men and women speaking foreign tongues they did not learn. I have seen cripples healed in the name of Jesus of Galilee. I have seen knowledge of the very thoughts and intentions of men's hearts granted to those who were servants of the *Kristos*. And what I have seen," he finished, raising his voice to carry above the mounting hubbub, "I cannot but repeat, that you, too, may believe in the *Kristos* and have life in His name." And with that, Nicolas abruptly sat down, calmly awaiting whatever might follow.

The rabbi, visibly shaken, tottered back toward the lectern. Gripping it like a crutch, he raised a shaking hand for quiet. "My brothers, today we—we have heard many words that are hard to understand." He took several deep breaths, then gathered himself. "Let us depart in peace from this place, and ponder what our—what our brother Nicolas has said. He is—" the rabbi glanced at Nicolas, then away— "is an honest man, and has a good heart. And, he has been obedient to the covenant of our fathers."

Tacitly, every eye glanced at Trochaion, who kept his gaze studiously lowered.

"Therefore, let us not be too quick to judge what we have heard today. And now," the rabbi said, raising his hands in benediction, "may the Lord bless you, and keep you. May He make His face to shine upon you, and be gracious unto you. Amen."

"Amen," responded the congregation. Slowly, the worshipers began to rise from their seats and drift through the door. Linus saw Trochaion and Miriam go to Nicolas, then hover around him as together they started for the door.

Linus felt, suddenly rising within him, the urge go to Nicolas, to demand of him what he had seen. Perhaps to catch a tenuous gleam—or even a proof!—of the truth that had so far evaded his perplexed, questioning mind. Could it be that admitting the possibility of the Nazarene's resurrection was no more mad than shutting himself within the prison of his own despair?

"Miriam! Trochaion! Wait!" he called, and hurried after them.

17

Tell me, then," Nicolas asked Linus, when the three men had seated themselves on the cushions in Trochaion's house, "when did you leave Jerusalem?"

"I left on the day of his...the day just before the beginning of the Passover Sabbath," Linus replied, unable to meet Nicolas's intense gaze.

Nicolas studied the bowed head of the carpenter, his dark, heavy eyebrows arching as he contemplated what Linus had said—and not said. In a moment, he asked softly, "So then...you were in Jerusalem during the time he walked among us, weren't you?"

Linus's eyes darted about like a trapped swallow—seeking a way out, any place to go other than toward the dark, honed eyes of this single-minded proselyte, this bold messenger of a hope beyond imagining. But at last he could avoid it no longer. He met Nicolas's stare. "Yes, I was there."

And then the question he had been nursing silently began to hammer at Linus's mind until, despite his fear of either answer, he could contain it no longer. "Did you see...Did you see him, after—"

"When he arose?"

Linus nodded, holding his breath. If this man had first-hand knowledge of—

"No," answered Nicolas, momentarily downcast. "I didn't come to Jerusalem until the following festival of Pentecost. I heard of him through the preaching of his disciples in the Portico of Solomon and other places in the city." A silence followed.

"But you," Trochaion asked Linus in a moment, "did you see him? Did you ever speak with him?" The eager rush of words was an echo of Phoebe's breathless queries, that evening by the fire.

Linus pulled himself back to the present. "Yes, I saw him—on several occasions. I never spoke to him, nor he to me."

Unless you repent, you too will all perish...

"How did he seem, to you?" Trochaion asked, after several moments.

The piercing eyes, the fathomless, knowing expression...

"He was like...like no man I have ever met," Linus murmured. "Though I have thought long on it, tried to put better words to it, I have been unable to arrive closer to an understanding than that."

Trochaion's eyes traveled to those of his brother, receiving in them the silent confirmation of Linus's assessment.

Nicolas heaved a sigh. "Though I have sat at the feet of those who traveled with him throughout Galilee and Judea, and heard them speak intimately of their days and hours with him, I deeply envy you the experience of having seen him with your own eyes. How I wish I could make a similar claim!"

Linus reflected a moment. "The curious thing is," he said, an ironic, bemused smile testing the corners of his eyes, "those I met on the way—those who had seen him, spoken to him—seemed no more specific in their opinions about him than I. How is it, do you suppose, that a man can have such an extraordinary effect on those he meets, yet leave them all at such a loss for words?"

"Ah, but you should have heard his disciples on the first day of the feast!" Nicolas assured him, the gleam returning to his eye. "Those who saw the risen Lord were by no means at a loss for words. 'This Jesus, whom you crucified,' they said, 'God has made both Lord and *Kristos!*'"

Pain lanced Linus's heart at the victorious words from the proselyte's lips.

His emblem, smeared with the Galilean's blood…

A small, unruly bundle of tangled garments and thrashing limbs came from nowhere, tumbling with a giggle into Linus's lap. "Uncle Linuth! Father! Uncle Nicolath! Mother want to know whether you're ready for thomething to eat!"

Secretly glad of the interruption, Linus tousled little Chloe's bushy auburn hair, then tickled her until she gasped for mercy.

Trochaion stood, beckoning to his wife to bring the victuals while he went to a nearby corner, where the board leaned against a wall.

"Come here, little one," beckoned Nicolas as Chloe wriggled free of Linus's grasp. "I haven't greeted you properly since coming home." Gaily she skipped into his warm embrace.

Trochaion carefully placed the board in their midst, and Miriam set down upon it a basket of fruits and cheeses. They gathered about the table, waiting expectantly, watching Trochaion. The master of the house raised his open palms to waist height. "May the Lord, the Master of Creation, bless this simple food and those who surround this table." He sat down, followed by the rest of them.

"Tell me then, brother," Trochaion asked as he helped himself to a handful of grapes, "what made you stay in Jerusalem for so many months after the feast was concluded? When you left, your intention was to attend the Pentecost festival, and then return home."

Thoughtfully, Nicolas tore a hunk of cheese from one of the larger cakes in the basket. He took a bite, chewed it carefully, then swallowed. He looked at his brother and said, "I can't answer your question, my brother, without talking about the power of the Almighty and its manifestation through the disciples who believed in the name of the *Kristos.*

"On the first day of the feast, I was gathered with a large group of pilgrims near the Sheep Market by the Bethesda Pool. As we milled about in the gathering heat, we heard a sound like a roaring storm, or one of the sandstorms of the Arabah. In wonder—for the sky was cloudless and benign—we gathered toward the source: an ordinary-looking house close at hand. As we listened and wondered, we heard shouting coming from inside the place, exclamations of surprise and awe—in Greek, Aramaic, Latin...every tongue I knew, and many I didn't! In a moment, the house's occupants came outside, and their faces..."

Nicolas's words failed as his eyes stared outward, past the faces intently turned toward him, past the baked-brick walls of the house in which they sat, past the gates of the city...Back, back his mind roamed, to that day in Jerusalem when everything had changed—a day whose events were so profound that afterward his former life seemed separated by a veil from the brilliant clarity he now experienced.

Watching the memory take possession of him, Linus shifted uncomfortably on his cushion. The look on Nicolas's face reminded him of another face, another set of eyes whose penetrating gaze had torn forever a rift between his soul and his will, between the unknown and safety, between the forever and the here-and-now. Nicolas was clearly being transformed into an image uncannily reminiscent of the Nazarene. Could he afford to remain in the presence of such an assertive summons? What would happen to him if he allowed himself to truly abandon his zealous guardianship of his security—if he, as Nicolas had plainly done, gave himself unreservedly to this savior whose resurrection was commended only by the power in the words of its advocates? What guarantee could there be for such an uncertain, irrevocable choice?

"Their faces glowed," Nicolas resumed, "as if, like Moses, they had been granted a momentary vision of the hinder parts

of God. And they began speaking—a hundred-odd of them—
in all the tongues of the wide world. As I looked about me, I
saw pilgrims from every nation under the sun, and I saw the
amazement on their faces when they realized these Galilean
peasants were speaking the tongues of their distant home-
lands as if they had learned them from the cradle!

"One of them—I later came to know him as Simon Peter
of Bethsaida, in Galilee—stood on the steps leading to the
upper room of the house where they had been gathered—"

Another memory ambushed Linus's mind. *I knew a man of
Bethsaida—Simon by name*, the robber John of Gischala had
said, *A man who knew how to use his knife and his fists...He fell in
with the Nazarene, Jesus...*

"Peter motioned for attention, and eventually the crowd
quieted," Nicolas recounted, "even though a few jeered at the
disciples, accusing them of drunkenness.

"But Peter, in a voice bedazzled with truth, refuted them.
'These men aren't drunk,' he said. 'It's far too early in the day
for that!' And then, as he quoted the prophet Joel, I felt something stirring deep within me—something that made me
want to hear every single word that came from his lips."

In the days and weeks that followed, Linus heard more of
Nicolas's strange saga: how, upon hearing Peter's announcement of the Galilean's elevation by the Eternal, hundreds of
his listeners—Jews from birth and gentile converts alike—had
taken, like new-made proselytes, the symbolic washing of
repentance—but in the name of Jesus the Anointed One! How
they had lingered on in Jerusalem, taking lodging among the
believers who lived there, exchanging words of instruction
and listening to the Nazarene's twelve principal followers
speak of his life and teachings. How the community's over-
whelming love and gracious generosity to strangers began to
attract a broader interest among the populace, even drawing a
number of the Temple functionaries into its orbit. How the
apostles performed signs and wonders, a source of awe
among the Nazarene's believers and a further reason for the
spreading fame of this strange, exultant, enthusiastic sect.

Nicolas told of how the wrath of the religious establishment found its unlikely weapon in Saul of Tarsus, a Pharisee.

At the mention of this name, Linus felt a chill shrouding his heart. Saul of Tarsus! The one who had summoned him from sleep to build the fateful instrument of the Galilean's death!

He is a rabble-rouser, an inciter of rebellion...

Now this same man hunted from house to house for those in Jerusalem and Judea who put their faith in the Nazarene messiah. He dragged them into the street, said Nicolas—men, women, and children—and lashed them shamelessly before the eyes of passers-by. He crammed them into dank prison cells and left them there to recant their faith in Jesus of Nazareth—or rot. And he aided and abetted the death of Stephen, a comrade of Nicolas, a fellow-worshiper at the Synagogue of the Freedmen.

With tears glistening on his cheeks, Nicolas told them of Stephen, a brother whose heart burned with a holy fire. How he refused to disown his confidence in the *Kristos*, though hailed before the stern, disapproving faces of the Sanhedrin. How, even as the stones flung by his rabid murderers struck him with mortal force, he sang a song of praise to his Lord and Savior, and prayed for the salvation of the men who were killing him.

* * * * *

Caius walked from the shop into the brittle winter sunlight of the work yard, peering thoughtfully at the mortised joint between the two pieces of cypress wood. "Will this fitting do for the thwarts, do you suppose?" he asked. Linus straightened from his work and turned to inspect Caius's sample.

The spine and ribs of a boat lay on the packed earth of the work yard. Linus had been busily pegging the last rib of the keel in place when Caius spoke to him. Now he eyed the joint critically, pulling it apart and placing it back together several times, tugging it this way and that to test it for stability. He handed it back to his younger cousin, smiling his approval.

"That joint is as well-fashioned as any I could have done. Thwarts joined like that should stand up to any weather the Orontes can toss at our fishermen friends, eh?"

Caius grinned, basking in the the glow of what he knew, by now, to be Linus's supreme compliment: I couldn't have done it better myself. "Good," he said. "Then I'll get the rest of them cut. How many, again?"

Linus turned back toward the boat's frame, eyeing each place where a thwart would be positioned. "Five," he said at last, turning back toward Caius. "Cut five of them—just like that one. But before you go, hold this rib in place while I peg it to the keel, would you?"

"Where is Chrestus?" Caius demanded, looking about in consternation for the manservant. "I told him—"

"It's all right," Linus said. "I sent him to the blacksmith's. Drilling the holes for all these pegs blunted my drill bit. He's gone to order me a new one."

At the word "blacksmith," Caius had ceased listening to Linus's words. Instead, he stared in the direction of that artisan's premises with a dreamy, preoccupied expression.

Linus glanced up at him. "Here, boy!" he shouted, snapping his fingers loudly in Caius's face. "Keep your mind on pegs and joints, not on kohl-darkened eyelashes!"

Caius reddened, then gave a guilty half-grin. Without another word, he picked up the rib and held it in place as Linus drove home the dowel pins which fastened it to the keel beam.

"Has Nicolas been by here today?" Caius asked as Linus paused his mallet blows to reach for another peg.

"I haven't seen him. Why do you ask?" queried Linus, positioning the dowel over its hole in the rib.

"Oh...I was just—wondering," the younger man said in an offhand voice. "We've been talking..."

Linus peered up at his cousin. "About the Nazarene? Is Nicolas seeking to recruit you to his sect also?" As soon as he spoke, Linus realized his words had come out sharper than he intended.

Caius's eyes shot toward Linus's face. "Would that be such a bad thing?" he demanded. "Many from the synagogue have heard Nicolas's words—and more than a few have believed in the *Kristos*. He proves from the writings of the Prophets that Jesus of Nazareth is the Anointed One. I've even heard Nicolas speak of going to other synagogues in Antioch to spread the word."

"To spread what word?" retorted Linus. "That a foolish Galilean got himself at odds with the High Priest and the Romans, as well? That he promised hope and life to the rabble, then proved unable to rescue himself from the net he wove? That some loose-tongued peasants saw a weird dream and preached it to a crowd of Pentecost pilgrims as fact? That the words of the Prophets can be twisted by fools to prove their folly?" All the rage, frustration, and confusion, simmering within him for so long, suddenly reached its boiling point. Linus, unable to help himself, spewed the acrid froth of his bewildered, tortured soul into the wide, unsuspecting face of his younger cousin, hating himself even as the stream of cruelties left his lips. "Is this the word that Nicolas spreads? That hope exists in a world that slays all hope? That eternal life is possible in a universe that displays nothing but death at every turn? That—that God truly sees and cares about us, pathetic vermin that we are? For I have seen nothing to convince me of such hope, such life, such caring." His sudden wrath spent, Linus fell silent, panting with the exertion and pain of the words he had just spilled.

Caius, eyes round with shock and fear, involuntarily backed away. "Linus, I...I have never heard—" His voice was a strangled whisper as he struggled to express his feelings. "What of the resurrection? Does this mean nothing to you?"

Linus glared sullenly at the other. "Those whom death has taken from me, it has never given back. The rules of life and death have not changed. This talk of resurrection says nothing to me."

"You...your grief has made you mad!" Caius stuttered. "Or perhaps...perhaps I only thought I knew you." Caius wheeled and paced quickly back toward the shop.

———————————

Dear Mom and Dad,

Well, school finally let out for the summer! All things considered, I guess it was a pretty good year for a beginning term at a new campus. Still—I'm glad it's over and that I've got June, July and most of August to recoup and regroup.

How are you guys? Good, I hope. I'm sorry I haven't written in awhile, but it seems there's always something that bumps letter-writing, if I let it. Today, I decided to get a few lines to you, to let you know what my plans are for the Fourth, and so forth— no pun intended (hah!).

I guess the main thing I've had on my mind is my friend Maude. She's about your age, Mom, and we've gotten really close, because of...well, just because. She works at the public library here, and I run into her a lot there—doing research for my book, and all that. Yes, I've still got delusions about getting a book published, and no, I haven't gotten any official encouragement from a publisher—not yet.

Anyway, I met Maude at church. Can you believe it—the prodigal daughter at church? Well, it's true. And the thing is...I don't exactly know how to say this...Maude and I have a lot in common.

My pen hovers over the last sentence. I stare at it, willing it to vanish—willing the thoughts it has spawned to dissipate. By dint of effort, I struggle to return to the safe inanities of my opening sentences. And then my hand moves again, almost with a will of its own.

You see, growing up, she got about as much encouragement for her dreams and personhood as I did. Which is to say not much. She was ignored, or punished, or at best tolerated. Rarely loved, rarely nurtured. Her aspirations didn't count for much, either. Her goals weren't considered—after all, children are to be seen and not heard, right? She's one of the walking wounded, kind of like me. She goes to the nursing home where her father stays—'stays', not 'lives'—and desperately begs him to come out of his senile dementia long enough to acknowledge her, to atone for his past sins. She longs for completion, for absolution—but it's beyond her. She tries to believe, to have faith in God, and gets a lot closer than I probably ever will. For some reason, she's been able to hang in with a church and find a measure of comfort there. But she isn't at peace—not by a long shot.

And that's why I've been putting off this letter. I know I should come see you on the Fourth, but I'm not sure I'm strong enough to come home. Isn't that an interesting observation? I don't think I have the strength to endure a day of tacit disapproval, of veiled barbs, of tight-lipped anxiety about my day-to-day choices and my eternal soul. Like Maude, I feel incomplete, hurt and confused. Love and acceptance aren't things I remember as major features of our family.

I realize I've been writing furiously for several minutes, my pen scratching nonstop across the stationery. I drop the pen and read what I've written, intimidated by the venom, the harsh insistence of these words which seem to have tumbled unfiltered from my mind onto paper—an impromptu tangle of acrimony, sprung to life beneath my fingertips.

I get up from the table and walk to the refrigerator. Opening a can of cola, I remember the way Shake looked as I spilled my guts onto his bedside table. The quiet, hurt-filled sheen of his aged eyes as he took my confession, there among the disinfectant-scented cloisters of the Shadybrook Convalescent Center.

I can't respect my father...I didn't want him to care only about my soul, I wanted him to care about me...My mother never stood up for me...Where was the church when I needed help? I always thought God was the great Hall Monitor, except he could see through the restroom walls... For minutes that seemed to last hours, I gushed this sort of invective at him, spouted all the bitterness I had kept contained all these years. Maybe I was trying to disgust him, trying to get him to shout at me.

trying to make him abandon me as I felt I'd always been abandoned before. But Shake just sat there in his wheelchair, looking at me in that pained, pitying way, listening and listening and listening.

Without any resistance to brace against, I soon ran out of steam. My words wound down, and I sat on the edge of the bed, sniffling and mumbling, "I don't know. I just don't know..."

A handful of tissues appeared beneath my nose. I wiped my face and looked up at him. When he knew I was finished, he shook his head sadly and said, "Honey, it sounds to me like your biggest trouble is puttin' your trust in the wrong place."

"Ummm...Excuse me?" I stammered.

"Um-hmm," he agreed with himself, nodding sagely. "That's what I said, sugar. All this time you been all tore up and mad inside, and the people you been mad at—your daddy, your mama, whoever—they couldn't have given you what you was lookin' for in the first place. You blamin' the wrong people, that's all."

I heard Maude's voice, remembered her tentative explanation—*Only God can do what you and I need done, honey...*

"But...but," I sputtered, "what they did—or didn't do—it was wrong! It was unfair!"

He cocked his head and peered sideways at me from his leathery, cream-and-coffee-colored face. "Now, honey," he said in a warning tone, "I'm old, I'm crippled, and I'm black. I seen a lot of wrong in my life, even before I got stuck in this chair—and you gonna try and talk to *me* about unfair?"

I quickly changed course. "Well, then...whose fault is it? If not theirs, whose?"

Instead of an immediate answer, he fixed me with a long, serious, probing look. "Until you let God into your heart, sugar," he said in a quiet, firm tone, "there ain't gonna be room in there for nobody but yourself. And that gets mighty lonesome."

A crosshatched wave of contradictory emotions ricocheted through me at hearing my own secret speculations voiced by another. Recognizing the truth of what he said, I got angry. "You mean I should give in!" I said in a voice that was almost a shout. "You want me to roll over and play dead for my parents—like none of it ever happened! I'm sick of hearing about God," I ranted. "I've heard all the Bible stories a thousand times each, heard all the passages quoted backwards and forwards, heard all the sermons—and I didn't find any answers there, Shake! I just got punished, that's all!"

"No, honey, you got it all wrong," he said in the same soft, compassionate, inflexible voice. "I ain't talkin' about your mama and daddy. I want you to roll over and play dead to sin. I want you to give in to Jesus, sugar. Until you do that, the rest of it don't make no difference."

I stared at him, unable to reply.

"I don't care how much you think you know about God. That don't matter a bit if you don't know God. You tryin' to make your own way, tryin' to be in charge and figure it all out for yourself." He shook his head. "You cain't do it. I learned that much, the hard way—a long time ago. You got to let it go. Let the Lord have it—all of it. All of you. It's the only way, honey. The *only* way."

"But, what about my dad?" I asked, clawing at the last shred of justification I could lay hands on. "Doesn't he owe me...*something?* Does he get off—just like that?"

He shook his head again, and I saw tears in his eyes. But his voice was as firm and gentle as ever, when he spoke. "I cain't tell you what to do about him, honey. Only God can help you there. The same God we all gonna answer to, someday. You got to let God in, baby. That's all there is to it." He leaned forward in his chair and gripped my arm. There was nothing left to say. I got up and left, the unfinished domino game still on the table.

Only God can do what we need done...

I walk over to the table and look again at the letter I've written. I pick it up, crumpling it in my fist, and toss it into the trash can. I pick up the phone, dialing an eight-digit number from memory.

"Hello?"

"Hi, Mom—it's me."

"Hi, honey…" Her voice is doubtful. "Is everything okay?"

"Yeah, I'm fine," I reply, telling most of the truth. "I just wanted to let you know…I plan to be there on the Fourth, if that's okay."

A pause. "Why, of course it is, dear! I haven't called because I wasn't sure if you already had plans—"

"Well, I just wanted to let you know," I say, suddenly needing desperately to finish the call. "I'll see you in a few weeks, okay?"

"All right, sweetheart. I'll tell Daddy."

"Great. Well…bye, Mom."

"Bye, honey."

I replace the handset in its cradle, staring at it as I try to calm my breathing. "Okay, God," I say finally, "what do I do now?"

———

Linus was planing the side of a newly made door. This was one of his favorite tasks: he enjoyed the crisp sound of the blade, the way the shavings curled ahead of the tool, then fell off to pile in fragrant, resinous profusion at his feet. He enjoyed the smooth, finished feel of the wood when he was done.

So pleasurably absorbed was he that he received a severe start from the boy who raced shouting, through the open doorway of the carpentry shop. To his annoyance, Linus realized that his flinching had caused him to slightly gouge the door's edge.

"Have you heard? Have you heard?" the youngster was shouting, leaping up and down in his agitation. The child was a waif who roved this area of the city, sleeping where he could, stealing if he must. Linus and Caius often used him to run simple errands, paying him a copper or two for his aid. Consequently, he spent more than a little time loitering about the shop.

Caius caught the boy by the arm and said, "Softly, lad. No one in here is deaf! Your shouts are wasted."

The boy calmed slightly. "I was in the marketplace when I heard the news. Have you heard? Do you know what has happened?"

"Surely nothing worth such a row as you have caused," groused Linus, running a hand over the gouge.

"So *you* say," remarked the boy with a knowing smirk on his dirty face. "But there are those who might even pay to have such information as I carry in my head." The lad peered from Caius to Linus with a brazenly expectant look.

Linus, hiding a smile despite his chagrin, turned away, rummaging in his wallet. "I can't imagine anything in that head of yours," he growled, "that would be worth even a single copper. But to stop your racket, here—" he flung two small coins at the boy's feet. The lad scooped them into a grimy fist and wheeled as if to bolt out the door.

Caius grabbed him by the back of his clothing, then held him suspended by his shoulders, his feet pumping uselessly in the air.

"Let me down! Let me down, you big ox!" the boy squealed.

"Extort money from my partner with the promise of news, then try to leave without delivering?" Caius growled threateningly. "I ought to hang you from that spike, yonder."

"All right! I'll tell! I'll tell! Only put me down!"

Caius dropped him to the dirt floor—none too gently—and placed himself in the doorway.

The boy gathered himself and dusted his clothing—uselessly, Linus thought—before staring significantly at the two men. Puffing out his chest, he announced, "The emperor is dead!"

The two men stared at each other for several breaths. Sharply, Caius questioned the boy. "Who told you such a big lie, boy? Where did you hear this rubbish you call news?"

"It's the truth!" the lad protested, a hurt expression on his face. "I was in the market, and I heard one of the officials of the legate talking about it."

"Why would an aide of Lucius Vitellius bother making such an important announcement to the likes of you?" Linus teased.

"Well…" the boy admitted, shrugging, "it wasn't *exactly* an official. It was one of the legionaries. But I heard him, plain as plain, and you can believe me or not. I don't care a fig, either way."

Caius moved out of the doorway. "Scurry along out of here, then, you little rodent, before I take a mind to step on you."

The boy vanished through the doorway as quickly as he had entered.

"Tiberius Claudius Nero Caesar—dead," Linus mused, arching his eyebrows as he considered the information. "What will this mean, I wonder?"

"Little enough for us, most likely. I don't think the caesars, nor the senate and people of Rome, trouble themselves over-much about Jewish carpenters," Caius returned, smiling.

Linus gave the younger man a sidelong look, then allowed his face to crack into a grin. "True enough, cousin. Still…Tiberius has ruled the empire of his grandfather Augustus for more than a score of years. When he came to the throne I was but a beardless boy, with breast-milk still wet on my lips. Much has changed with the passing of the time. The world is a smaller place, in many ways. And in some parts of the empire, a much hotter place." Linus remembered the fierce promises of violence in the words of John of Gischala, the highwayman of Galilee, and the relentless incitements of the Judean zealots. How much time would pass before the simmering kettle of Palestine boiled over?

But unless you repent, you too will all perish, the Nazarene had said. Was this a veiled prophecy about the fate of his homeland?

Barabbas! Give us Barabbas! the rabble had chanted, as if to hasten the fulfillment of their victim's words

"Hello, there! Is anyone hungry?" sang a lilting female voice. Caius turned to look, and a foolish grin spread across his face.

It was Agrippina—Caius's wife these two months past. The lovely young woman came into the shop carrying a basket covered with a linen cloth. Watching the fond glances passing between the two young lovers, Linus had to smile. Agrippina could have reached into the basket, handed Caius a stone, and he would have tried to bite it. The food she brought held not nearly so much interest for him as the face of his beloved.

He had married the gentile girl over the silent remonstrations of his mother. Like Trochaion, Agrippina was dutiful to Anna and strove conscientiously to be a good daughter-in-law. But the widow of Matthias, while not overtly hostile or rude, nevertheless managed to display her disapproval in subtle, disguised ways.

For his part, Linus could not help but be happy for the young couple. After all, this was not Jerusalem, nor Judea. He glanced at the shining faces of the young lovers, they way their eyes drank each other. If only…

"Well, then," he interrupted his thoughts, speaking in a gruff tone. "Is a man to starve while you two make moon-eyes? If there's food in that basket, let's have some!"

Agrippina blushed and hurried to him. "I'm sorry, cousin Linus," she said in a flustered voice. "Here—have some of this cheese. And I made the bread only this morning."

Later, as the two men polished off the last scraps, Agrippina asked Linus, "When you were in Jerusalem, cousin, did you ever meet a man named Nicanor?"

"No, Agrippina, I don't recall ever having met a fellow by that name. Of course, Jerusalem holds many folk I never met, even though it's smaller than Antioch by more than half. Why do you ask?"

"Oh, I was just wondering. This Nicanor is a friend of Trochaion's—or at least of his older brother Nicolas. He is just arrived here from Cyprus, and I—"

"From Cyprus, you said?" interrupted Caius. "Why then should Linus have known him from Jerusalem?"

"Oh! I'm sorry!" she laughed "I forgot to say that Nicanor had only been a short time returned to Cyprus from Jerusalem. He had gone there for some feast or other." She glanced at her husband, smiling. "You Jewish folk have more feasts and holidays than I can keep in my head."

"Is Nicanor a Jew, then?" asked Linus.

"Yes, but Cypriot by birth," she explained.

"How come you know so much about him?" insisted Caius.

"She's already told you," Linus admonished, "between her words. He is a friend of Trochaion's—hence a friend of Miriam. Do you imagine the women sit in the house all day while we're here playing in the sawdust?"

Caius looked sheepish. After a pause, Agrippina continued.

"At any rate, this Nicanor speaks strange, new words—such things as I have never heard before. And Nicolas seems to approve of what he says. Nicanor says that the resurrection of *Kristos* makes it possible for everyone to know the God of Abraham and Isaac, or that is what I suppose from the little I've heard. He says that everyone should believe in him, should pledge obedience to him. Trochaion understands more than I," she said presently, with a sigh. "But, then...he has longer knowledge of the faith of the Jews."

Linus scowled at the floor. Since his outburst in the work yard months before, he and Caius had gingerly avoided the topic of Nicolas and the beliefs of the Nazarene sect. Linus had often regretted the tenor of his words, but Caius had seemed willing to allow the matter to be forgotten. It had been easier to let time dull the sharpness of their exchange.

But now, the bewitching talk of resurrection and eternal hope again trickled into the shop—on the innocent lips of Caius's gentile bride. It was one thing to make pronouncements about the ill-fated Galilean messiah among the synagogues of Antioch, but it now seemed that Nicolas and his Cypriot friend were seeking converts among the uncircumcised as well!

Living in peace and respect among the *goyim* was one thing—but this! If God had been unable, in all the generations since Moses, to convince mankind of the justice of the Levitical ordinances, why should he now throw the gates open to the gentiles at large? Had so many ages of obedience meant so little that God's favor was now to be sprayed among the nations like cheap wine at festival-time? What point was there in being Jewish?

It smacked to him of the same sort of fond thinking that no doubt accounted for the resurrection-talk of the Nazarene sect. But wishing something to be so and truly having it so were two different things. How many times, as Heracleia's tortured screams from the birthing-bed ripped at his nerves, had he fervently begged God not to take the lives of his wife, his child?

But, something whispered to his soul, was it really his zeal for the Law that constrained his consideration of the Nazarene doctrine? Or was it fear that held him back? Fear that this resurrection-talk might be true? The differences between Jews and *goyim* were less than nothing compared to the differences between the living and the dead. If Jesus of Nazareth had truly arisen from the tomb in Jerusalem, then everything was changed. Moorings he had once thought sufficient were instantly obliterated. If death was not the end, then...

He got to his feet and strode toward the door. "Thank you for the delicious food," he said to Agrippina in a voice he hoped was civil, at least. "I'm going to the timber market," he tossed over his shoulder to Caius as he left. "We'll need the wood to begin those racks for the wine-merchant."

Agrippina, wide-eyed with concerned surprise, looked at her husband. "What did I say to offend him?"

"Nothing," Caius replied. "The fault lies with what he heard."

*****

Strato moved toward Linus, smiling easily. Things were much better for the manager of the timber market since the arrival of the new legate, these two years past. Many of the public building projects cancelled or postponed by Quirinius had been reinstated by his successor, Lucius Vitellius. The deadly silence that had greeted Linus and Caius on a previous visit seemed impossible now—the yard was a tumult of shouting, sweating men and braying beasts. "Grace to you, Linus," the overseer said in the habitual shout that he used in the busy compound. "What brings you to me today?"

Linus gave the cheerful man a sour glance, then looked away, pointing toward a stack of cypress logs. "I need ten planks of ten cubits each. The width needs to be at least four spans. And don't try to give me any of that worthless stuff with knots every other finger's width, like the last time."

Strato, taken aback by Linus's acid tongue, gave the carpenter a surprised look. "I will have the wood delivered to you," he said, "and I hope my man finds you in a more civil mood." He turned to give the order, then wheeled back toward Linus. "I just remembered. A fellow is looking for you. There." Strato jerked a thumb over his shoulder toward the lean-to.

As the disgusted manager strode away, Linus ambled toward Strato's headquarters—angry with himself for his curtness and angry with the cosmos for his anger. He was staring at the ground just ahead of his feet as he walked, so he didn't see the man who stepped out of the lean-to to await his approach. Finally looking up, Linus was startled, after a moment's recollection, to recognize Praxos, Phoebe's contentious servant. The carpenter's eyes darted about, half-expecting to see Phoebe herself.

"You are Linus, the carpenter, are you not?" Praxos was asking.

When he found his tongue, Linus said, "Yes, I am. But—"

"My mistress suggested I begin by looking here," the man said, shaking his head in amused respect, "and, as usual, she was correct. For my part, I might have wandered for a week among the streets of Antioch, inquiring after every carpenter in the entire city. But not my mistress. No, no, she is far too clever for that—"

"Where is she?" Linus blurted impatiently. "Is she in Antioch?"

Praxos gave him a strange look. "Why, of course! Where else might you imagine her to be? Would I be here if she weren't in Antioch? Would I leave the side of my gracious mistress, who—"

"What message are you to give me?" Linus interjected.

Again, the curious stare, as if a mushroom had suddenly sprouted from Linus's forehead. "Why, no message at all, sir! My mistress asks you to accompany me to her presence. What makes you think she would allow one such as myself to speak for her? Why should anyone presume to speak for one as—"

Linus feared he would either be mazed into a dull trance by Praxos's insurmountable prattle—or that he would throttle the loquacious servant with his bare hands.

As Praxos rattled on, Linus's mind spun along the paths of choice before him. Should he go to her? Though this was the answer to many a wishful night-dream, the sudden daylight prospect made him skittish. Would it not be better to refuse to come—to ask Praxos to tell his mistress the carpenter could not be found?

But, no—Praxos would never do such a thing. Such was his stubborn loyalty that he would cut out his own tongue rather than lie to his beloved mistress. The only way to prevent his telling her of finding the carpenter would be to slay him—which, Linus thought, listening to the endless stream of chatter falling from the servant's lips, might be a mercy for all.

But he knew he longed to go, longed to see once again the raven shower of curls, the ivory smoothness of cheek and neck, the dark joy flashing in her eyes. The image of her filled him, pulled at him, overpowered him. Though the sight of her would pierce his soul with a thousand shards of incurable want, he would go to her.

"—as quick a mind as any trader *we're* ever likely to meet, I told him, and besides—"

"Praxos!"

The servant paused in mid-word, his mouth hanging open in renewed surprise at Linus's exasperated shout. "Yes?"

The carpenter made a neat little bow toward the gate of the timber market. "Shall we go, then?" His voice was dangerously polite.

"Well, of course," replied Praxos without taking a breath. "What else would we do? After all…"

Phoebe and her retinue were quartered in a newer section of Antioch, in a spacious hostel across one of the straight, paved Roman thoroughfares from a gleaming, recently constructed temple erected to Jupiter the All-Knowing.

She was in the courtyard of the inn, with Lysander and another of her servants flanking her on either side. She was haggling with a spice buyer who had not, it appeared, properly estimated her prowess.

"Your price for frankincense is far too dear!" the fellow was saying as Linus and Praxos entered. "Neither I nor any spice merchant in Antioch will pay ten *sesterces* per half-shekel-weight! You must lower your price!" the merchant exclaimed, with great, theatrical waves of his pudgy, bejeweled hands.

"Theocrates, we go through this same exercise every year, you and I," Phoebe said in a voice whose courteous tones belied its biting message. "I bring you the only frankincense you will see all season, ask a fair price for my wares, and listen to your zealous rhetoric while the sun moves halfway across the sky. In the end, the result is always the same; you pay my price for the frankincense which you will then sell to your hapless patrons for fivefold what you pay me—or you do without." She held his eyes until he looked away, blubbering something under his breath which sounded like "other sources for frankincense."

"Other sources?" Her question was dagger-swift, but couched in the same tones a mother might use with a wayward child. "Be reasonable, Theocrates. Think! Is Rome's treaty with Parthia so unstable that you can trust your desert scavengers to continue smuggling their tiny packets of contraband spices across the eastern border? Without the Parthians to trouble them, what will Vitellius's patrols have to occupy their time, other than capturing your ragamuffin henchmen as they try to sneak their untaxed wares into Syrian territory? How long can you live on the pathetic bits of product that will dribble into your hands if I refuse to sell to you? And how will you explain that hardship to the other spice merchants of this city?"

In all this exchange, her voice had not risen above the reasonable, conversational tone she had begun with, nor did the patient smile leave her lips for an instant. But as she spoke, Linus saw the fat buyer flinch, as if each of her words were a tiny scourge to his cheek. She finished speaking, then shook her head slowly, like a fond teacher whose pupil has, once again, failed to memorize his lessons.

Linus grinned, despite his nervousness. Praxos, for all his annoying verbosity, was right: she was as clever as any trader she was likely to meet—and more. As anyone within earshot knew would happen, the heavy-jowled buyer conceded defeat with a weak nod and a wave of the hand. Graciously, as if he had just paid her a handsome compliment, Phoebe made arrangements for the delivery of the spices. The transaction concluded, she wished the hapless Theocrates a good day and rose to face Linus.

At the sight of her face upon him, he felt his knees go weak. She was still as radiant as her name suggested. "Linus!" she was saying. "I'm so glad Praxos found you! I...I had so

18

Folks, he's still standin' on his front porch, shadin' his eyes with his hand. Can't you see him? He's lookin' down the road, just hopin' against hope his lost child will come home…

I stir uneasily against the upholstered back of the pew. It's Sunday morning, and I've allowed Maude to talk me into coming with her to church. I felt a twinge of trepidation agreeing to it, but—she's my friend, right?

I've felt weird for the last eighteen hours or so…ever since last night when I made the mistake of listening to Shostakovich's *Fifth Symphony*.

I hadn't heard it in quite a while. But for some reason, last night, the bottomless agony of the opening bars pierced me like a sword. A two-edged one. And again, in the third movement—the slow and poignant "Largo"—I felt as if all the pain and confusion of humanity were pouring in a scalding flood from my stereo speakers. I mean—I sat on my couch and bawled like a homesick day-camper.

He wants you back—and it doesn't matter to him where you've been, what you've done. He loves you—so much that he died for you. He's waitin' for you, longing to welcome you with a hug—and with all the love in his heart…

And then, in the blazing conquest of the "Finale," I felt as if the brass section had exploded inside my chest. The victorious crashes of trumpets and percussion, the unmitigated triumph of the closing chords—and in the back of my head, that annoying, know-it-all voice, laughing aloud with elation as it said, "See? This is what I meant! Disaster doesn't win! Can't you hear it? Doesn't your heart teach you to believe it? Despair isn't forever unless you let it be! Give in! Let go! Release yourself into joy! Joy alone is permanent!" And I wept glad tears. Me! Of all people!

"Cut it out!" I told myself. "Get real!"

"This is real," the voice rejoined. "As real as you will ever have a chance to become."

"Shostakovich was a loyal Communist!" I scream at the stereo. "Where do you get off, ascribing all this Christian hyperactivity to a dialectical materialist? Haven't you read your Marx?"

"Truth cannot be contained by the intentions of the vessel. Joy uses arrows from many quivers to find His mark. This music is your summons. How will you respond?"

How long are you gonna keep him waitin'? How long are you gonna break his heart?

So imagine my inner state when the very capable, somewhat predictable, completely likable, not-too-inspiring minister climbs into the pulpit and delivers a down-home, razor-eyed, eloquent, straight-from-the-heart message that comes right at me, high and inside. It's the story of the Prodigal Son, and every word clings to me, burns and anoints like a gracious baptism of boiling oil. He's deep into his closing sequence, and I'm feeling things inside my head that I can't explain, much less control.

"Won't you come home to him, today?" he urges, leaning into his words like a miner wielding a pickaxe. "Don't let him keep hopin', keep waitin'. He wants to give you that ring, that robe. He wants to give you that love. Come home, while the Father invites you."

My Jesus, as Thou wilt!
Oh, may Thy will be mine!
Into Thy hands of love I would my all resign...

The opening strains of the altar call barely register in my consciousness. My heart is too busy with the crashing, leaping, exultant "Finale" of Comrade Shostakovich. "This!" the voice is saying. "Now! This is where it is to be found! In the place where He has brought you!"

Only God can do what we need done...

I feel my mouth moving, but I don't think I'm singing. I think, instead, I'm talking to the voice. "But...I'm not sure. If I do, there will be nothing left in reserve. I will have committed everything—"

"There's already nothing left in reserve!" the voice shouted above the pounding of Shostakovich's tympani, above the pounding of my heart. "You have already expended everything in the battle against yourself. Only here, only in Him can you find rest and replenishment."

I want you to give in to Jesus, sugar. Until you do that, the rest of it don't make no difference...

"But...don't I have any choices? None at all?"

Mr. Barton's dried, feeble fingers—sorting through a random pile of life's flotsam and jetsam, placing them in homogeneous, comfortless piles...

I feel my feet inching toward the center aisle. I see the threadbare pile of the sculptured, out-of-date, cranberry carpet. Leading me toward the front. Leading me toward surrender. Toward escape.

> *Through sorrow and through joy,*
> *Conduct me as Thine own;*
> *And help me still to say,*
> *My Lord, Thy will be done...*

Someone greets me at the front. Someone places a card in my hands. Someone asks me what I want to do. How should I know what I want to do? "I'm ready," I say—not to the people at the front, but to the voice. To the hymn of praise blaring inside my head, carried along on the wave-crest of Shostakovich's victory song.

271

A while later, as the tepid baptismal water runs down my face, Maude clasps me in a bear-hug of sisterly affection. We're standing in the women's dressing room, a dank, grade-school-green cubicle just offstage left from the baptismal pool.

"Maude! Watch out!" I warn her. "I'm soaking wet!"

"Oh, Janice, I don't care! I'm just so happy for you—" Emotion chokes off her voice, and I can see the proud tears of joy standing at attention in her eyes. "Is…is there anyone you want to call? Anyone who—who needs to know about your decision?"

I reach thoughtfully toward the towel hanging on a nearby hook and begin sponging my wet hair, face, and neck. Going behind the curtained dressing partition, I begin pulling off the soaked baptismal garment.

"Yes. I guess there is someone who needs to know about this." Seating myself to begin dressing, I smile to myself. "Mr. Walker, your dad's roommate."

We drove out to the nursing home as soon as church was dismissed. My hand was throbbing from all the handshakes, and I felt as if my face might be sunburned by all the beaming smiles I'd received. But, for some reason, I didn't mind. It was even…welcomed, if that makes any sense. I felt oddly pleased to know that so many people agreed with what I'd done— even on a superficial level. Acceptance wasn't something I had often associated with church, but I was hoping to form a new habit. And something within me gave quiet notice that such things were now possible.

We parked out front and walked inside. Even the smell was different today. Oh, the slack faces were still there, the blank stares and the useless limbs. But today I also saw the smiles, scented the content ripeness of those whose long lives had been well-spent, who knew the calm assurance of impending rest and the promise of resumed, imperishable vigor. How had I missed these people before? I wondered. How had I failed to realize that old age need not be an admission of defeat—could, instead, become a badge of victory? Crumpled into a wheelchair, a wrinkled, cherubic old woman grinned gaily at me, and I winked back—feeling like a co-conspirator, feeling as if we shared a secret, a communion granted to those who await a common deliverance.

We entered Shake's room, and as soon as he looked up at me, he knew...something, at least. He could see something in my eyes, and he began to grin.

"Well, looky here! Hello, there, sugar!" he chortled, his teeth looking as big and white and joyful as the dots on a double-six from the boneyard. "I'm sure glad to see you! You been on my mind this mornin'!"

"Shake, I've got something to tell you!"

His eyes fastened on me, but the smile never left his lips. I felt almost as if he knew what I was going to say.

"Shake, I...I thought a lot about what you said before. About—you know...what was really wrong with me. And... you were right."

His head began to nod—barely enough to notice at first, then in wider and wider arcs, until, by the time I finished talking, he almost looked like he was sitting in a rocking chair.

"Something happened to me—inside me, really—at church this morning, and...Shake—I did what you said. I surrendered to Jesus."

He threw back his head and laughed aloud—big, round, coffee-colored bubbles of laughter that originated from somewhere around his belt. He laughed, even as tears streamed down his face.

"Yes, indeed! Yes, indeed, Lord!" he cried. "I knew you could do it, Jesus! I knew you could!" He shook his head and slapped his thigh as if he had just heard the best punch line in the universe. Then he reached toward me and pulled me into a hug that brooked no resistance.

When he finished with me, he beckoned toward Maude, who stood fidgeting at the back of her father's wheelchair. "Come on over here, Miss Barton. You a part of this, too." Shake grabbed her hand and pumped it in an exuberance of gladness. "I knew, from the first time you brought this young 'un in here," he grinned at her, "that the Lord brought the two of you together. He did it for a purpose, and I'm mighty proud of this day. Yes, ma'am…mighty proud, indeed."

Maude smiled at Shake, but I saw the shadow that flitted across her expression when she turned to look again at her father. I'm not sure whether Shake noticed or not, but he gave her hand a final squeeze and turned back to me, a more serious expression on his face.

"Now, honey, you beginnin' the most important time of your life, right now. The devil don't like what you done this mornin' and he's gonna pull out all the stops to try and get you to take it back. But you got the Holy Spirit livin' inside you now, and you don't have to take nothin' off the devil, no more!"

I grinned shyly at him, feeling a little like a prizefighter, crouched in the corner of the ring, getting the final instructions from a trainer.

"All that mess inside you 'bout your mama and daddy—I figure that's where he's gonna come at you first," Shake went on earnestly. "A family is a wonderful thing," he said, and I didn't miss the minor-key inflection in his voice. "Families can help each other—or they can hurt. I know. I seen it a lot—in lots of folks. Both ways. Devil knows that, well as I do."

Though Maude appeared to be attending her near-catatonic father—straightening his collar, fussing with his hair—I could tell Shake's words had more than one recipient. Whether he intended it that way or not, I wasn't sure.

"Now, sugar, I cain't tell you just what to do or say when you talk to your daddy. But you got to talk to him," he said, jabbing the air with his index finger. "Somehow, you got to get all that poison out of you that's been buildin' up all these years. You got to get it out, without hurtin' somebody—'cause hurtin' is what the devil specializes in, see? You cain't play by his rules no more."

"But, Shake!" I protested. "What you just said…it's impossible!" I was appalled, panicked by the thought of confronting my father with the blistering resentments I had cherished through the years. If stubborn silence had bought me his disapproval, what in the world would my candor summon from him?

"Impossible for you, maybe," Shake said, squinting one eye at me, as if he were taking aim. "But they ain't found nothin' yet that's too hard for God, honey. He does the impossible, all the time. When you and me cain't see no way 'round a situation, why—that's right when God gets down to business!"

I must have had a doubtful look on my face, because Shake kept on selling. "Once I heard a preacher tell it this way: if God tells you to jump through a wall, it's up to to you to do the jumpin'. It's up to God to make the hole."

W ell, then," said Phoebe into the uneasy silence between them, "what do you think of the news from Rome?"

Linus took another slow bite from the fig in his hand. "About the death of Tiberius Caesar? Well, however the succession goes, I don't think it will affect our—"

"Oh, haven't you heard?" Phoebe interrupted. "Caius, the son of Tiberius's adopted son Germanicus, is now emperor."

"Caius, the son of the great general? The one the soldiers in Germany nicknamed 'Little Boots'?"

Phoebe nodded. "Yes, Caligula. He has already been confirmed by the senate. Many in Rome have high hopes for his reign. At least, it is said, he may be less despicable than his adopted grandfather became in his later years."

Linus nodded. "Caius Caesar Germanicus," he said, slowly sounding out the full name of the new emperor as he carefully studied the carvings on the side of the fruit bowl and gave his best imitation of a thoughtful expression. He tried desperately to think of something else to say about the imperial succession, in order to stave off the uncomfortable quiet that would prod him to look at Phoebe—or saying something to her he could not afford.

But Phoebe was again the first to speak, broaching the treacherous quiet with a series of questions. "How goes it for you here, Linus?" she asked in Hebrew. "Does your trade prosper? Did you find your people well? Are you..." her voice faltered, then resumed. "Are you happy?"

He shifted uneasily on his cushion, then looked away. "It goes well enough," he said in Greek. "The legate's building commissions make enough work for a good carpenter to live in adequate fashion."

He could feel her eyes on him. He dared not meet them. Perhaps she was troubled by his insistence on Greek, by his refusal of the intimacy of Hebrew. He must steel himself against such considerations. She is gentile, he lectured himself. You cannot, must not—

"There is something I must tell you," she said in Greek, sighing as she acceded to his implied demand. "While I have been away, I have learned more of the teachings of Jesus, the Anointed One. I and my entire household have given our allegiance to him. We have called him Lord and have taken the proselytic washing in his name."

Linus could not restrain himself from an incredulous look at her. "But—you are already a proselyte! Or so you implied on the way from Damascus. Why then did you—"

"It was needful," she replied gently. She paused a long moment, an expression of amazed reverie passing across her features. "As you may have realized by my earlier conversation with the buyer outside, I am returning from a buying expedition among the bedouins of the Arabah. On my way here, I came by the coast road rather than the inland route I took when I made your acquaintance.

"When we came through Caesarea, I chanced—if, indeed, it was truly chance—to meet a most interesting man—"

Linus felt a tiny twinge of annoyance. Had he not left his own shop to escape talk of just this sort? Now, here was Phoebe, the fond object of his fruitless desire, appearing almost as if from nowhere—and on her lips was the same foolishness!

"He is a devout man, Linus—a God-fearer—like myself. And then, one day, a vision came to him."

She proceeded to relate a bizarre tale of angelic visitations, an interview with one of the Nazarene's twelve deputies, and the same sort of ecstatic outbreak among the centurion and his household as at the Pentecost festival.

"And so you see, Linus," she concluded, leaning forward in her urgency, "Jesus *Kristos* did not come just for Jews, but for all mankind. He—he calls all men unto himself, as I heard him say, shortly before his death."

And I, if I be lifted up—

Linus shoved the scene in the Temple courtyard from his mind.

He looked about at Phoebe's men—at Praxos, beaming in silent agreement with his mistress's speech. "So then, Praxos!" he asked, more to avoid the eyes of Phoebe than for any interest in the slave's words, "what caused you to embrace the teaching of the Nazarene? Is this, too, a mark of your loyalty to your mistress that you toss aside the charms of Lady Luck for the untried teachings of a slain Jew?"

"Whatever do you mean, Linus?" Phoebe began, a confused, hurt look on her face. "I would never force my—"

"Please, mistress," Praxos interjected. "May I answer him in my own way? Please?"

Her eyes flickering from the drawn, despairing face of the carpenter to the beseeching, earnest face of her manservant, she nodded, watching tensely to see what sort of exchange would follow.

"Friend of my mistress," Praxos began, "it is true that for many years I made the luck goddess my patron. I prayed to Tyché, ascribed to her the happy circumstances of my life— which were few enough—and pleaded for her mercy when things didn't proceed so well. And if I made Luck my goddess, well…perhaps it's because chance seemed to be the only observable difference between those who got on and those who didn't.

"Philosophy was so much useless blather, as far as I was concerned—after all, I couldn't see that its adherents had appreciably more ease or greatly improved circumstances than those who sacrificed to the gods. If luck was the ruling principle of existence, I reasoned, then it was Luck I would worship. After all—she made no demands nor promises. Either she was there, or she was not. Clean and simple, I thought."

Linus stirred restively, believing he was trapped by another of Proxos's long-winded orations.

"Oh, my lady Phoebe had tried for years, without much success, to teach me the ways of the Jews. For long hours she would expound to me the advantages of the Law. She would urge me to renounce my belief in Tyché and all the other gods and accept the doctrines of Moses and all those others whose names were so strange and whose teachings were so strict and dusty-dry. To be sure, the ethics of the Jews are admirable in theory, and the code of conduct recommended by their law is laudable—but what need had I of such things? I had the luck, you see—and if the luck ran out, I would be dead, and beyond the concerns of Moses and his scrolls. Besides, I could hardly justify self-mutilation on the mere grounds of adopting a better form of ethics.

"But all that changed," the slave said in a voice of quiet emphasis, "when I heard the teaching of the *Kristos*."

Something in Praxos's voice drew Linus's eyes to him. Something in his expression held them there.

"When I heard of the *Kristos*—of his healing of the sick and blind, of his compassion for all people, Jews and non-Jews alike, and especially of his death and *anastasis*—something began to change within me," the slave said, his eyes peering unfocused into the middle distance. "When Gaius Cornelius told us of the things he had learned from Peter of Bethsaida—"

Again! Once more the name of the Galilean fisherman whacked against Linus's ears. This fisherman, it seemed, was not content to remain in Jerusalem. Apparently, he was travel-

ONCE UPON A CROSS

ing all over Judea and Galilee—even to the capital in Caesarea—spreading the name of Jesus of Nazareth. How could a man so bold be one of the dirty, bewildered twelve whom he had seen following the Nazarene into the Temple courts? Were such men truly capable of feats like those Linus had heard ascribed to them since the supposed resurrection of their leader? *He fell in with the Nazarene, Jesus...*

"—when he told us of the love of God, which caused him to send the *Kristos* as payment for the transgressions of mankind," Praxos was saying, "when he told us of the life beyond death which is promised to all who are faithful followers of the *Kristos,* who himself was the first to be delivered forever from death; when he told us that all mankind—Jews, Greeks, Romans, Parthians, everyone—was now able to approach this Holy One through obedience to the *Kristos*... something, or Someone, spoke strongly to my heart, telling me that my soul had at last found its true home. I knew that I need no longer depend on the whims of a luck goddess or the powerless pronouncements of philosophy. I was, in that instant, delivered from aimlessness, from the meandering path of faithless Fate. And it is because of this that I freely joined my lady in pledging my life to the service of the *Kristos,* Jesus of Nazareth."

Praxos fell silent, his eyes shifting from the closed, distant face of the carpenter to the concerned, troubled eyes of his mistress.

Phoebe smiled gently at Praxos and nodded, then turned again to Linus.

"I know you are a good man, Linus," she said softly, trying again in Hebrew to summon some spark of response from this strange, unpredictable man for whom she held such unaccountably resilient feelings. "I know that you carry some pain within you that presses hard on your soul. But having seen the *mashiach* face-to-face as you have, why can't you—"

"I saw no *mashiach* !" he exclaimed suddenly, the words bursting from his lips like stones flung from a sling. "I saw only a wandering rabbi who said good things and got himself killed for his trouble! I saw no deliverer, no savior! Nothing but a hapless preacher who knew no better than to allow others to make of him something he could never be! A foolish kindler of dreams he could never hope to fulfill!"

He pushed himself up from the table and turned toward the door. "I'm sorry, Phoebe," he said, unable to look at her, unwilling to see in her face what he knew he must see if he beheld her. "I wish I could believe in your *Kristos*. I wish more than anything in the world that I could believe in this, this resurrection." He limped toward the portal, each step away from her an admission of defeat, a sacrifice on the altar of the implacable past. When he reached the doorway, he turned about to face them again, his jaw trembling with helpless anguish.

"Dead is dead! Can't you understand that?" he said in a voice hoarse with loss. "People don't come back from the dead—neither wives, nor children...nor messiahs! The sooner you realize this, the better for all!" Suddenly clutching his chest, Linus left.

Phoebe watched him go, her eyes big and dark with shock and grief. "May the Lord have mercy upon him," she whispered, tears coursing down her cheeks and onto her lap.

19

L ooks like you got de bid, Shake. Dadburn your no-good hide!"

Shake chuckles and his whole torso moves in undulating waves of mirth. He and I are partners in a vicious, no-holds-barred game of forty-two. Our opponents are Maude, seated to my left, and Grady LeTournier, a crusty, rail-thin old Cajun who lives down the hall. Mr. LeTournier is a double amputee who takes his dominos very seriously. But he's also sweet—in an abrasive, old-fashioned sort of way.

" 'Scuse my language jus' now, ladies," he apologizes, "but I can't figger out how in de world why, ever time I get a decent hand, Shake always outbid me. Den he gets to call trumps, and dat make all my dominos a bunch of no-count trash."

"Three's are trumps!" Shake sings out in a delighted voice.

"See dere? Dat's just what I mean! Dadburn it! 'Scuse me again, ladies."

"Mr. LeTournier, you'd better start thinking more about what you've got in your hand," Maude admonishes with mock seriousness, "and less about losing the bid. If they make one more mark, they win."

"Don't I know it!" he groans. "I tell you, Shake Walker, you jus' about de luckiest man alive—today, at least."

"What you talkin' about, Grady?" Shake asks in a hurt voice. "Luck ain't got nothin' to do with it! It's my partner over there! She and I on the same wavelength, see?"

Grady mumbles something under his breath, while I frantically try to figure out if the domino I'm looking at is a six in the three's suit, or a three in the six's suit. Forty-two always does this to me. The function of any given domino within a hand of forty-two is mostly a matter of semantics.

Maude glances away from the game toward her father, hunched over the table in front of his wheelchair, sorting a fresh shipment of assorted buttons. As always, he's somewhere on the back side of the moon, as far as anyone else is concerned. But his presence still maintains its pernicious power over Maude.

Since my baptism, she's been—different. More contemplative, if that's possible. Just now, I see her eyes moving back and forth between her father and Shake, almost as if she's evaluating or comparing or...measuring. Weighing odds—like a convict in the prison yard, eyeing the distance to the wall. Her eye catches on the corner of my look. She blushes slightly and, with an effort noticed by no one but me, returns her concentration to her dominos.

The hand opens. Shake leads with a three-five, taking the first trick. I'm still trying to figure out if my hand is an asset or a liability, and I make a stupid play on the next pass, enabling Maude to take the trick.

"Dere you go, Miss Maude!" Grady applauds. "Dat's de way to do it. We gonna get dese dirty rascals, yet. You watch and see!"

Fortunately, there aren't any counters in the trick—no dominos which add to multiples of five—so they only get one point. She leads back with a trump—the three-four—and Shake pauses long before playing. His hand moves toward his dominos, then back, then forward again. I can tell he's unsure what to play. Finally, with a sigh, he lays down a double-three. Grady chortles with delight.

"Well, well, well! Looky here at dis! Shake, what you doin' biddin' thirty-four wid a no-count hand like you got?"

Shake grins and shrugs. "Make your play, Grady. We ain't got all day."

Grady squints at his dominos a moment, then selects a tile. "I think we gonna get 'em right here, Miss Maude," he announces. "I think ol' Shake jus' run out of luck." He lays down the double five. The trick is now worth eleven points—more than enough to keep us from getting our bid if they win it.

I stare at my dominos. The only thing I have in my hand with three spots is the three-six. Still unsure if I'm doing the right thing, I place it gently in the center of the table. Shake's cackle of glee, followed closely by Grady's disgusted moan, tells me it was indeed a six in the three's suit.

"I want you to jus' look at dis trash!" Grady grouses. "My luck is so bad it'd kill knee-high cotton, I tell you dat for sure." He shakes his head helplessly as I shove the dominos across to Shake.

"That's my girl, sugar!" he grins at me. "That's my girl. And now, folks, I got a 'nouncement to make. This game is *over.*" He turns his tiles face-up, showing that he has the rest of the trumps.

"Now if dat don't beat all!" exclaims Grady. "A lay-down hand, on top of everyt'ing else! Well, dat's it for me, I reckon," he says, wheeling himself back from the table and pivoting toward the door. "I gonna go back to my room and watch TV. Maybe my luck'll change. Bye, y'all."

"Goodbye, Grady," Shake waves. "Come back tomorrow and I'll give you another forty-two lesson."

"Dat's mighty sorry, Shake," he admonishes, "kickin' a fella when he down. Mighty sorry."

Shake laughs as Grady wheels himself briskly out the door.

"That Grady," he chuckles, shaking his head in amusement as the door swings shut. "I ain't never seen nobody that hated as bad to lose, nor looked forward to the next game as much."

"Well, you sure had the shuffles falling right for you today," Maude observes.

"Yes, ma'am, I guess I did. That, and my partner there." He gestures toward me.

"Oh, come on, Shake," I demur. "You carried us and you know it." I'm gathering the dominos, placing them back in the box.

"Well…maybe just a little bit," he concedes with a shrug. "But I don't reckon I minded the load."

"My goodness, look at the time!" Maude exclaims, staring at her wristwatch. "They'll be coming soon to get Papa for supper. I need to comb his hair and get him presentable." She snaps open her handbag and takes out a barber's comb, going to Mr. Barton and briskly stroking the few strands of hair around the perimeter of his bald pate.

"Maude, why don't you let it go for today?" I suggest, seeing her determined, Puritanical mask of martyrdom. Maude is engaging in an act of self-flagellation—I know it, and she knows it, but she won't admit it.

"Got to get you looking nice," she says to her father, ignoring me. "Don't want you going in the dining room looking like no one cares about you, do we? Of course not."

There is a thin edge of hysteria showing in Maude's voice and manner, and it starts to scare me.

"After all," she continues, combing the same few hairs again and again, "you were my father! That constitutes a debt that must be paid, doesn't it?"

Jonas Barton's features never move, never alter from the unliving stare, the crablike motions of his fingers as he sorts the buttons into piles. I feel the blood draining from my face as she continues.

"You put a roof over my head, and food on the table, and that's any Christian man's duty, right?" she grates, her breath starting to come in short, labored bursts. "You clothed me, provided for me—so naturally it was my job to stay out of the way and be no trouble, isn't that so? Well, here I am, Papa. Taking care of you now. I would have liked to stay out of the way, but I couldn't, could I? Somebody had to come up to this miserable room and see that you had toys to play with and someone to care about you and a blanket on your shoulders. So here I am, Papa! The dutiful daughter. Your little Maudie—all grown old. Old and useless and drab—but out of the way, and no bother to anybody. What do you think of that, Papa? Aren't you proud of me?"

The comb falls from her fingers and she sways, bringing her hands up to her face.

"Watch out!" Shake yells. "She's gonna fall!"

I jump across the bed and grab her upper arm, trying to steer her onto her father's bed to break her fall. She sits down heavily on the mattress, then doubles over, sobbing into her hands. I'm there beside her, my arm around her shoulders—at a loss for words, as usual. And then I hear Shake's voice.

"Get up, honey. Move him out of the way."

I look up, and he's motioning toward Mr. Barton's chair, then pointing a finger at the corner of the room.

"Go on!" he urges. "Back Jonas up and get him out of the way!"

I get up and steer Mr. Barton away from the table and his buttons. A look of confusion crosses his features for a moment. Then his fingers, suddenly unemployed, fall still in his lap. He stares into the corner, as passive as a piece of furniture.

Meanwhile, Shake has wheeled himself between the beds and taken one of Maude's hands in his own. His voice is low and urgent. In the caring slope of his shoulders, his acute focus on Maude, he reminds me oddly of a physician—or a midwife.

"It ain't your fault, Missy. Ain't none of it your fault, and you got to believe that. I seen the way you done for him, the way you tried to take care of him. And I seen the way he turned it all back on you—when he still could. I seen the way he done you, when you done nothin' but good for him. It ain't your fault, honey. You done all a body could, and that's the truth."

She's still weeping, but the sounds are softer, more controlled. I can tell Shake's words are having an effect—but I'm not sure yet what the effect will be.

"Now, your daddy wasn't a bad man—you got to know that, too," he says, patting her hand softly. "He done the best he could in hard times, and he made plenty of mistakes. I..." his head drops a moment, and his voice stumbles just a bit, tripping over some regretful memory, perhaps. "I guess we all made some mistakes, some time or other. Tryin' to raise a family, tryin' to keep body and soul together the best way we knew how."

I sense he is peering into his own past, into certain recollections that pain him still. But, I realize, that sort of retrospection doesn't hold the same liabilities for Shake that it does for Maude or me. Shake has made peace with his yesterdays. That is what sets him apart, equips him. He has learned the futility of regret and the freedom that comes on the wings of grace. He has forgiven himself, becoming a channel of forgiveness to others.

"But that ain't no excuse for doin' you wrong, is it?" he says, his hand slowly patting hers, his voice coming in a silken, assured murmur. "You tried to be what you thought he wanted you to be, but it hurt you, didn't it, honey? There's a part of you that ain't never gonna get over that...but you got to keep on livin', anyway. You got to go on with your life, and make the best of the days that God gives you. You got time, honey! Precious time. Don't keep on payin' for what he done to you. Let God have it, sugar. Your daddy can't tell you he's sorry—it's too late for him. But it ain't too late for you."

She uncovered her face and slowly raised her eyes to look at him. And I saw something in her face that, given enough time and encouragement, might evolve into hope.

Caius Germanicus Caligula had ruled for less than two years when ill news of events in Rome began to trickle back to Antioch. Some said the emperor had suffered a grave illness which, though sparing his body, took its gravest toll on his mind. Still others opined that the son of Germanicus, far from being a man of the measure of his father, was now as he had always been—a vain, conceited, and eccentric demagogue whom the robes of empire fit but poorly. In any case, it became clear that his reign would not be remembered for its equanimity and even-handedness. Antioch was spared the worst of his depredations only by dint of distance.

Linus, along with the rest of Antioch, had had certain misgivings when the able and even-handed legate of Syria, Lucius Vitellius, was recalled to Rome by the new Caesar, to be replaced by Publius Petronius. But the new legate proved himself to be capable and fair-minded as well, and most folk in the province of Syria had no reason to complain of the substitution. Even less regretted by those in the southern reaches of the province was Caligula's deposition of Pontius Pilate as procurator of Judea. More and more complaints of Pilate's cruelty and cavalier disregard for the opinions and sensibilities of his subjects—Jew and gentile alike—had reached the ears of the legate in Antioch. So much so that Lucius Vitellius had, before his own recall, ordered Pilate to Rome to account for his actions. No one in Judea was sorry to see him leave. If Marullus, the newly appointed prefect, was no better, he was at least no worse.

More disturbing news reached Antioch a few months later, but this news came from the east rather than the west—and its weight fell most heavily on the Jews of the region.

The gentile citizens of Babylon and its environs rose up against the Jews living among them, angered by the depredations practiced by two Jewish brothers who styled themselves lords, but were really little better than highwaymen, even if brave and daring ones. So harsh was the anger and repression of the gentile majority that many Babylonian Jews relocated to Seleucia, a city on the coast, not far from Antioch. But their reception by the Greeks and Syrians living there was far from hospitable. Many of them journeyed inland to Antioch, to seek refuge among the larger Jewish community there.

Linus began to hear his cousin Caius and other followers of the Nazarene who frequented the shop discuss certain *logia*—sayings attributed to Jesus of Nazareth. Linus gathered from their talk that many of these aphorisms circulated in written and oral form among the loose network of synagogues and believing gentiles throughout Antioch.

Though Linus resolutely gave out the impression of ignoring these earnest huddles, he could not stop himself from trying to catch wisps of words as they discussed the latest ideas about the Nazarene. They seemed eager to learn all they could of the life and thinking of this man they had never met. Not only Caius, but Agrippina, Caius's wife, and Chrestus, their servant, had taken the proselytic bath in the name of their professed Lord and Anointed One. Even Anna, was evidencing a grudging interest in the teachings of this supposed messiah. So widespread had the Nazarene cult become in Antioch that it had attracted the attention of the gentile population at large. More than once in his journeys among the marketplaces and streets of the city, Linus had heard Syrians, Greeks, and Romans alike discussing the *Kristianos*—"the people of Kristos." By the way they used the term, Linus could tell they thought *Kristos* to be the name of some political or spiritual master-figure. Though he thought this usage laughable, he saw no need to correct it.

Among themselves, he knew, the adherents of the Nazarene cult referred to themselves as "followers of the Way." The way of folly, he was prone to mutter to himself as he listened, despite himself, to their talk.

"A letter has come to the synagogue of the Sons of Righteousness," one of them enthused, "from Joseph of Cyprus—he who is called the Son of Comfort."

A soft gasp passed among the group. Linus surmised that this Joseph fellow must enjoy some notoriety among the Nazarene's followers. He kept on with his bow drill. Someone had to work around here, he groused to himself. Perhaps

Caius could afford to sit idle and chatter with his friends all day; Linus could not.

"In his letter, he says that he is coming from Jerusalem as soon as possible to meet those of the Way in Antioch, and to encourage and strengthen them."

"Joseph Bar-Nabas," one of them breathed. "Here—in Antioch!"

"I have heard," said another, "that he is a true Levite of pure lineage!"

Linus had to restrain himself from snickering aloud as the speaker and Caius tried to explain the meaning of Levitic ancestry to the puzzled gentiles among the group.

"I have also heard," added Caius, "that he is—or was—a wealthy landowner, but that he sold most of his land and gave the money to Peter of Bethsaida, for distribution among the poor of the Way in Jerusalem."

Whose ranks he is destined to join, thought Linus, checking the width of the hole he had just drilled against the diameter of the peg that would occupy it.

"Did our Lord himself not say," put in another, "that we should store our treasure in heaven and not on the earth? Surely Joseph Bar-Nabas has a great trove laid up by the Lord for such acts of kindness as these."

A murmur of agreement came from the group.

A tangle of dirty rags and tousled hair tumbled into the carpentry shop. The nameless street urchin, by this time too old to be charming in his dishevelment, scrambled to his feet, pointing frantically out the door.

"Quick! Linus! Caius! They're coming!" he warned in a voice breaking with the treachery of adolescence. "There are many of them! You'd better get ready!"

The huddled conference broke up instantly as Caius and Linus strode toward the shop door, grabbing whatever implement lay close to hand in preparation for whatever real or imagined threat approached.

But the boy had spoken truly. A scowling, cursing mob of perhaps a dozen men stalked in their direction, gesticulating angrily with much clenching of fists. One of them spied Linus and Caius, standing in the doorway of their shop. He pointed at them.

"There's two of them! Look at the filthy Jewish traitors! That's the sort of trash that's causing all the trouble!"

The mob surrounded the carpenters, facing them in an angry semicircle as its members flung bitter, foul-mouthed accusations at the two men.

"Jews are a curse upon the peace of the country!"

"Dirty, traitorous wretches! Ought to be exiled! Don't deserve the protection of the law!"

"What right have they to flaunt their religion in the face of the emperor? What right, I ask you?"

One of Linus's friends, a gentile, stepped past the two men guarding the doorway and faced the angry group. "Portullus! Philopater! What are these ill-fated words with which you accuse these two men—men I myself know to be honest, hard-working citizens of this city?"

"Haven't you heard the news?" one of the others growled. "The legate Petronius marches for Judea, with two legions. There is to be war, in which good Syrian blood will be spilled—and all because of some cursed Jewish superstition!" A loud chorus of angry agreement spilled from the throats of the mob.

So, Linus thought, matters had come to this pass—and all because of the hot-headed Zealots in Jamnia.

Most of the Syrian province was aware of the disturbance created by these characters: how they had pulled down and desecrated a statue of the emperor. Word of the disrespectful vandalism had reached Caligula's ears, and his anger was said to be great. It had been hoped that the recent delegation of Alexandrian Jews would be able to explain to the emperor the Jewish viewpoint on graven images, and also to assure him of the continued loyalty of the empire's Jews. After all, didn't the priests in Jerusalem offer daily prayers and sacrifices for his health?

But apparently such efforts had proved futile. Swords would be drawn, and Linus knew that men such as John of Gischala would not be loath to enter such a fray—probably drawing many others with them.

Gradually, it came out that Caligula, in punishment for the actions in Jamnia, had decreed that Petronius was to erect an image of the emperor in the temple of Jerusalem. Hearing this, Linus and Caius, along with the other Jews present, felt the cold tendrils of fear. Like the desecration of Antiochus Epiphanes, some four generations past, Caligula's appalling action would spawn an open rebellion among the Jews of Judea, and perhaps a fierce backlash against Jews everywhere in the empire. Judea would be knee-deep in blood—Jewish and Roman.

Linus's knuckles stretched taut across the grip of the mallet he held. Striving to keep the tension in his arm absent from his voice, he said, "You men should disperse. Caius and I have done you no harm, nor will we purposely do so. But you will come to harm if you are here when my messenger returns with the legionaries."

Caius, taking his cue from his older cousin, joined in. "That's right. Why be punished as rioters? Why permit the troubles in the south to cause bloodshed here today?"

One by one, the members of the mob began to drift away, grumbling and threatening as they went. Finally, the only ones left were Linus, Caius, and his Nazarene friends. Linus watched as they looked at each other with eyes made big by fear and confusion. What would be the outcome of these events? What would become of the budding religion of the Nazarene if the gentiles among them were forced to choose between the ill favor of Rome and the teachings of an executed Jewish criminal? This crisis would display in unmistakable fashion, Linus thought, the impossibility of a lasting union between Jews and non-Jews. As Linus studied the worried faces about him, he was surprised to find pity stirring about beneath his apprehension and uncertainty. Pity for himself and his countrymen...and pity for these poor gentiles who had just had the cold water of reality thrown on the tender flame of their hope.

As days and weeks passed into months, an uneasy truce settled over the city of Antioch and the province of Syria. Eventually, word trickled down to the provinces that, through the good offices of Herod Agrippa and the favor he continued to enjoy with Caesar, the plan to erect the statue in Jerusalem was aborted. Following close on the heels of these good tidings was the news that Caligula had been assassinated by a group of senators and knights, and that his uncle, the scholarly but somewhat befuddled Claudius, was elected Caesar.

Not only this, but because of the good reputation Herod Agrippa enjoyed with Claudius, the territory of Judea and Samaria was given him to rule as an *ethnarch*—a client-king. Further, Claudius Caesar published an edict throughout the empire that the suspicion under which the Jews were held was due not to their own calumny, but to the madness and injustice of the deceased Caligula. The nations of the empire were instructed to respect the religious practices of the Jews, and the Jews were likewise admonished to respect the practices of other peoples. Thus, in Syria and elsewhere, a measure of calm returned.

It was in these days that the news came which the Nazarenes of Antioch had been anxiously awaiting: Joseph Bar-Nabas had arrived as a guest of the House of the Covenant—the synagogue of Caius and his friends and, formerly, of Linus. So many of the synagogue's members had gone over to the Nazarene belief that Linus scarcely bothered to attend any more. There were almost as many *goyim* there now as Jews, and the situation galled him, reminded him continually of the irreparable rift between his beliefs and that embraced so gladly by Caius, his associates...and Phoebe.

But today Caius begged and pleaded with him, and Agrippina made such insistent eyes at him, that he grudgingly agreed to go to the synagogue. He had to admit, he was slightly curious about this storied fount of generosity nick-named Bar-Nabas. He wanted to see the sort of fabric such a pious figure might be cut from.

The congregation was singing a psalm when they entered:

Give thanks to the Lord, call on his name;
Make known among the nations what he has done.
Sing to him, sing praise to him;
Tell of all his wonderful acts.
Glory in his holy name;
Let the hearts of those who seek the Lord rejoice.
Look to the Lord and his strength;
Seek his face always…

Linus craned his neck this way and that, searching for the unfamiliar face of the guest from Jerusalem. But there were so many unfamiliar faces that the exercise accomplished little. Finally the psalm ended and the rabbi stood and faced the congregation, a pleased smile showing through his gray beard.

"My brothers and sisters," he said, "we have among us today a guest whose name and reputation I think you already know. Joseph Bar-Nabas is come to us from our brethren of the Way in Jerusalem, and I have asked him to give us the teaching from the Law, and make the exposition. Brother Joseph," he said, beckoning with his hand to someone seated on the front row, "will you come?"

The man who stood and walked to the lectern was tall and carried himself with a natural dignity that attracted rather than intimidated. His hair was steely-gray, as was his beard. He had a high forehead and thin lips. He bent to reverently kiss the scroll before him, then unrolled it to find the place where he wished to begin. He read in the rich overtones of a trained orator, but the sincerity in his manner could not be feigned.

" 'See, I have taught you decrees and laws as the Lord my God commanded me, so that you may follow them in the land you are entering to take possession of it. Observe them carefully, for this will show your wisdom and understanding to the nations, who will hear about all these decrees and say, "Surely this great nation is a wise and understanding people." What other nation is so great as to have their gods near them the way the Lord our God is near us whenever we pray to him? And what other nation is so great as to have such righteous decrees and laws as this body of laws I am setting before you today?' "

Bar-Nabas looked up and his smile embraced them all. "My brethren," he said, "I greet you all in the name of Jesus the *Kristos,* whom God has appointed as the fulfillment of this and all other blessings for mankind.

"Is it not apparent that Moses, in his admonition to the children of Israel, contemplated the witness to the nations that Israel's obedience to the Lord might present? Why else would the Lord our God have said to Abraham, so many ages before, 'all peoples on earth will be blessed because of you'? Why else would he have said, through the blessed prophet Isaiah, 'Nations will come to your light, and kings to the brightness of your dawn'?

"My brothers and sisters, we are favored by the Most High to be living in the very days when the Lord our God fulfills his gracious promises to Israel and the nations. For through Israel, and through the lineage of David, has come that Light which illumines all the world—the blessed light of our Lord and Messiah, Jesus of Nazareth."

It was just as Linus had feared—he would have to endure a diatribe on the Nazarene. He looked about him. Everyone else seemed to be eagerly drinking the words of Joseph BarNabas. He was, as far as he could see, the only island of skepticism in this sea of fatuous gullibility.

"As you may know," the tall Cypriot continued, "I have come to you from Jerusalem, from among the Lord Jesus' twelve apostles, the men who walked with him and knew him. We have heard of your confidence in the Lord Jesus, and that is why I have come. I have met many disciples of the Way

in Antioch—both Jew and gentile—and my heart is glad-
dened because of the faith I have witnessed. This faith, this
bond of belief that reaches across the chasm dividing Jew and
gentile, is that very light that Isaiah preaches. Jesus of
Nazareth, born of the house of David, is that very Root of
Jesse who stands as an ensign, as a rallying banner to the
goyim, as the blessed prophet Isaiah has said. You yourselves
are the evidence of that fulfillment. As I look out upon your
faces, I see those who are of the seed of Abraham, and those
who are not. I see those who wear the phylactery and prayer
shawl, and those who do not. I see those who have spent long
years studying the *Torah* and *Tanakh,* and those who only yesterday were offering libations to Cybele or Jupiter.

"But the blessed Lord Jesus has brought you all together.
He has given you a common cleansing, a common inheri-
tance. He has brought about in you that circumcision of the
heart that the blessed prophet Jeremiah urges. He has made
you a light to the world, as he promised his followers while
he walked among us. He has founded in you a hilltop city
which cannot be hid."

So! This was the tack of the Nazarenes, Linus thought.
That somehow the purported resurrection of Jesus tran-
scended the covenant of Abraham; that because of this event,
God might now make covenant with anyone who pledged
faith in this *Kristos.* "And now, my children, I urge you to live
lives worthy of the Lord who has called you into his light. You
must keep yourselves pure. You must be chaste and sober, not
given to the passions and profligacies of those round about
you. You must not run after harlots, nor debauch yourselves
with wine and strong drink. Each of you must deal honestly
with his neighbor. Obey the authorities, for they reign because
the Eternal has so appointed them. Love and cherish those of
your household so that God may be honored in your homes.
Do all within your power to earn the respect of all men,
whether or not they are followers of the Way.

"We are living in the day of the Lord, that time spoken of
by the prophets, when God writes his name on the hearts of
his faithful ones. Soon I will go away from you for a time, but

I will return. And when I come back, I will bring with me a mighty servant of God, a man raised up by God for a great work in the name of Jesus the *Kristos*. He will gladden your hearts and will give you many teachings which will strengthen you in the faith of our Lord. Grace and peace be with you all."

As Joseph Bar-Nabas sat down, Linus could hear the rustling all about him, could hear the excited whispers and speculations as to the identity of the "mighty servant of God" Joseph would bring to Antioch. Despite himself, Linus was intrigued by the reference. Ah, well, he grumbled to himself, I'm sure it will only present another excuse for Caius to drag me back here for more talk.

———————

The letter falls from my fingers. I'm staring straight ahead into a blinding, exhilarating unknown which rushes toward me at the speed of sight. And then the thought: call Maude! She's the one person who might have a clue what I'm feeling right now. After a moment or two of blind fumbling, I manage to find my phone and stab out her number.

"Hello?"

"Maude, it's Janice, and you're not going to believe this!"

"What's wrong?"

"Nothing! Absolutely, unbelievably—" a semi-hysterical peal of laughter mingles uncontrollably with my words "—nothing! Something is right!"

"Janice, what in the world are you talking about? Are you okay?"

"I'm fine! Glorious, enraptured, scared to death, blown away, euphoric, thrilled, and even okey-dokey!"

"Janice—"

"I got a letter of interest from a publisher."

There's a long pause. "Janice! Are you serious?"

"Of course not! Who in their right mind could be serious at a moment like this?"

A badly distorted cackle rattles the earpiece of my receiver. "Oh, Janice! That's—that's...What did they say? Who's it from?"

"Wesley House. They say, and I quote, 'After reading the sample chapters you sent and carefully considering the outline included with your query letter, we would like to see additional chapters of the book, and a complete manuscript as soon as possible.'"

"Janice! They want to publish your book!"

"Easy there, girl," I say, reaching with outstretched toes toward *terra firma*. "This is a preliminary expression of interest. No publication commitments are made or should be inferred."

"Oh, Janice," she scoffs, "quit talking like a lawyer! They're interested in you or they wouldn't have taken the trouble to respond to your query."

"Well..." I grab the letter from the floor and stare fixedly at it, afraid it might evaporate. "I just don't want to get carried away."

"Sounds like it's a little late to worry about that."

I grin. "I guess you're right, there. Anyway, you were the first person I thought of when I opened it."

"Well, I'm honored," she replies. "And I hope you know how pleased I am for you. One of these days, when you're famous—" She laughs. "Anyway, I'm glad you called. It so happens I was about to call you."

"Oh?"

"Yes. I had...had something I wanted to share with you."

"What's that?" I can sense a quiet pleasure in her voice that I don't remember before.

"I've started writing again."

"Really? Maude, that's great! No kidding!"

I can feel her beaming through the earpiece. "Well...I've been thinking a lot about...a lot of things. And, I've written down some of it, and...it helps, somehow. I think I'll keep on."

"Oh, you should! When can I see some of it?"

"Well, I'm not too sure about that," she hedges. "Maybe someday…"

"Whenever," I say. "I'm just glad you're writing. Like somebody told me one time: don't ever let anyone tell you you can't do it—because you can!"

She chuckles. "Well, does this change your holiday plans? I'd imagine you'll chain yourself to that word processor until you've got the manuscript ready to send to Wesley House."

My mind sticks a toe in the waters of Maude's suggestion. If ever I needed an out, this is it. A real letter of interest, from a real publisher…Get the manuscript whipped out, sent to them…Surely Mom and Dad could understand, and if not— just think of the vindictive pleasure it would give me to explain to them…

"No, I guess not," I say, amazed at my own response. "I think they're sort of counting on me. I imagine I'll probably go ahead."

"So…you'll be back on Thursday?"

Thursday. A shiver runs down my back as I realize that the Fourth is Wednesday—three days away. "Yeah. Thursday."

"Well…" A long pause. "I hope it goes well for you."

"Thanks, Maude," I say, hearing what she means but doesn't say.

"I'll be…I'll be praying for you, Janice," she adds quietly.

"I know. Thanks. Really. Well…I guess I'll let you go, huh?"

"All right. And Janice—congratulations! You earned it!"

"Thanks. Thanks so much. Goodbye."

A letter of interest. A real publisher. Thursday. I stare at the letter, then at my word processor.

20

C ome along, you." Linus tugged at the lead line as he weaved his way along the crowded Street of Horses. Behind him the donkey, two medium-sized cypress timbers lashed across its back, picked its way along, its head hanging forlornly down.

The donkey was getting long in the tooth, Linus knew. He had had the beast for, what? almost twelve years, was it? It was really too old to continue working, but Linus hated the thought of putting it away. When he had a lighter load, such as this one, he brought the donkey along rather than have the timber delivered to the shop. One day he would go to the tiny stall behind the shop and the beast would no longer answer his call. But that day was not yet arrived.

Linus felt a hand on his shoulder. "Grace to you, Linus," someone was saying. Linus looked about to see who had addressed him.

It was Lukas, the physician. "Grace and peace to you, Lukas," he returned gravely, without breaking his stride.

"It appears we are bound for the same destination. I happened to catch a glimpse of your beast amid the crowds and worked my way toward you."

Linus made no reply other than a tacit nod. Lukas was a kind man, a good man. Linus had even seen him visit the House of the Covenant in the days when he had still been a regular attender. But he made the carpenter uncomfortable, for Lukas was a visible reminder of the deaths of his wife and child.

Linus could not blame Lukas, of course. The physician had done all mortal man could attempt. But it had not sufficed.

Lukas blew on his hands and rubbed them briskly together. It was the month of Anthesterion—twelve days before the *kalends* of March, by the Roman reckoning—and the weather was brisk, the sky hung with tatters of gray, cold clouds. "I hope you have a fire built in your shop, Linus," Lukas chattered. "I think I must thaw out my hands, and soon!"

Linus took several paces in silence. "What brings you to our shop?" he asked finally. "Is someone ill?"

If Lukas noticed the reserve in Linus's manner, he gave no sign. "No, no, nothing like that," the physician laughed. "There is someone there, I am told, whom I very much wish to see."

Linus could not help glancing at Lukas. The physician was a few years older than Linus, but his face had the unlined enthusiasm of one who was boundlessly curious about the world around him—and consistently optimistic about his circumstances. His hair was cropped, his face clean-shaven—all in the Roman style—and his eyes held an inner spark, much like…Linus checked himself. It would do no good to remember now her whom he had forever thrust from his life and heart.

"Who is this person who awaits at my shop?" Linus asked. "I don't remember entertaining any guests."

"Someone just arrived in Antioch," Lukas replied. "Word came to me only a few moments ago, and I left my house as soon as I heard. Joseph Bar-Nabas has brought him here from—"

"The Cypriot is back in Antioch?" Linus interrupted. "I hadn't known this."

"They must have arrived while you were at the timber market," Lukas opined, glancing at the wood loaded on the donkey's back. "At any rate, the man Joseph brought with him needed a place to ply his trade, and Caius, who happened to meet them along the way, offered a corner of the carpentry shop. So, Linus, it appears you do, indeed, entertain guests."

The carpenter grunted and trod on.

When at last the two men arrived at the shop, Linus gestured toward the entrance. "Go on inside," he told the physician, "and warm yourself. I will be along after I've seen to the animal." Lukas was only too glad to obey. As he opened the door and ducked quickly inside, Linus caught a glimpse of Caius huddled with Bar-Nabas and another man, apparently deep in some discussion. Typical, Linus thought. Since his conversion to the Nazarene sect, Caius had spent more time talking and hearing the supposed *logia* of his Galilean messiah than he had spent in work. Linus shrugged it off and led the donkey toward the stall at the rear of the shop.

Moments later, after leaning the timbers against the wall by the back entrance, Linus ducked beneath the low doorway and went inside. The four men seated by the fire looked up at him. Caius leapt to his feet and came toward Linus, talking excitedly.

"Cousin, this is the man Joseph Bar-Nabas was talking about when last he was here—the mighty servant of the Lord Jesus! Joseph has brought him here from Tarsus in Cilicia, and his name is—" The younger man broke off, for Linus was staring at the small, stoop-shouldered stranger by the fire, staring with the expression of one who has seen the very last thing in all the world that he expected to see.

As he turned to look at his guest, Caius was even more surprised to see him returning Linus's scrutiny, with a look of dawning recognition on his face.

"Come to the fire, wood-butcher," said Saul of Tarsus. "You must surely be cold." A tiny smile was playing across his features as he spoke.

Linus's tongue broke free from the bondage of his astonishment. "You!" he stammered. "The one who—"

"Yes, the one who woke you from a sound sleep on the night before Passover Eve, and commissioned you to build an additional cross," Saul smiled. "It is I—the very same fellow. Do you remember your anger so well, all these years? Perhaps I shall have to find other quarters for my tentmaking."

"What...how...you know each other?" stuttered Caius.

"Come to the fire, Linus," repeated Saul, a more serious look replacing the amused one of moments ago. "There is much to be said—much that you should hear."

Linus staggered toward the fire like a road-worn wayfarer who had just felt the world tilt beneath his feet. Bar-Nabas and Lukas shifted to make room.

The condemned is a blasphemer...a rabble-rouser, an inciter of rebellion...

How could such words have come from one who was now hailed by all as a mighty servant of the Lord Jesus the *Kristos*? Linus was stunned, but his whirling mind at last coalesced around a single thought, a single question his tongue could form into words.

"How? How is it that you, of all people, have come to believe in the Nazarene?"

Saul of Tarsus gazed into the heart of the blaze for several heartbeats, then looked at Linus with eyes that burned with a fire not of human kindling.

"I saw him," he said.

The words fell on Linus's ears like hammerblows. If he had been confused before, he was hopelessly so now. Saul, of all people! Not the yearning, suffering Tabit, nor Janneus, who claimed cleansing from leprosy, nor the remorse-riddled Jude, nor even the fiercely dedicated Nicolas could make the declaration now asserted by this man.

"I was on the way to Damascus," Saul was saying, "to find and arrest followers of the Way..."

As Linus listened along with the others to Saul's tale of his vindictive mission to Damascus and the blinding, searing light which had altered both the mission and the messenger, he realized he was faced with a terrible choice, the more dreadful because it was unavoidable. He could refuse to believe, could reject the incredible tale and remain in the world he had constructed for himself—a world where pain was kept at an acceptable distance, along with joy.

Or he could believe the truth of Saul's vision of the resurrected Messiah, and be forced to reevaluate every assumption, every action and decision of his life in the shattering glare of the One who had so radically altered the course of Saul's life. He could, like Janneus and Tabit and Nicolas, admit that he would never be complete until the Nazarene made him so. He could embrace his deepest fear—utter dependence on another person.

And yet...what else besides a resurrection could account for such a radical, irrevocable change in the heart of Saul of Tarsus? Why would this man, who had nothing to gain and everything to lose, determine to become like one of those he had journeyed from Jerusalem to arrest? Linus could never forget Saul's implacable conviction of the necessity for Jesus' execution, would always remember with chilling clarity his ruthless insistence that the Galilean troublemaker must die. What power, other than that from beyond the circles of this world, could instigate such a fundamental change in a human soul?

"And so," Saul was saying as he finished his tale, "I have, from that day until this, not stopped telling those I meet about the grace that is granted to us through the power of the risen *Kristos.*" As Saul spoke, the simple, unadorned honesty of his belief shone like burnished gold. And as Linus listened, something deep within him began to respond. "He is the fulfillment of all the prophets," Saul was saying, "and through him God calls the nations unto himself." The former Pharisee, who had been staring into the fire as he spoke, now turned his eyes again upon the dumbfounded carpenter. "Do you believe this, Linus? Will you accept the testimony of my eyes and heart?"

Linus felt the eyes of everyone in the room, of everyone in the world, upon him. He felt as if he stood tiptoe on a mountain pinnacle, surrounded by shadowed chasms too deep to plumb, even in imagination. And Saul was asking him to step forward, into the empty air. Telling him he might fly, if he wished.

"But," Linus stammered at last, "I am guilty—directly guilty of his blood! I knew, felt he was innocent, and yet I—" He could not make himself say the words, his mind absorbed by the blood of an innocent man, soaking into an emblem carved in wood.

"I built the cross on which he was killed," he whispered at last, in a voice choked with shame and confusion. "I knew, and yet I consented—"

Caius's brow furrowed deep with surprise and concern at Linus's words, but Saul leaned over and gripped his forearm. "Surely you cannot imagine you have more guilt in this than I, carpenter," he said in a low, earnest voice. "But none of us can escape a part in his death. Don't you understand, Linus? He is the Passover Lamb, slain once for the sins of the whole world—of everyone who has ever lived or who will ever live."

Hot tears began to seep from Linus's eyes. He shook his head, unable to see, unable to permit himself to accept—

"Think of it this way, my friend," Saul continued. "If your work contributed to his death, it has also contributed to a new life for the whole creation. You didn't just build a cross, Linus. You also built an altar."

Linus clenched his jaw against the inexplicable gush of emotion welling upward within him. He held the rushing flood inside until it grew too strong, until the pain and confusion of years burst from him in a raw, keening wail of purest anguish.

"I long to believe what you say!" he cried in a tortured voice. "I wish, with all my heart, to have hope, to have a reason for living, to trust something other than what I can see and touch. But it is hard for me, don't you see? It is so very hard."

He rocked as he wept, like a woman in mourning. And then he felt arms encircling his shoulders, heard the voice of Saul, close and comforting in his ear. "Very well, then, Linus the carpenter. I have heard your words and I have felt your pain. I will teach you how to believe."

In the days and weeks that followed, Linus became a different man. Saul plied his tentmaking trade in a corner of the carpentry shop, and as he sewed hides together or measured poles for Linus to cut, the two men talked. And as they talked, Linus felt the irresistible warmth of Saul's message melting the frost of pain and doubt that had clenched his heart for so long.

Time after time, Saul cited the prophets, as Bar-Nabas, Nicolas, and the Damascene tanner's son had done, to demonstrate that Jesus of Nazareth was the long-awaited messiah. Saul related details of the Galilean's life, ministry, death, and resurrection to myriads of references in the Torah and Tanakh.

As Saul spoke of how the death and resurrection of Jesus had provided a path to God for all nations, a shaft of remorse smote Linus's soul. He thought of all the stubborn and hateful words he had spewed on Caius—and even on Phoebe. Words spawned by his inability or unwillingness to admit the possibility of the fundamental change ushered in by the *Kristos*. He went immediately and apologized to Caius. But even as he did so, he thought with regret of the one apology he would never be able to offer, of the sadness and regret in her dark, weeping eyes as he had turned his back on her forever.

And then came the day when, before the proud and happy faces of Caius, Trochaion, and their families, he waded into the swirling brown waters of the Orontes, accompanied by Saul, his teacher and newfound friend. In the name of Jesus the *Kristos*, he took the bath that proclaimed his willingness to repent of his sins, the watery burial that replicated, as

Saul explained, the interment of Jesus in the tomb and the glo-rious resurrection that followed. As he burst through the surface of the river's waters, Linus sensed a new life thrum-ming within him, a life whose source he could no more explain than he could duplicate by his own efforts.

———————————

I push myself away from the desk and turn off the word processor. I've put off packing as long as possible. It's late, and I need to get an early start tomorrow to get to Mom and Dad's by lunchtime. I go to the bathroom, dig out my vanity case, and start tossing in the essentials.

I wish I felt better about tomorrow. I wish that my new-found commitment would carry me over the hounding feelings of inadequacy and guilty. Don't new Christians get byes past some of these opponents?

I realize I'm going to have to pay one more visit to Shake before I can face this gauntlet. In the morning, I decide. I'll go talk to him in the morning.

He's sitting in his bed, the covers pulled up around his waist. He has on one of those frayed, faded blue terry cloth robes that everybody's grandfather used to wear around the house in the mornings. At first, I think he's praying, because his head is bowed and his right hand is covering his eyes. Then I notice the crumpled letter in his left hand. He looks up at me, and I can see he's been crying.

"Shake, are you okay?"

He looks at me a long time, and for the first time I can remember, he can't locate a smile. "Well, honey, I been better. That's for sure."

"What's the matter?" I'm beginning to wish I hadn't come.

"Oh, just..." Weakly he flicks the letter in his left hand. "Letter from my daughter."

"Is something wrong with her?"

"No, no. She's fine, her family's fine…" He gazes out the window, and I know he's talking around a gaping hole in his heart.

"Well? What, then?" Nice lead-in, Janice. Real smooth.

"She keeps me up-to-date on what my boy's doin'," he says in a voice that echoes with sadness. "And that's good, 'cause he ain't gonna tell *me* nothin'…"

I sit beside him on the bed, and without my consciously willing it, my hand covers his and begins to pat.

"Like I told Miss Maude the other day," he says, "ain't none of us done it all perfect, when it comes to raisin' kids. I don't know what it was about me and that boy, but…" He swallows several times around trembling lips. I don't know what to say, but for once I don't clutter my ignorance with inanities. I wait until he's ready to talk some more.

"I remember when he was a baby," Shake says, fresh tears welling in his eyes, "that boy wouldn't sleep a lick, it seemed like." A wistful smile of remembrance wafts briefly across his features. "Me and the wife would take turns gettin' up with him. I can remember sittin' up with him at two, three in the mornin'…warmin' bottles, walkin' him around the house, changin' his diapers, doin' anything I could think of to get him to settle down.

"And then he got older. I don't know just how it started, but we got off on the wrong foot, some way or other. I'd get mad, and then he'd get mad, and before you know it, we both painted ourselves into a corner with our anger. I know I'm to blame for a lot of it," he says, shaking his head. "I spent a lot of time prayin' about that boy. I'd be awake at two, three in the mornin', just like when he was a baby. Only this time, he wasn't there with me. This time, a bottle wouldn't fix it; a dry diaper wouldn't make no difference."

"Shake," I say around the lump in my throat, "I just know you did everything you could. He's grown now. He's got to take responsibility, too, you know." I realize what I've just said, and I'd laugh if I weren't so busy feeling ashamed.

"I know that, honey," he says. "I've thought about that a hunnert times. And I know that God can forgive me for my part in it. But my boy…" He looks at me with a face gashed by anguish. "What about my boy?"

I can feel the tears spilling down my cheeks. All I can do is look at him and cry for him—and for myself—and pray for him and pat his hand and be there. Just be there. In the final analysis, what else can a human really do?

After a long time, he sniffs and daubs his eyes with a thumb. "Well, now. You goin' to see your folks today, right?"

I nod. "I wish I knew what to say to them. I wish I knew things would be better."

"I know what you mean," Shake says. "Just 'cause you followin' Jesus don't always mean you get a lay-down hand, does it?"

I grin through my tears and shake my head. "Nope. And I don't even know how high to bid."

Shake gives a quiet little chuckle. "You in trouble, girl. You startin' to sound like me."

I shrug, wiping my nose on the back of my hand.

"Still, honey, you got a lot goin' for you. Even if—" he broke off, looking troubled and unsure.

"Go ahead and say it, Shake."

He looks at me a moment, as if evaluating. "Even if you cain't ever see eye-to-eye with your daddy," he said slowly, "you got God livin' inside you now. And that makes a difference."

I nod. "It makes a difference, all right. I wouldn't even have attempted this little trip before."

Shake smiles, then his face gets serious again. "But, honey," he says, holding up the crumpled letter, "promise me you at least gonna try. You got to promise me that."

I look at the letter, then at Shake. I think about all the ways I've failed, all the times I've fallen into traps of my own setting. I reflect on a lifetime spent in useless flight from the god I assumed was my father's ally. How I ran headlong, looking over my shoulder in loathing and self-satisfied conceit, never realizing my flight was carrying me straight toward the God who never moved, who inhabits the ends of all ways of escape. The God who cannot be avoided.

And then I think of all the broken promises, all the lonely disappointments, all the guilty, heartbreaking failures to live up to a standard that was as impossible as it was inflexible. I think of the ways my father could have assuaged my fears— but didn't. Is this God big enough to cover all that? I wonder. This God who has captured me—can he bring a new beginning to the relationship I never had with my father?

Shake is still looking at me, pleading with his eyes, the crumpled record of his pain still held between us like a flag of truce, like an appeal for help. I clear my throat, but it's still a couple of minutes before my voice will work. "I promise, Shake," come the croaking words. "With…with God's help, I promise."

"That's my girl," he breathes, shining with approval. "Just remember—ain't nothin' too hard for God. Nothin'."

I look closely at him, then reach out to take the wrinkled letter from his fingers. "I'll remember that," I say, holding it up, "if you will."

He looks at me, his eyes widening slightly in surprise, then down as I drop the letter into his lap. As I rise to give him a hug before leaving, he slowly begins to nod.

I'm on the interstate, my car pointed toward a confrontation and—who knows?—perhaps the beginnings of a healing.

My fingers find again, lying in the passenger seat, the note that was taped to my door when I returned from the nursing home. I hold it up and reread it as I drive.

Janice,

I wanted to see you in person before you left, but you weren't here and I couldn't wait—

I'm praying for you and for the success of your visit with your parents. Thank you for your friendship, which has become

very precious to me. Be careful. Call me when you get back.
Happy Fourth of July!

Maude

Happy Fourth of July. Independence Day. What will this day commemorate for me, I wonder? Freedom—or frustration? God, please help me to…to…Just help me. In Jesus' name. Amen.

Music. I need music. I select a tape, plug it into the slot, and the shimmering evanescence of Debussy trickles in sparkling rivulets from my stereo speakers. As I drive, I begin to reflect upon the finale of my manuscript.

It was spring, and Linus and Caius had received, within the space of a few days, a handful of orders, all direly needed by their patrons within a brutally short time.

"Depend on it," Linus groused as they trudged toward the timber market, "when the jobs come in, they come all at once—and each is an emergency."

"But cousin," Caius reminded him, "thank God for the work. With Agrippina due to give birth any day, I can ill afford to turn away commissions."

"True enough," Linus agreed, grudgingly. "Still, you might think folk wouldn't always need everything at the same time."

"You sound like the apprentice, and I the master," Caius laughed. "Why this sudden impatience on the part of my teacher?"

Linus grinned guiltily and made no answer. Caius was right; he had been inexplicably edgy lately, for no reason that he could discover. Perhaps it was the coming of spring—or perhaps it was his subconscious apprehension over the imminent birth of Caius's first child. Or it could be nothing more than the day-to-day stresses of managing the carpentry shop around the added complications posed by Saul's tentmaking.

Linus recalled his surprise, mirrored in the face of Caius, when they had learned of Saul's Roman citizenship. "Nothing remarkable about it," he had assured them with an amused shrug. "My grandfather performed some service—which I've quite forgotten—for one or another of the Roman generals who sojourned in Tarsus. In gratitude, one of them nominated him for citizenship. Nothing more than that." His Roman name, Paullus, was easier for the Greek tongues of Antioch than the Hebrew "Shaul." Therefore, the tentmaker-preacher was becoming most widely known as Paullus.

Lukas the physician had taken to spending much time at their shop, conversing with Paullus and scribbling notes of their discussions. He had, some time before, become a follower of the Way, having been baptized by Nicolas. From time to time, Linus overheard them, together with Joseph Bar-Nabas, making plans for journeys to other cities and provinces of the Roman dominion.

They arrived at the timber market and delivered their order to one of Strato's minions, then settled back to wait until the manager could come to them to set a price for the wood. Squatting in the shade of Strato's lean-to, Linus dabbled in the dust with his finger, thoughtfully tracing a design that had lately engaged his mind.

He had been thinking much lately of Heracleia and the child. He had pondered the meanings and possibilities of his new-found belief in the resurrection of Jesus of Nazareth, and with joy had come to realize that this faith had delivered him of remorse when he considered the death of his beloved wife and her stillborn baby. Without diminishing by a single iota his cherished memories of Heracleia or his profound grief at her untimely passing, his new-found hope enabled him to release her and the child into the loving arms of a delivering God. This gratitude was balm for his troubled soul.

Such thoughts had occupied much of his mind in these last days. He was considering the resumption of a trademark for his completed work—but wondered how to incorporate his ripening faith into such a statement of identity and purpose. He looked down at the pattern his finger had traced in the dust:

Two symbols, whose meanings demonstrated, in Linus's mind, all the disparate threads of his tangled life, now woven together by the work of the *Kristos*. Two shapes that preserved the symmetry of his remembrance of Heracleia and the child, but showed also the transformation from grief to hope that the resurrection of Jesus had made possible for him.

The first was the Greek letter *sigma*, the first letter in the word *soter*—Savior. So did Linus show the source of his confidence, the wellspring of his faith. His gratitude for the life, death, and new life of the Galilean messiah.

The second symbol was the Hebrew character *kaph*, the initial consonant of the word *chaiyim*—life. Thus did Linus blend the two streams of the world: the nations God had called unto himself in the person of Jesus of Nazareth, and Israel, through whom God had produced the *Mashiach*, the *Kristos*—the Anointed One who was the fulfillment of Israel's promise and the nations' hope. The Anointed One who brought peace in the war between Linus's heart and his mind.

Linus nodded, studying the two symbols. The Savior who gave Life. It was just. It was proper. It was the meaning he had been searching for in his blind confusion, all these weary years.

A shadow fell across the dust at his feet. He looked upward, expecting to see Strato. Instead, his heart leaped into his throat and his jaw gaped.

Phoebe looked down at him, her eyes dark pools of ardent joy.

"Grace to you, carpenter."

After a long search, he found his tongue. "Grace and peace to you, my lady."

"Haven't I told you that my name will do quite well?"

"You have," he smiled, feeling a pleasing, giddy warmth rushing into his heart, his belly, the tips of his fingers. "Phoebe, I have...I want to say I am deeply sorrowful for the things I—"

"Be still," she said, laying a finger across her lips. Again he noticed the pleasing fullness of her lips, the profusion of curls now graced with a few glistening strands of silver, the ivory slenderness of her neck.

"I have spoken with Lukas and with Paullus. I know of your decision," she said with a smile.

"How did you—" he spluttered, "that is...how could you know where—"

"It doesn't matter," she said with a shake of her head. "I did, and I'm here." She beckoned him with an outstretched hand. He scrambled to his feet, hurriedly dusting himself. Only when he stood did he realize that Praxos and the others stood grinning about them. Seeing the direction of his glance, she said in Hebrew, "I am on my way south, to buy spices and spread the news of the *Kristos* to any who will listen. And it seems my oxcart is in need of some repair."

Caius forgotten, Linus walked with her toward the gate of the timber market. Feeling her nearness, intoxicated by her presence, he replied in Hebrew, "Come back to the shop. The walk will give us time, and there are things that must be said."

"Indeed there are," she smiled.

Caius, watching them go with an amazed smile on his face, saw Linus's hand reach shyly toward that of the woman who had materialized from nowhere. Just then, Strato came up to him.

"I have your order for the wood," said the harried overseer. "It will cost you ten sesterces per cubit-length. I can have it delivered—"

"Seven," replied Caius, pulling his eyes away from the departing Linus and his lady. He met the surprised gaze of Strato. "I will pay seven sesterces per cubit-length."

Strato looked about in frustration. "Where is Linus? Surely he will be more reasonable…"

Caius, peering above the crowd milling about the timber market and seeing them gone, turned his attention back to Strato. "Linus has, I believe, left the shop," he said with a calm smile on his face. "You will be dealing with me from now on."

Strato opened his mouth, then shut it. What else was there to say?

I pull up in the driveway, put the car in "park," and turn off the engine. My folks must be in the back of the house, since no one's coming out to meet me. I lean my head forward onto my forearms and pray a wordless prayer for guidance.

Is this going to work? Is it possible for something as dead as my relationship with my dad to be resurrected? Can hope really co-exist with defeat? Has such a thing ever happened?

And then I realize…it's happened once—upon a cross. With a sigh, I open the car door and start up the walk. The front door opens, and my dad is there. "Happy Independence Day," he says, trying to smile. "Glad you could make it."